GREAT

AMERICAN

CRIME

STORIES

LYONS PRESS CLASSICS

GREAT AMERICAN CRIME STORIES

EDITED BY
BILL BOWERS

GUILFORD
CONNECTICUT

An imprint of Globe Pequot

Distributed by NATIONAL BOOK NETWORK

Copyright © 2017 by Rowman & Littlefield

British Library Cataloguing in Publication Information Available

Library of Congress Cataloging-in-Publication Data available

ISBN 978-1-4930-2937-2 (paperback)
ISBN 978-1-4930-2938-9 (e-book)

♾™ The paper used in this publication meets the minimum requirements of American National Standard for Information Sciences—Permanence of Paper for Printed Library Materials, ANSI/NISO Z39.48-1992.

Printed in the United States of America

CONTENTS

INTRODUCTION

Why is true crime one of the most popular nonfiction genres? I suspect it comes down mainly to two things: fear, or rather the adrenaline rush that fear gives us; and our innate desire to understand the human mind, particularly the criminal human mind.

Evolution has hard-wired into our psyches a fight-or-flight adrenaline reaction to fear, which goes hand in hand with tragedy or calamity, crime included. While the adrenaline rush improves our chances of surviving dangerous situations, it is also just plain *exciting* . . . whether or not we wish to admit this to ourselves. Reading (or viewing) stories of frightening events—fictional or true—provides this adrenaline rush without posing any actual physical danger.

In addition to the excitement, stories of crime offer at least the possibility of understanding what might drive someone to commit terrible deeds in which most of us cannot even imagine ever being involved. Perhaps reading about terrible events might give us some inkling of an answer to the eternal question: "How could anyone *do* that?"

While assembling the classic stories in this volume, I soon realized there's nothing new under the sun. Though the crimes recounted here took place long ago, many of them (with the possible exception of the story of Rachel Wall, hanged for piracy—see Chapter 10) sound uncomfortably similar to stories you might see today in your online newsfeed.

Some people still commit crimes out of blood lust or in the hope of material gain (see, for example, The Colt-Adams Affair, Chapter 1; The Bloody Benders Family, Chapter 3; Laura Bullion and the Wild Bunch, Chapter 7; The Antoine Probst Ax Murders, Chapter 13; or The Loomis Gang, Chapter 19). Some criminals are unimaginably cruel toward those over whom they have power (see Madame Delphine Lalaurie, New Orleans Monster, Chapter 11; or Harry T. Hayward, the "Minneapolis Svengali" in Chapter 16).

Still others kill over family matters with which they feel otherwise unable to deal, or because of some possibly misplaced desire to defend their loved ones (see The Murder of Grace Mae Brown, Chapter 5; the Mansfield Walworth Parricide, Chapter 6; or The Beadle Family Murder-Suicide, Chapter 12).

Brothers Felipe Nerio Espinosa and José Vivian (see Chapter 18) might be called terrorists if they operated today. And in some cases criminals' motivations are unclear, the perpetrator is unknown, or it's not certain whether a crime even occurred (see Henrietta Robinson, the Veiled Murderess, Chapter 8; or Abraham Lincoln's Remarkable Case, Chapter 15).

Some engage in a lifelong pursuit of criminal activity, as though almost unable to help themselves—or simply indulge their personal enjoyments of doing wrong and fooling others, including the lawmen who tirelessly pursue them—often starting this sort of life at a very young age (see The Loomis Gang, Chapter 19; or Jimmy Logue and Alphonso Cutaiar, Career Criminals, Chapter 20).

Bizarre as they may be, all the stories in this modest volume are true. Whether you read them for the thrills they might provide, because they may offer insights into the minds of otherwise incomprehensible criminals, or because you love American history, I hope you enjoy perusing them as much as I have collecting them, and they provide many hours of pleasurable reading.

—Bill Bowers, somewhere in New England

Editor's note: Because the stories in this volume were written long ago, some spellings, word choices, typographical errors, and punctuation may seem odd or even offensive to modern readers. Nonetheless, every effort has been made to preserve the "flavor" of the originals. This, after all, is what makes them classics.

1

THE COLT-ADAMS AFFAIR (1841)

After John C. Colt (1810–1842) brutally murdered Samuel Adams—a printer who claimed Colt owed him $1.35—in New York City on September 17, 1841, the high-profile case created a tremendous national sensation. Colt was from a prominent and well-connected family. His brother, Samuel Colt (1814–1862) was a manufacturing magnate, founder of the famous Colt Firearms Company of Hartford, Connecticut. John Colt claimed he'd killed Adams in self-defense, but the trial jury did not believe him. Convicted of murder and sentenced to die by hanging, Colt married his mistress Caroline Henshaw in jail just before his scheduled execution, but then cheated the hangman by stabbing himself in the heart with a smuggled knife.

The story did not die with John Colt, however. Conspiracy theories swirled about who brought him the knife in jail, with some maintaining he had somehow faked his death and substituted another man's body.

Colt's Case.—The Murder Of Samuel Adams.—The Death Grapple In Colt's Office.—Shipping The Body To New Orleans—Detection, Arrest, The Tombs.—The Wedding In The Cell.—Suicide Of Colt.

The hand had shut upon it tight, with that rigidity of grasp with which no living man, in the full strength and energy of life, can clutch a prize he has won. They dragged him out into the dark street, but jury, judge and hangman could have done no more, and could do nothing now. Dead, dead, dead!

—*Charles Dickens, in* Martin Chuzzlewit

On the afternoon of Friday, the 17th day of September, 1841, Mr. John C. Colt, a professional book-keeper, and teacher of ornamental penmanship, was sitting in his office, which was in the granite building at the corner of Chambers street and Broadway. The building still stands, and is occupied by Delmonico as a restaurant. Mr. Colt's office was on the second floor, looking out upon Chambers street In an adjoining room a Mr. Wheeler, also a book-keeper, was sitting at work. With him was a young lad, a pupil of his.

It was between three and four o'clock, and at that very moment there was walking to the building a man who was walking to his death. That man was Samuel Adams, a printer. Colt was engaged in writing a work on book-keeping and Adams was printing it. There was a balance of money due by the author to the latter, and Adams was coming to see Colt about the accounts.

On he came—into the entrance, up the stairs, into the room. He sat down on the opposite side of the table to Colt, and the two began an argument about the amount of money due from one to the other. A small hammer, or axe, lay upon the table. The different opinions held by the two about the debt led to ill feeling. Argument became abuse.

"You are a liar!" This from Adams, followed by a blow. They grappled; it was the struggle of death! Adams held Colt by the neck, and shoved him up against the wall.

As quick as a flash Colt seized the hammer and rained blow after blow upon the head of his assailant There was a groan, a heavy fall, and the fiend Murder had added another name to his crimson catalogue of votaries.

Mr. Wheeler, in the next room, looked up from his work, and said to his pupil, "Did you hear that? What was it?"

Stealthily he crept to Colt's door and peered through the key hole, displacing the cover, which was down, with the handle of his pen.

What did he see? He saw a man, with his back to the door, stooping over something, and quietly raising it There was no noise—all was still as the charnel house.

After the fatal blows Colt staggered into a chair, sick unto death, almost; but, although he looked out into the gay street, that form on the floor was always before him. Where the head rested there was a fearful, hideous stream, crawling out over the floor.

Something must be done. It wouldn't do to leave this dead man on the floor, with the blood soaking into the planks. But what?

First out into the open air. His brain was on fire, and he wanted the cool evening breeze. Noiselessly he opened the door and peered out on the landing. It was all dark and still. He crept down, turning pale when the stairs creaked. The street once reached he took a walk in the City Hall Park. It was a beautiful night, and the stars never looked more lovely; but to him their soft light was a baleful blaze. The round moon rose on the metropolis, but to the red handed man walking among the trees it looked as if it had come dripping from a sea of blood. That fearful pool in his room, that crimson snake, crawling along in the dark, had flooded the universe, and everything was incarnadine.

Colt walked down to the City Hotel, corner of Cedar street and Broadway, where a brother of his was stopping, with the intention of telling him about the deed he had done.

He looked through the window into the reading room. His brother was talking to a gentleman, and Colt retired.

He went back again to his room. On the way he thought of many things. First he determined to fire the building and burn the corpse up. This plan he gave up.

Once more he was alone with his dead. It lay there—that hideous corpse—limp, lifeless. The tongue would never again utter a word; but how eloquent that dead clay was! It spoke with a thousand tongues.

In a closet in that room was a box; in the box was a piece of cord and some canvas awning. He first tied the cord around the dead man's neck, for the purpose of stopping the flow of blood; then he wrapped the body up in the awning, and proceeded to pack it in the box. It was merchandise now, and he had determined to ship it away to some distant port, and after cramming it in he salted it.

Then he began to wash up the floor and the walls of the room. That done it was necessary to cleanse his shirt, which had certain fearful stains on it This was done at the Washington Bath House, in Pearl street. From that establishment he went to his home, where his mistress, Caroline Henshaw, awaited him. He struck a light, undressed and went to bed. As Tom Hood says, in his poem of "Eugene Aram," did "Death, the grim chamberlain, light him to his couch?"

The next morning he shipped the body of Adams to New Orleans, putting it on board a vessel lying at the foot of Maiden lane. Fate held that vessel back. It was delayed a week. A horrible stench came from the hold. "Break the cargo!" That was the order of the skipper. They came upon this mysterious box; it was opened, and there what remained of Adams was found.

The Superintendent of Carts advertised for the carman who brought the box to the ship. In the meantime the strange disappearance of Adams was the town talk. The carman appeared, and told who gave him the box. Colt was immediately arrested and locked up in the Tombs.

THE TRIAL.

While in prison Colt lived like a prince. His respectable connections and the wealth of his relatives made him an immense sensation. The papers were full of the murder and the coming trial. The case was the town talk.

The trial began, and lasted some ten days. Colt appeared un concerned and careless. He was always neatly dressed, and created a favorable impression by his appearance.

District Attorney James R Whiting conducted the prosecution. Colt was defended by an array of the brightest legal talent of that day. The line of defence determined upon was that of man slaughter in self-defence. At last the jury retired, and, after being out several hours, brought in a verdict of "Murder in the first degree."

Unusually strenuous exertions were made to save the doomed man. The case was carried from court to court, but all in vain. Money was also lavishly used, but it could not buy this man's life from the outraged law. Eventually he was sentenced to be hanged on the 18th day of November, 1842—over a year from the perpetration of the murder.

COLT'S CONFESSION.

Shortly after his arrest Colt wrote out the following confession:

"Samuel Adams called on Friday at my office, as near as I can recollect, between the hours of three and four o'clock. Whether he had any especial object in view in coming at that time or not I cannot say. When he entered my office I was sitting at my table, as usual, and was at that time engaged in looking over a manuscript account book, as I had been engaged in this work for one or two days previous—that is, I was reading over the entries, and reconsidering the arithmetical calculations belonging to the entries, etc. Mr. Adams seated himself in a chair near the table, and within an arm's length of myself—so near that had we both leaned our heads forward towards each other, I have no doubt but that they would have touched. I spoke of my account, which he had, at my request, handed to me ten or twelve days before. I stated to him that his account was wrong, and read to him at the same time the account, as I had made it out on another piece of paper, and requested him to alter his account as I had it He objected to it at first, saying that I did not understand printing. He however altered his figures as I read them from my account, as I made the remark that I would give $10, or some such sum, if I was not right; after he had altered his figures, and on looking it over, he said he was right at first He made the remark that I meant to cheat him. In the meantime we both had been figuring on separate papers parts of the account Word followed word until we came to blows. The words 'you lie' were passed, and several slight blows, until I received a blow across my mouth, and more, which caused my nose slightly to bleed. I do not know that I felt like exerting myself to strong defence. I believe I then struck him violently with my fist We grappled with each other at the time, and I was shoved against the wall, with my side next to the table. There was a hammer on the table, which I then immediately seized hold of, and instantly struck him over the head. At this time I think his hat was nearly in my face, and I think his face was downward. I do not think he saw me seize the hammer.

The seizing of the hammer and the blow were instantaneous. I think this blow knocked his hat off, but will not be positive. At the time I only remember of his twisting my neck handkerchief so tight that it seemed to me as if I lost all power of reason, still I thought I was striking away with the hammer. Whether he attempted to get the hammer away from me or not I cannot say. I do not think he did. The first sense of thought was, it seems, as though his hand or something brushed from my neck downward. I cannot say that I had any sense or reflection until I beard a knock at the door, yet there is a faint idea remains that I shoved him off from me, so that he fell over, but of this I cannot say.

When I heard the knock on the door I was instantly startled, and am fully conscious of going and turning the key so as to lock it I then sat down, for I felt very weak and sick. After sitting for a few minutes, and seeing so much blood, I think I went and looked at poor Adams, who breathed quite loud for several minutes, threw his arms out, and was silent I recollect at this time taking him by the hand, which seemed lifeless, and the horrid thrill came over me that I had killed him. About this time some noise startled me. I felt agitated and frightened, and I think I went to the door to see if I had fastened it, and took the key out and turned down the slide. I think I stood for a minute or two listening, to hear if the affray had caused any alarm. I believe I then took a seat near the window. It was a cold, damp day, and the window had been closed all day, except six or eight inches at the top, which I let down when I first went to the office, and which remained down all the time I occupied it I remained in the same seat for at least half an hour without moving, unless it was to draw close the curtains of the window, which were within reach. My custom had been to leave the curtains about one third drawn from the side of the window towards Broadway. The blood at this time was spreading all over the floor. There was a great quantity, and I felt alarmed lest it should leak through into the apothecary store. I tried to stop it by tying my handkerchief around his neck tight This appeared to do no good. I then looked about the room for a piece of twine and found in a box which stood in the room, after partially pulling out some awning which was in it, a piece of cord, which I tied tight around his neck, after taking his handkerchief off, and his stock, too, I think.

It was then I discovered so much blood, and the fear of its leaking through the floor caused me to take a towel and gather with it all I could, and rinse it in the pail which stood in the room. The pail was, I should think, at that time about one third full of water, and the blood filled at least another third full. Previous to doing this I moved the body towards the box and pulled out part of the awning to rest it on, and covered it with the remainder. I never saw his face afterward. After soaking up all the blood I could, which I did as still and hastily as possible, I took my seat near the window and began to think what it was best to do. About this time some one knocked at the door, to which, of course, I paid no attention. My horrid situation remained at this time till dark—a silent space of time, with still more horrid reflection. At dusk of the evening, and when some omnibuses were passing, I carefully opened the door and went out as still as possible, and was, as I thought, unheard. I crossed into the Park and went down to the City Hotel, my purpose being to relate the circumstance to a brother who was stopping at that house. I saw him in the front reading room, engaged in conversation with two gentlemen. I spoke to him; a few words passed between us, and; seeing that he was engaged, I returned to the Park. I walked up and down, thinking what was best to do. I thought of many things, among others of going to a magistrate and relating the circumstance to him. Then I thought of the horrors of the excitement, the trial, public censure, and false and foul reports that would be raised by the many that would stand ready to make the best appear worse than the worst for the sake of a paltry pittance, gained to them in the publication of perverted truth and original, false, foul, caluminating lies. All this, added to my then feelings, was more than I could bear. Besides, at this time, in addition to the blows given, there would be left the mark or evidence of a rope drawn tightly around the neck, which looked too deliberate for anything like death caused in an affray.

Firing the building seemed first a happy thought, as all would be enveloped in flames and wafted into air and ashes; then the danger of causing the death of others, as there was quite a number who slept in the building, the destruction of property, etc., caused me to abandon the idea. I next thought of having a suitable box made, and having it leaded, so the blood would not run out, and then moving it off somewhere and burying it; then the delay of all this, and the great liability of being detected. After wandering in the Park for an hour or more I returned to my room and entered it as I had left it, and, as I supposed, unobserved. Wheeler's door was open, and he was talking to some one quite audibly. I went into my room, entering undetermined, and not knowing what to do. After I was seated in my room I waited silently until Wheeler's school was out and his lights were extinguished—and during this suspense it occurred to me that I might put the body in a cask or box and ship it somewhere. I little thought at this time that the box that was in the room would answer; I thought it was too small, and short, and unsafe, as it was quite open. Wheeler's school being out I still heard some one in his room, and, as I then thought, whoever it was lay down on the benches. The noise did not appear exactly like a person going to bed; there was no rustling of bed clothing. I felt somewhat alarmed. The thought then occurred to me that it might be the person who Wheeler had stated was going to occupy the room which I then held as a sleeping room as soon as I gave it up, which was to be in about ten days.

The party in question was temporarily occupying Wheeler's room. Relieving myself by this thought I soon lit a candle, knowing that something must be done; there was no time to lose. This was about nine o'clock, I should think. Having closed the shutters I went and examined the box to see if I could not crowd the body into it.

I soon saw that there was a possibility of doing so, if I could bend the legs up so it would answer, and if I could keep some of the canvas around the body, so as to absorb the blood and keep it from running; this I was fearful of. It occurred to me, if I bury or send the body off, the clothes he had on would, from description, establish his identity. It became necessary to strip and dispose of the clothes, which I speedily accomplished by ripping up the coat sleeves, vest, etc. While doing so the money, keys, etc., which he had in his pocket, caused a rattling; I took them out and laid them on one side, and then pulled a part of the awning over the body to hide it; I then cut and tore a piece from the awning and laid it in the bottom of the box; then cut several pieces from the awning for the purpose of lessening its bulk, supposing it was too much to crowd into the box with the body; I then tied, as tight as I could, a portion of the awning about the head, having placed something like flax, which I found, in the box with the awning; I then drew a piece of rope around the legs at the joint of the knees and tied them together; I then connected a rope to the one about the shoulders or neck, and bent the knees towards the head of the body as much as I could, which brought it into a compact form.

After several efforts I succeeded in raising the body to a chair, then to the top of the box, and, turning it around a little, let it into the box as easy as I could, back downward, with head raised. The head, knees and feet were still a little out, but by reaching down to the bottom of the box, and pulling the body a little towards me, I readily pushed the head and feet in. The knees still projected, and I had to stand upon them with all my weight before I could get them down. The awning was then all crowded into the box, excepting a piece or two, which I reserved to wipe the floor. There being still a portion of the box next to the feet not quite full, I took his coat and, after pulling up a portion of the awning, crowded it partially under him, and replaced the awning. The cover was at once put on the box and nailed down with four or five nails, which were broken, and of but little account. I then wrapped the remainder of his clothing up, and carried it down stairs to the privy and threw them into it, together with his keys, wallet, money, pencil cases, etc.; these latter things I took down in my hat and pockets, a part wrapped in paper and a part otherwise. In throwing them down I think they must have rattled out of the paper. I then returned to the room, carried down the pail which contained the blood, the contents of which I threw into the gutter—into the street I pumped several pails of water and threw them in the same direction. The pump is nearly opposite the outer door of the building. I then carried a pail of water up stairs, and, after rinsing the pail, returned it clean, and two thirds full of water, to the room, opened the shutters as usual, drew a chair to the door, and leaned it against it on the inside as I closed it, locked the door, and went at once to the Washington Bath House, on Pearl street, near Broadway.

On my way to the bath house I went to a hardware store, for the purpose of getting some nails to further secure the box. The store was closed. When I got to the bath house, I think, by the clock there it was eight minutes past ten o'clock. I washed out my shirt thoroughly in parts of the sleeves and bosom that were somewhat stained with blood from washing the floor; my pantaloons, in the knees, I also washed a little, and my neckhandkerchief in spots. I then went home. It wanted, when I got home, about five minutes of eleven o'clock. I lit a light as usual. Caroline wished to know why I came in so late. I made an excuse, saying I was with a friend from Philadelphia, I think, and that I should get up early in the morning to see him off. I went to the stand and pretended to write till she became quiet or went to sleep, then put out the light and undressed myself, spread my shirt, etc., out to dry, and went to bed. In the morning about half past five, I got up, put my shirt and handkerchief, which were not yet quite dry, in the bottom of the clothes basket, under the bed. I always change my shirt on going to bed. In the morning put on a clean shirt and handkerchief, and was nearly dressed when Caroline woke up. I stated to her it was doubtful if I would return to breakfast; did not return; went to the office, and found all, apparently, as I had left it.

I went after some nails and got them at Wood's store. The store was just opened. I returned to the office, nailed up the box on all sides, and went down to the East river to ascertain the first packet to New Orleans. I then returned to the room, marked the box, and moved it, with great difficulty, to the head of the stairs. I did not dare to let it down myself, but went to look for a carman. I saw a man passing the door as I was going out, and requested him to help me down with the box. He got it down without any assistance, preferring to do it himself, and I gave him ten or twelve cents. I then went down Chambers street for a carman whom I saw coming towards Broadway, and hired him to take the box to the ship at the foot of Maiden lane. I went with him.

While he was loading the box I went to my office for a piece of paper to write a receipt on, and wrote the receipt to be signed by the captain on my way down the street I did not offer the receipt to be signed; requested one, which the receiver of the box gave me.

The clerk was by at the time, and objected to the form of the receipt, and took it and altered it, wishing to know if I wanted a bill of lading. I at first remarked, as there was but one box it was not very important, adding, however, that I would call at the office for one. I did not go for the bill of lading. I tore up the receipt before I was two squares from the ship. I returned to my office by way of Lovejoy's Hotel, opposite the Park. I went to the eating room and called for a hot roll and cup of coffee; I could not eat, but drank two cups of coffee. Went to my office, locked the door, and sat down for some time. I examined everything about the room, wiped the wall in one or two places, and then went home and to bed."

Caroline Henshaw, although not married to Colt, was true to him. During his incarceration she was a constant visitor to the Tombs. It was the doomed man's desire that he should marry her before he was hanged. Consent having been obtained, the marriage ceremony was performed at noon on the fatal day, the time of execution having been fixed four hours later.

The bride was at the cell at 11.30. She was attired in a straw bonnet, green shawl, claret colored cloak, trimmed with red cord and a muff. She was accompanied by Colt's brother and John Howard Payne, the author of "Home, sweet home." The Rev. Mr. Anthon performed the ceremony. The mistress became by law the wife, and the same law had decreed that in four short hours she should be a widow. Colt bore up like a man, and was even cheerful and chatty. It was his wedding day, and when should a man be in good spirits if not then? The marriage was solemnized in presence of David Graham, Robert Emmett, Justice Merritt, the Sheriff, John Howard Payne and Colt's brother. After it was over the bride and groom were allowed to be alone one hour.

What could have been their conversation—what their thoughts. A husband of an hour, with his valet, Death, making his wedding toilet! A bride whose orange flowers would soon be cypress leaves, and whose trousseau was the weeds of widowhood!

FIRE! FIRE!

After his wife had gone, and the honeymoon of an hour was over, Colt requested to be left alone. His wish was respected.

In the meantime the excitement in and around the Tombs was tremendous. The gallows was erected—all the preparations were completed. The time was slipping away, and the dread hour was near at hand. Just as the clock trembled on the verge of four—the boundary moment between brief time and endless eternity—the cry of fire was raised. The greatest commotion immediately prevailed.

It was found the cupola of the prison was all ablaze. Engines thundered down the street, the bells rang, and the light of the conflagration cast its lurid glare over the horrid scene.

"DEAD, FOR A DUCAT—DEAD!"

But the man must be hanged all the same. At a few minutes before four o'clock the Rev. Mr. Anthon went to the cell to notify Colt that all was ready. He opened the door and entered. In a moment he staggered out with a wild cry, and his face as white as the snow. The cell was crowded in a twinkling. There, dead upon the bed, with a knife in his heart, lay the man for whom the rope was waiting outside. His hands were composedly crossed upon his stomach. The gallows was cheated, and the ghastly execution in the prison yard was anticipated by the suicidal knife in the prison cell!

PUBLIC EXCITEMENT.

The excitement created by this remarkable and fearful affair was naturally great In the *Herald*, the next morning, appeared the following editorial:

"THE LAST DAY OF JOHN C. COLT.— HIS EXTRAORDINARY SUICIDE AND DEATH."

In another part of this day's paper will be found the extraordinary suicide and death of John C. Colt, before the hour appointed by law for his execution, and the no less extraordinary circumstance of his marriage to Caroline Henshaw, his final separation, and the firing of the cupola of the Halls of Justice about the hour at which he committed the fatal act that closed his course on earth.

We hardly know where to begin, or how to express the feelings and thoughts which rise up in the mind in contemplating this awful, this unexampled, this stupendous, this most extraordinary and most horrible tragedy. The death of Adams, and the circumstances attending that fatal deed, can only be paralleled by the trial, sentence and awful suicide of Colt. The history of the case cannot be equalled in its horror by that of any criminal trial on record.

Yet it will not probably end here. The public will demand a full investigation of the circumstances through which such a catastrophe was permitted. How came Colt to ask for religious consolation from a clergyman and yet to commit suicide? The prayers said over him by the Rev. Mr. Anthon seem to have had little influence upon his mind when we look at the horrible termination of his life. Christianity had not penetrated or pervaded the last moments of his existence in the remotest degree. Taking all the horrid circumstances of his end into consideration, we have every reason to believe that Governor Seward will order an investigation into the facts, and ascertain that no one is to blame for such a death but the unfortunate being himself. Toward him that was, none can have any feeling but that of pity, commiseration, and deep anguish of heart. From the first moment of his trial to the last pulsation of his existence he seems to have been under the influence of a false system of morals, a perverted sense of human honor, and a sentiment that is at utter variance with the mysterious revelations of Christianity, or the sacred institutions of justice in civilized society. The perverted principles of honor and respectability that spring from modern philosophy and human pride have precipitated him upon the fatal precipice. These principles, arising from materialism in philosophy and unbelief in all revelation, are too rife in the world, and may be looked upon as the principal cause of all the licentiousness, private and public, which seems to overwhelm the whole institutions of civilized society in one mass of uproar, confusion and despair.

We cannot say more to-day, nor could we say less at this momentous crisis. "We have no doubt Governor Seward will order an investigation at once into this most unheard of—most unparalleled tragedy."

In a further allusion to the subject, the *Herald* says: "Who gave him the knife? Persons who were alone with him in his cell yesterday: Rev. Mr. Anthon, Dudley Selden, Samuel Colt, Caroline Henshaw, Sheriff Hart.

"In addition to the above, David Graham and Robert Emmett visited him together, when no other persons were present. Also, John Howard Payne and Lewis Gaylord Clarke visited him with Samuel Colt. Who gave him the knife?"

There were at the time, and are now, many persons who believe that during the excitement consequent to the burning of the Tombs cupola, Colt was allowed to escape, and a body substituted by his friends to convey the impression of suicide.

2

DR. VALOROUS P. COOLIDGE

Valorous P. Coolidge was a well-known and fairly prosperous medical doctor in Waterville, Maine. He was also the rare murderer who performed the autopsy on his own victim. Though he made a good living and had a sterling reputation, Dr. Coolidge also had the unfortunate habit of living beyond his means. Edward Mathews, a wealthy cattle dealer, agreed to loan the good doctor $2,000, but also demanded $500 in interest. So Coolidge offered Mathews a drink—whether it was brandy or whiskey is unclear—spiked with prussic acid (aka hydrogen cyanide). Then for good measure he struck him in the head with a hatchet, several times. Convicted and sentenced to hang, he managed to get more prussic acid smuggled into his jail cell, which he used to commit suicide, thereby cheating the hangman.

TRIAL OF DR. COOLIDGE.

The trial of Dr. Valorus [sic] P. Coolidge, for the murder of Edward Mathews, took place the 14th of March, 1848, at Augusta, in Maine, before Chief Justice Whitman, and two associate justices.

The respectable position in society held by the prisoner, and the singular atrocity of the crime with which he was charged, excited unusual interest; so much so, that to accommodate the large number desirous of hearing the trial, the court was induced to transfer its sittings from the court-house to a very capacious church, which was filled as soon as the doors were thrown open.

The trial lasted an entire week, and the number of witnesses examined amounted to about seventy. From this voluminous mass of testimony it appeared that Dr. Coolidge was a physician in the town of Waterville, in a very successful practice; notwithstanding which he was always in need of money, and borrowed it wherever he could, and commonly at usurious interest. More than a dozen witnesses stated that he was indebted to them for money lent, from fifty to three or four hundred dollars, and that about the time of Mathews' death, he offered $500 for the use of $2,000 for six months, and even for a still shorter time.

It further appeared that the prisoner knew that Mathews had gone to Brighton with a drove of cattle; that he made repeated inquiries of the amount Mathews would receive, and requested the barkeeper of the house where Mathews boarded, to let him know when Mathews returned. Mathews arrived on Saturday, the 25th of March, but Coolidge did not see him until the following Wednesday. There were several private interviews between him and Coolidge on Wednesday and Thursday. In the afternoon of the latter day, he received $1500 from the Taconic Bank, and after eight o'clock at night, remarked that it was time to go to Dr. Coolidge's office, and was seen to go in that direction. The next morning he was found dead, in the cellar in which Dr. Coolidge kept his fuel. Two deep cuts were found on his head, some black and blue spots about his throat, and his boots were clean, though the streets were muddy at the time.

At the Coroner's inquest, Coolidge was examined with other witnesses, and stated that Mathews had been at his office twice the day before, for the purpose of borrowing $200, which he wanted to make up the sum of $2,000 he had promised to raise. The last time it was a little after eight o'clock at night when he received the money of which one hundred dollars was in a note he had received of W. R. Doe. Denied that he had written any note to Mathews the day before, or at any time.

There was then a *post-mortem* examination of the body, when Coolidge, remarking that they could not tell whether the wounds in the head were sufficient to produce death, unless the scalp was turned back, cut and turned back the scalp. It being then proposed to examine the stomach, it was taken out by Coolidge, and the contents emptied into a basin. They smelt strong of brandy. A few minutes afterwards he re-marked to a bystander that they had better be removed, as they might scent the room. They were accordingly taken out, and after remaining awhile behind an old hogshead, were locked up in an icehouse; whence they were taken, on the following Monday, and delivered to Professor Loomis for examination. When Coolidge was asked, on Friday evening, if the contents of the stomach had not better be examined, he inquired of the witness if they had been preserved; and on being told that they had, he replied, they had lain so long, nothing could be ascertained from them.

These contents were carefully analyzed by Professor Loomis, and found to contain prussic acid by several tests. Several physicians, who were present at the post-mortem examination, also testified that the liver, lungs, spleen and brain, indicated the action of prussic acid, and that they perceived its peculiar odor.

The medical men further thought that the wounds in the head not having been attended with inflammation, were probably given after death, with a view of preventing suspicion of the real cause. From these indications of the presence of prussic acid, and other circumstances, Coolidge was now strongly suspected of the murder, and was accordingly taken into custody. It was then found, and it was proved in court, that, on the 17th of September, he had written to Boston for an ounce of hydrocyanic (prussic) acid, "as strong as it can be," which he received: and that, on the 19th of September, he also wrote to Hallowell for an ounce of the same acid, "as strong as it is made." This acid, when used in medicine, is commonly diluted to 2 per cent. The pure acid is seldom called for. Dr. Coolidge previously had by him some of the diluted acid.

On Monday, after the murder, a boy found in the top of Coolidge's sleigh, a gold watch and chain, which were proved to be the same as those worn by Mathews the Thursday before. They were wrapped up in white paper, which was of the same description as some found in Coolidge's office.

Coolidge endeavored to persuade two witnesses to conceal from the coroner's inquest that he wished to borrow money of them—having himself stated to the jury that, so far from wishing to borrow money, he had lent Mathews $200, and to one witness he proposed to give fifty dollars, and declared he was a ruined man, when he could not succeed.

Many minor circumstances corroborated the inference from the preceding strong facts, but the testimony of Thomas Flint removed every shadow of doubt of the prisoner's guilt.

The witness was a student in Dr. Coolidge's office, and he stated that, about nine o'clock on Thursday night, when he was going to bed, at his boarding-house, he met Dr. Coolidge, who requested the witness to go to his office with him. When there, he said, "I am going to reveal to you a secret which involves my life; that cursed little Edward Mathews came in here, and went to take a glass of brandy and fell down dead; he now lies in the other room. I thumped him on the head to make people believe he was murdered." After some consultation, they decided on carrying the body to the cellar, to remain there until it was discovered the next day. The next day he found in the office a note from Coolidge; requesting him to sweep the office carefully, which he did, and removed some signs of blood. About noon he saw Coolidge charge Mathews with $200 lent. Coolidge handed him a sum of money, requesting him to keep it, saying the jury might ask to see his pocket book, and he did not know but there was too much money in it. After the examination of the body, Coolidge told the witness, while in the office together, that there was $1,000 under the carpet, beneath the iron safe, which he wished witness to take care of. In the evening the prisoner seemed to be greatly agitated. He took the money he had given witness, selected some of the bills, put them into his pocket book, and gave the witness others from the pocket book. The money was put in one of a number of jugs in the office, and the prisoner requested the witness to sleep with him that night. The next day he seemed unwilling to receive back the money he had given to the witness, but afterwards went to the office, broke the jug and threw the notes into the stove. He stated that a letter produced to the coroner's jury (from Coolidge to Mathews, requesting the latter to call at his office on Thursday night), he had withdrawn "from the bag" on Friday night and destroyed. He told the witness there was a bottle at his office that had contained prussic acid, which ought to be destroyed, and that the bottle which had come from Boston should be filled up, for some of it had been used. He also desired that the brandy bottle should be rinsed, and the water in the sink thrown out. He requested the witness to take the watch from his sleigh, and throw it into the river. Witness slept with the prisoner the two or three following nights, and when he did not, believes that Mr. Baker did. The witness admitted that when before the grand jury, he did not state anything about the money, the watch, or washing out the stains from the floor. He had partly disclosed to his father the facts stated to-day, and also to Mr. Baker. General Simons, his father, had encouraged him to testify in the case.

In consequence of this variance in Flint's testimony, the counsel for the prisoner endeavored to invalidate it; the jury, however, after a deliberation of twenty-four hours, returned a verdict of guilty, and the prisoner was sentenced to be hanged, after the expiration of a year spent in hard labor. The law of Maine, by a seeming compromise between those who would abolish, and those who would retain capital punishment, has thus postponed the execution of the sentence of death, that the person convicted may profit by subsequent evidence, so as, if not to establish his innocence, to raise sufficient doubts of his guilt to obtain a pardon; or he may effect his escape by force or artifice, or finally escape ignominious punishment by disease or suicide.

3
~

THE BLOODY BENDERS FAMILY

Between about 1871 and 1873, the Benders, a family of two men and two women, murdered and robbed at least eleven people who had stopped for the night at the small inn and general store the Benders operated in Labette County, Kansas. Most of the victims had their skulls crushed—most likely with a large hammer—and their throats cut. The Benders were never brought to justice. Apparently fearful their terrible crimes would soon be discovered, they fled, and their ultimate fates are unknown.

DEVILISH DEEDS.

FEARFUL AND DIABOLICAL BUTCHERY IN SOUTHERN KANSAS.

A FARM PLANTED WITH CORPSES – EIGHT BODIES ALREADY DISCOVERED – FOUR PERSONS IMPLICATED – HOW A FAMILY OF HUMAN HYENAS PREYED UPON THE PASSERS BY.

What follows in its facts may read like the recital of some horrible dream, wherein nightmare mirrors upon the distempered brain a countless number of monster and unnatural things, yet what is set down in the narrative is as true as the sun.

From the information furnished to us last night by a gentleman just from the

SCENE OF THE BUTCHERY,

and from dispatches and accounts already published, we are enabled to give a tolerably detailed account of the monstrous series up to date.

THE BEGINNING OF THE END,

came about in this wise: On the 9th of March Dr. William H. York, the brother of that other York famous now for his penetration of the guilty secrets of Pomeroy. and his betrayal in the supreme moment of the senatorial crisis, of the trusts confided to his keeping—left Fort Scott on horseback for his home in Independence. Kansas. He did not come home. His friends watched and waited for him, his family prayed for him, the talk of the town dealt day after day with him, expectations at last deepened into downright earnestness about him, until, on the 28th of March, the Lawrence *Tribune* gave a brief account of the mysterious disappearance. All at once thereafter all the papers in the State took up the tale of his journey, of his non-arrival, and of the fears of foul play. He was traced to

CIIERRYVALE

Cherryvale is a small town on the Leavenworth, Lawrence and Galveston Railroad, and is in Lalbette County, about fifty miles from the south line of the State. To the smith of Cherryvale, some two miles or less, stands a frame house, having in front a large room where the meals are served, and in the rear a sleeping room furnished with two beds and some scant additional furniture besides.

WILLIAM AND THOMAS BENDER

lived in this house with their wives. To the right of the dwelling house was an outhouse, as the diagram shows, and in the rear was an enclosed garden of possibly two acres. The search seemed to suddenly end at Cherryvale.

One day early in April some men from Cherryvale rode over to the Bender house to inquire concerning Dr. York, and to learn, if possible, some tidings of his fate. They learned nothing, however.

WILLIAM BENDER,

the eldest of the brothers, had a wife who was a Spiritualist. The balance of the Benders called her a medium, the neighbor a she devil. She was forty-two, with iron-gray hair, ragged at the ends and thin over the temples. Her eyes were steel-gray and hard. The light that came from them was sinister and forbidding. She had not a single prepossessing feature. Her form, angular and tall, seemed to lift itself up when the Spiritual influences took possession of it, and to become not only gigantic in height, but super-natural as well. At times she dealt in incantations, and the boiling of herbs and root that had charms and spells about them. Her will was indomitable. All the household feared her, dreaded her, obeyed her, and, as the sequel proves, they did the

DEVIL'S WORK FOR HER

beyond all the atrocious devil's work ever done in Kansas.

Time went slowly by, and a man riding in one day from the prairie saw no smoke arising from Benders' chimney. The windows were down, the doors were closed, there was no sign of life anywhere. These evidences of emigration did not even interest him. This man, however, in riding by a pen to the left of the house, saw a dead calf in the lot, and upon further investigation, and with the practical eye of a practical farmer, used to guessing the weight of live stock upon the hoof, he knew that the calf had

DIED OF STARVATION.

Then the truth came, as an overflow comes often to a Kansas creek, all of a sudden and over whelming. Such a death suggested flight, flight meant guilt, and the nature of the guilt was surely murder. He galloped into Cherryvale and related what be had seen. The town aroused itself. A party was organized instantly and set out for the Bender mansion.

In the rear, as we have said, was a garden. This, at first, was not examined. The front room of the home was next carefully searched, every crack and crevice being minutely looked into, and subjected to the application of rods and levers to see if the floor was either hollow or loose. Nothing came of it all. No blood spots appeared. The floor was solid—the walls were solid. Then came the back room. The beds were removed. In his flight the elder Bender had left everything untouched. After the beds had been removed, one of the party noticed a slight depression in the floor, which, upon closer examination, revealed a

TRAP DOOR

upon hinges. This was immediately lifted up, and in the gloom a pit outlined itself, forbidding, cavernous, unknown. Lights were procured and some of the men descended. They found themselves in an abyss shaped like a well, some six feet deep, and about five feet in diameter. Here and there little damp places could be seen as if water had come up from the bottom or been poured down from above. They groped about over these splotches and held up a handful to the light. The ooze smeared itself over their palms and dribbled through their fingers.

IT WAS BLOOD

thick, foetid, clammy, sticking blood—that they had found groping there in the void. The party had provided themselves with a long sharp rod of iron, which they drove into the ground in every direction at the bottom at the pit, but nothing further rewarded the search, and they came away to examine the garden in the rear of the house. Shovels were set at once to work, and in a few moments a corpse was uncovered. It had been buried upon its face. The flesh had dropped away from his legs. There was no coffin, no winding sheet, no preparation for the grave, nothing upon the body but an old shirt, torn in places and thick with damp and decay. The corpse was tenderly disinterred and laid upon its back in the full light of the soft April sun. One look of horror into the ghastly face, festering and swollen, and a dozen voices cried out in terror:

"MY GOD, IT IS DR. YORK!"

And it was. He had been buried in a shallow hole, with scarcely two feet of dirt over him. Had he been murdered, and how! They examined him closely. Upon the back of his head and to the left and obliquely from his right ear, a terrible blow had been given with a hammer. The skull had been driven into the brain, and from the battered and broken crevices a dull stream of blood had oozed, plastering his hair with a kind of clammy paste, and running down upon his shoulders.

It seems as if the winds carried the tiding to Cherryvale. In an hour all the town was at the scene of the discovery. A coffin was procured for Dr. York's body, and his brother, utterly overwhelmed, sat by the ghastly remains as one upon whom the hand of death had been laid. He could not be comforted. But the

HORRIBLE WORK WAS NOT YET COMPLETED.

The iron rod was again put in requisition, until six more graves marked (E) were discovered, five of which contained a corpse and the sixth, that in the second row, (E) containing two, an old man and a little girl. Some were in the last stages of decomposition, and others, not as far gone, might have been identified if any among the crowd had known them in life. Coffins were provided for all, and again was the search renewed. It was past midnight when our informant left, but three more graves had been discovered, each supposed to contain a corpse, although they had not been opened. The

WHOLE COUNTRY IS AROUSED.

Couriers and telegrams have been sent in every direction with descriptions of the Benders, and it is not thought possible that they can escape. With the crowd at the grave was a man named Brockman who was supposed to know something about the murders. Furious men laid hold upon him at once, and strung him up to a beam in the house. His contortions were fearful. His eyes started from their sockets, and a livid hue came to his face that was appalling. Death was within reach of him when he was cut down.

"CONFESS! CONFESS!"

they yelled, but he said nothing. Again he was jerked from his feet, and again was the strong body convulsed with the death throes. Again resuscitated, he once more refused to open his mouth. He did not appear to understand what was wanted of him. The yelling crowd, the mutilated and butchered dead, the flickering and swirling torches spluttering in the night wind, the stern set faces of his executioners, all passed before him as a dreadful phantasmagoria which dazed him and struck him speechless. For the third time they swung him up, and then his

HEART COULD NOT BE FELT TO BEAT,

and there was no pulse at the wrists. "He is dead," they said. But he was not dead. The night air revived him at last, and he was permitted to stagger away in the darkness as one who was drunken or deranged. Six butchered human beings were brought forth from their bloody graves, and three others are to be uncovered. It is thought that more graves will yet be discovered. One corpse was so horribly mutilated as to make the sex even a matter of doubt.

THE LITTLE GIRL

was probably eight years of age, and had long, sunny hair, and some traces of beauty on a countenance that was not yet entirely disfigured by decay. One arm was broken, and the breast bone had been driven in. The right knee had been wrenched from its socket, and the leg doubled up under the body. Nothing like this sickening series of crimes has ever been recorded in the whole history of the country. It is supposed they have been following their

HORRIBLE WORK FOR YEARS.

Plunder is the expected cause. Dr. York, it is said, has a large sum of money on his person, and that he stopped at the house either to feed his horse or to get a drink of water. While halting for either he was dealt the blow which killed him in an instant.

*****

THE KANSAS HORROR

FURTHER PARTICULARS OF THE SHOCKING AFFAIR.

The *Kansas City Times* gives the following additional particulars of the Kansas horror, furnished by its correspondent:

Dr. York's body being found, further search was made by thrusting a sharp pointed rod into the earth, which soon developed the fact that there were many more graves in this half acre of ground, and by nightfall eight bodies in all were exhumed, of which the following is a partial list, so far as they could be distinctly identified: W. F. McGronty, of the one hundred and twenty-third Illinois infantry, company D.—Brown; Henry McKenzie, of Hamilton county, Indiana, and a Mr. Lonchore and his little girl. The latter had recently buried his wife, and was about starting to Iowa.

THE SCENE THURSDAY

was too horrible to give even a faint description of. Seven bodies in various stage of decomposition were lying on the ground by the side of their open graves, their skulls broken in and their throats cut from ear to ear, except the girl, eighteen mouths old, who must have been strangled or else thrown into her grave alive. She was in full dress, as her grandmother had dressed her that morning. She was in the bottom of the grave and her father lying upon her. The child's body showed no

MARKS OF VIOLENCE.

The manner in which they accomplished these terrible deeds was this: on the house was posted the sign "groceries," but they kept nothing but some wines. This sign called in their victims. In the floor near the store was a trap door, two feet square, which opens into a rude hole in the ground, seven feet deep, six feet wide at the top, and three feet at the bottom. The earth outside of the house does not show any sign of excavation. In this horrible hole were plunged the unfortunate victims whom they

MURDERED IN DAYLIGHT.

The hammers used for breaking the skulls were such as are used by stone-breakers on our streets, and the handles are around twenty inches long. Upon examination it was found that the skulls were all broken at the back and right side of the head, showing that the desperate deeds have been done by a right handed man.

The bodies have all been identified but two. The Bender family have lived at this place for more than two years, yet all

THE BODIES FOUND

have been killed within the last nine months, and the skill shown in this terrible work and the neatness with which all traces of their crimes were blotted out, is the best evidence that their bloody work did not commence so recently. Several hundred persons were at the scene of horror yesterday, and the excitement is intense. Every one is confident that half is not yet unearthed.

THE WORK OF SEARCHING

the premises still goes on, and what may be developed none can tell, but the people are prepared for anything. In an old Bible which was found in the house. and on the family record page, was written in German the following memoranda: "big slaughter day, Jan, eighth (8.)" and another which read: "hell departed." These were interpreted by a German citizen who was present yesterday.

A CATHOLIC PRAYER BOOK

was also found in the house, which contained the following, written in German: "Johanna Bender, born July 30, 1848. John Gerhardt came to America July 1, 18—."

the deputy prosecuting attorney of Labette county, appeared on the ground at the beginning of the search, and for some time insisted on all these roles of "red tape," and did not want anything done until the coroner and other officials came. His desires were overruled very decidedly, and speedily the examination proceeded.

Great excitement prevails all over the country, and a strong effort is being made to discover this family of murderers.

SECOND DISPATCH.

Cherryville, May 8, 10 p.m. Parties just arrived from Parsons report that some persons supposed to be implicated have been arrested at that place; and there is a rumor that scours are on the trail of the Bender family, and only twenty four hours behind them, they being en route to Texas.

Numbers of people have been visiting the grounds from motives of curiosity.

ANOTHER RUMOR

reports a gang of horse thieves in the vicinity of the human slaughter-house, who are spreading rumors to throw the detectives off the track.

LATER FROM THE KANSAS HORROR.

Parsons, Kas., May 12. Col. Bondenot, who has just returned from the scene of the Bender murders, reports that three more graves were discovered yesterday. Over 3,000 people were on the ground, and a special train has just arrived with seven cars filled with people; that there was intense excitement all over the country and a firm determination to ferret out the parties engaged in the murders. It is understood that a large reward will be offered by the county, and state, for the arrest of the assassins. Nearly all the bodies of the dead are indecently mutilated, and it is considered certain that the little girl was thrown alive into the grave of her father, as no marks of violence can be found on the body.

★★★★★

THE DEVIL'S KITCHEN

The Tricks of the Professed Mistress of His Satanic Majesty—Fiendish Torture—An Invitation to a Supper of Double Edged Daggers—the Pursuit of the Human Butchers—How Armed Men were Fooled by a Woman—A Sunday Scene at the Graves.

The foul and dreadful series of murders lately brought to light in Labette county, Kansas, continues to be the all-absorbing topic of speculation and conversation throughout the State, and to excite wonder and amazed horror all over the nation.

Every item or circumstance connected with the horrid butchery is diligently sought after, and ears made credulous by the fearfully true story of the damnable deeds of the Bender family, are made to drink in rumors and stories which have their foundation only in the imagination, which vainly labors to invent something more strange and horrid than the reality. The *Times* has already published such fall and generally accurate account of the discovery of the affair, and the subsequent movements of the populace, officers and criminals, that little remains to be added, but the following facts, gleamed by the *Times's* special reporter, who returned from "Hell's Half Acre"—as the Bender garden will hereafter be known—yesterday, will be read with universal interest.

THE DEVIL'S KITCHEN,

otherwise the Bender house, is a small, rude frame shanty, without lath or plaster or intervening substance between its floor and the rafters of the pointed roof. In size it is 16x24 feet. Small uprights 2x4 inches are set to mark the house into two compartments, but no wall had ever been made other than a white cotton cloth hung in the rear apartment and against these uprights. The front apartment had in a counter, over which the butchers once pretended to sell groceries. In the rear room was a rude bed, a table, a stove and three chairs.

The table, to which the guests of the fiends were seated, was placed directly over the trap door, so that the guest's back was to and against the white curtain. In this position it was an easy thing for the male villains in the front apartment to strike the form clearly lined and resting against the white cloth, and when the blows of the sledge and hammer had knocked the victim, with a crushed and broken skull, senseless and helpless to the floor, for the female fiends in the back room to cut their throat. The execution was as simple as it was dreadful, but, though it would seem resistance to such well planned murder of the trusting and unsuspecting was impossible, the walls gave silent evidence that some of the murdered ones had not been sent to their doom without an effort to defend their lives. No less than a dozen bullet holes in the sides and roof of the house attest that armed men, when struck down so relentlessly, had attempted to shoot their murderers, but, unfortunately, the aims had been wild, and the murderers are reserved for the hempen halter.

THE SITUATION.

This building is located just on the rising edge of a beautiful narrow valley, circled on the south, east and west by a range of mounds or hills, fronting to the north in the mouth of the valley. The hills are distant from the house from a half mile to a mile, the closest being on the south, to the rear. The house fronted to the road just in the bend, sitting back about its own length from the roadway. From this point of the road can be had a full view of everything for a half mile in every direction, but not another house is within sight. It is about seven miles from Cherryvale, ten miles from Thayer, eight from Ladore, and two from Morehead, and just in the northwest corner of Labette county.

WHERE THE MURDERED NOW SLEEP.

With the exception of Dr. York and Henry F. McKenzie, G. W. Longcor and daughter, whose families took charge of their remains and buried them at Independence, the bodies of those found in the garden graves were quietly taken by silent men, who knew them not, yet longed for vengeance on their assassins, to the base of a high mound, about a mile to the southeast of the devil's kitchen, and there a second time returned to the earth to sleep until the final resurrection.

WHO THEY ARE.

The first of the eight bodies discovered was Dr. York, of Independence.

GEORGE W. LONGCOR AND DAUGHTER.

Mr. Longcor was a neighbor of Dr. York's, from whom be had purchased a team just before he started for Iowa, last December. He and his infant child were buried in one grave. He, as all the other men, had the back of the skull crushed in and broken and his throat cut, and the body stripped of nearly all its clothing. The child was placed at the father's feet, without a bruise or mark of violence, and with all its clothes on, even the hood and mittens, and many judge that the infant had been buried alive.

L. G. BROWN

was from Cedarvale, Howard county. He had recently traded horses near Ladore, and was supposed to have had about $60 with him. He was recognized by a silver ring on his finger, which was identified by the friend Johnson, with whom he had traded horses.

W. F. MCROTTY

lived near Cedarvale. He was en route to Independence to contest a land claim. One report says he had a large sum of money on his person, and another, judged to be more reliable, that he had but a small sum.

HENRY F. MCKENZIE

was from Hamilton county, Indiana, and was on his road to locate at Independence, where his sister, Mrs. J. Thompson, resides. He had but little money and was on foot, and had been missing since December last.

PETER BOYLE

resided in Howard county. His body was so mutilated as to be hardly recognizable, but his poor widow identified him by his peculiar shirt, which her own hands had made for him. He had started on foot for Osage Mission sometime last December.

THE UNRECOGNIZED.

The only one of the bodies not identified is supposed, and very reasonably, to be that of Jack Bogart, who started for Illinois, on horseback, about a year ago. The horse he rode has been found in the hands of a responsible man, who purchased him from one of the suspected confederates. This completes the list of those yet discovered on the grounds.

PISTOLS AND KNIVES FOR A SUPPER.

One of the most marvelous stories ever heard, but which is vouched for by reliable men, is the following: One evening about three months ago, a poor woman, footsore and weary, traveling to Independence, without money, stopped at the Bender den and asked for some supper and for privilege of resting awhile. She was invited in, and being nearly exhausted, she took her shoes and scanty wrappings off and laid down on the bed in the back room. She soon fell into a troubled doze, from which she was awakened by the touch of the old hag of the den, who, pointing to an array of pistols and double edged knives, of various sizes, lying on the table, said in the spirit of hellish malignity: "There, your supper is ready." The woman was motionless and breathless with terror, and as she sank back on the bed, the devil dame picked up the knives one by one and drew her finger along the sharpened blades at the same time glancing fiendishly at her intended victim.

How long this terror lasted the woman could not tell, but at last she, in the very desperation of fear, arose as though not alarmed, and made a private excuse for going out. She was permitted to do so, and moving around to the shelter of the stable, barefooted and scarce half clad, she darted off on the wings of fear, and ran for two miles to the house of one who protected her and gave her shelter. As she was running away, she turned frequently to see if she was pursued, but no one followed her, though she saw the light from the open doorway several times, as though the devils inside were awaiting her return. Even this story seems not to have aroused more than the before existing suspicion that the Benders were not exactly the right kind of people.

A BURGLING BUSINESS.

Although for the past three years this section has been infested with horse thieves and murderers, and this known to every one about the country, it is probable the same state of affairs might have continued for an indefinite period, had not the murder of Dr. York, man of family, friends and reputation, led to the exposure. Men have been missed and bodies found of murdered men for three years past, and "vigilance committees" have hunted and driven some men from the country; but it would now seem as though the leaders of these "regulators" were themselves the villains, and honest men had been falsely and foully suspected and driven from their homes. Known villains have for that time been sent to the penitentiary, only to be pardoned out out by governors.

And even the band of seventy-five armed and honest men who scoured the country in search of Dr. York, when it was learned he was missing, seem to have had very little judgment or discretion.

On the 28th of March last, Col. York and Mr. Johnson visited the Bender house to which place they bad tracked Dr. York, and endeavored to coax some information from them, but they would tell nothing. On the 3d of April this armed band visited the house with the sole object of finding the murderers of Dr. York, yet they did not notice the bullet holes in the house, and allowed themselves to be fooled by an assumed stupidity which was the disguise of most hellish cunning. The old hag sat mum and gloomy, pretending she could not understand or speak English; old Bender said nothing; Kate, she of the evil eye, denied all knowledge of the lost, and the younger male villain fooled them with a well made up story. He said that at about the time they say Dr. York was missed, he, Bender,

HAD BEEN SHOT AT

in a lonesome place near Drum creek, one evening, and it must have been by those who killed the Doctor. He described the place minutely, and then took them to it, and it was found as he said, and they half believed his story, and returned with him. Col. York repeated the story given above, of the supper of pistols and knives offered to the lone woman, when the old hag soon found her sense of the English language improved. She understood all that had been said, and flew into a violent passion. She denied the story of the supper, and said that that was a bad and wicked woman, whom she would kill if ever she came near them again; that the woman was a witch, and had bewitched Kate's coffee; and then she ordered the whole band away. While going and coming from the creek, John told Col. York that his sister Kate could do anything, that she could control the devil, and that the devil did her bidding. When they returned to the house, Col. York tried to induce this wonderful mistress of the devil to reveal where the body of his brother was. She positively refused her satanic aid at this time, giving as her reason therefor that she could not do so in the day time, and while there were so many men and so much noise about.

AN INVITATION.

The pretended sorceress and real fiend then told Col. York privately that if he would come the next night, Friday—when best she worked her spells—and bring only one man with him, she would take him to the grave of his murdered brother. Had the Colonel been so foolish as to believe the mysterious power of the creature, there is no doubt she would have proved her promise good. The whole band then left the house. They visited the house of Roach and Smith and Harness, at Ladore, and made many threats, but accomplished nothing. Their intent was good, but they lacked an experienced detective for a leader. So strong was their conviction, however, of the guilt of the

Roaches and of the Benders, that they would have hung them then had it not been for the persuasion of Col. York and a few others, who were determined that none but the known guilty should suffer. Of course this alarmed the Benders, and they fled. How, has been published in the *Times*.

MORE CARELESSNESS

It seems strange that no watch was put on the suspected Benders, and still more strange that they should have been gone three weeks before any knew of it. When they went to Thayer they left their team and wagon and dog on the public street of the town. On the street the team and wagon remained for two days without a claimant, when they were taken charge of by a livery firm there—Bear & Wheeler. No notice, other than an item in the *Head Light*, the local journal, was given of the finding of the team, and no description of the horses published, though they were peculiarly and similarly marked. Had such description been given it must have led to the speedy pursuit of the fleeing criminals. It is not suspected that there was any guilt in this neglect, but only carelessness.

THERE MUST BE A GANG.

No doubt is entertained that the Benders have not been alone in their damnable villainy. They must have had confederates to dispose of the stock and clothes of his murdered men, and suspicion has already pointed to a number of men, living throughout that section, in different directions, and to none with more evidence of justice than one

MIT CHERRY.

This fellow lives about three miles south of Parsons, and when Col. York was making search for his brother, he tried to induce the Colonel to employ him as a detective. Luckily the Colonel would have nothing to do with him. This man, it is said by two men who are generally credited, at different places and times, and separately, told them that he was a member of a band of "regulators" in the County, and that when they found a criminal they never troubled him with the law, or put the County to any expense about him; that the baud always knew their own work when they saw it, for every man they put out of the way they laid with his throat cut, his left arm across his breast, and his right by his side.

In such condition and position were found nearly all the Bender victims. As a further evidence against this fellow, it is known that soon after McCrotty's disappearance was known, and when there was about to be some action taken to look for him, he pretended to have a letter from McCrotty, telling of his safe arrival in Illinois, at his intended destination.

The other suspected parties who have been arrested are men of bad repute in general, and believed for some time to be horse thieves, if nothing worse. On Sunday, Sheriff Stone brought into Independence, under arrest, Addison Roach, of Ladore, and Wm. Buxton, a son-in-law of the elder Roach, both found near Cedarvale. This makes the number under arrest now on suspicion, so far as known, twelve. The names of the others have been published in the *Times*.

LAST SUNDAY AT THE GRAVES.

On last Sunday there were about one thousand men, women and children, at the Bender grounds, gazing with mingled emotions of horror and curiosity. The graves even yet sent forth a sickening stench, and women held their noses as they peered down into the narrow tenantless holes. Two special trains were run, one from Independence and one from Coffeyville, to a point on the railway line about two miles from the house, and teams were busy running to and from the cars to the grounds, while the greater portion of the crowd was compelled to walk. These trains brought about 600 persons. There were about six or seven hundred persons there from all parts of the surrounding country, in wagons, carriages, buggies and on horseback.

The curiosity of many seemed to master their repulsion, and hundreds brought away some memento of the dreadful place. The blood-stained bedstead was smashed to pieces and divided in the crowd, all the shrubbery and young trees were broken or torn up and carried away, and pieces of the house borne off by the curious. Such another raid would not leave much of the shanty. It was supposed that the grounds would be ploughed and scraped again this day to search for other bodies, but the intention was abandoned, and it is not probable any further search will be made until it is done regularly by the County authorities.

REWARDS OFFERED.

Rewards to the amount of $5,000 have been offered for the capture of the murderers, and there is not the slightest doubt but they will be recovered. On last Saturday the detectives were on the trail of the Benders, with the express certainty of effecting their speedy capture, and it is more than probable that they are already taken.

With the number under arrest and the others watched, no doubt some one will reveal the whole truth, when Kansas will be rid of the worst scoundrels that ever infested and cursed this country.

4

~~~

THE LAMANA
KIDNAPPING AND
THE NEW ORLEANS
BLACK HAND

Despite sensational American press reports (beginning in the late nineteenth century) depicting the Black Hand as an organized criminal enterprise, it was more precisely a method of extortion common to Italian-American criminal gangs. Typically, practitioners would send a letter to an intended victim, demanding that a specified sum of cash be delivered to a certain location at a certain time, and threatening beatings, torture, kidnapping, or even murder unless the target complied with the demand for money. The criminals usually decorated their letters with drawings of skulls, knives dripping blood, coffins, or other terrifying images, almost always including a human hand colored in with black ink, which gave the method its name. Not surprisingly, prominent and well-to-do Italian-Americans were most frequently targeted.

In June 1907, gangsters kidnapped seven-year-old Walter Lamana and sent his father, Pietro Lamana, a threatening letter demanding a $6,000 ransom (equivalent to about $145,000 today). But the elder Lamana refused to pay, and instead notified the police, who commenced a frantic search for the kidnapped child.

BLACK HAND KILLS KIDNAPPED CHILD

Head Severed, Body Cut Up Near New Orleans

PRISONER CONFESSES

Lays Bare Terrible Secret of Blackmailing Society.

All but Three of Gang in Parish Jail, and Lynching Is Threatened. Fear of Detection Leads to Strangling Victims – Intention Was to Return Body Piecemeal to Father, Who Refused to Pay Ransom.

New Orleans, June 23—The fate of the kidnapped Italian child, Walter Lamana, and the crime of the "Black Hand," here, was disclosed this morning, when the dead body of the missing child was found in a thick swamp, back of St. Rose, fifteen miles from New Orleans.

The boy's head had been cut off, and the body, chopped to pieces, was wrapped in a blanket and deposited in a box, which floated on a cane raft anchored in the swamp. The discovery was due to a vigorous sweating of the suspect, Ignacio Campi Sciano, in the Jefferson Parish woods, last night, by the sheriff's posse and members of the Italian vigilance committee.

After being put through a severe examination, the prisoner weakened and promised to lead the party to the place where the body of the murdered child was concealed. But for this guidance the body probably would not have been recovered. It was a tramp of nearly two miles through a dismal and almost impenetrable swamp, the slimy water of the morass reaching to the waist of the officers. The body when found, was in an advanced state of decomposition.

Child Strangled Ten Days Ago.

The child had evidently been murdered ten days ago by strangling, when the pursuit of the "Black Hand" became so hot that it looked as though the kidnappers would be run to earth. Fearing that the child knew too much and would betray them, the kidnappers murdered him Thursday, June 13, after they had him in captivity five days, and cut off the head and chopped up the body, intending to send it piecemeal to the father to prove that the "Black Hand" had kept its promise to return the child in pieces in case they did not receive the $6,000 ransom demanded, but the pursuit had lately grown so hot that the murderers dared not carry out their purpose.

Indeed, they were in such terror of arrest that they dared not return to the swamp, where the body of the child lay floating on the cane raft, to dispose of it and get rid of the dangerous evidence, for it now develops that the police and vigilance committee had struck the right trail at the very start, and had several times passed within a few yards of where the child was concealed. The trail pointed to Kenner or St. Rose as the place of his captivity, while the men arrested at the very beginning of the police investigation and afterward turned loose proved to be parties to this awful crime.

Released Suspects Were Murderers.

They were among the first arrested, but, with exception of Tony Costa, were released, as no direct evidence could be found against them. They were kept under surveillance, however, and the rearrest of Campi Sciano late last night, and his fear that he was going to be killed, finally broke the seal of silence and he told the whole story of the crime.

It was what had been supposed from the beginning. The conspiracy had been concocted in the Monteleone house, where the "Black Hand" met. Tony Costa led the boy from his home with promises of candy, and he and the barber, Charamonte, threw the child in the closed wagon on Saturday, two weeks ago. The boy was gagged and bound, driven through the streets of New Orleans at night and fifteen miles up the river, by Stefano Gianduza, and delivered by him to Campi Sciano at St. Rose. Here, Gianduza, Campi Sciano, and Mercurio Como, nicknamed "Morte," or "Death," held the boy a prisoner for the ransom.

CRIME OF THE "BLACK HAND."

On June 13 the "Black Hand" held its meetings at Campi Sciano's house, to determine what should be done, as things were getting threatening in New Orleans. There were present Antonio Gianduza, Campi Ceiano [sic], Stefano Monfre, and Francesco Incarearietra [sic]. The men agreed that the situation was bad. Lamana would not give up the ransom they demanded, and the police were hot on their trail.

During the conference the child, who was confined in the next room, constantly cried and begged to be taken back to his parents. This annoyed the kidnappers, and Frank Incarcarletra said that these cries would sooner or later bring the police on them. The child was ordered to shut up, and not doing so, Incarcarletra ran into the room where he was confined and strangled him to death.

The body was chopped up by Gianduza and then taken to the swamp for concealment.

GANG THROWN IN JAIL.

The police continued their arrests today, raiding the Monteleone house, where they got nine more members of the "Black Hand." They include Campi Sciano and his wife, Charamonte Costa, Nicolena Gibbra, a handsome girl of twenty and mistress of Francesco Incarcarletra, who strangled the child, and who confessed she knew of all the crimes of the "Black Hand." Carmelo and Vincenzo Incarcarletra, brothers of the murderer; Angelo Monteleone, his wife, sister-in-law, father and mother-in-law; Michael Fici, and Francesco Gibbra. It is thought that the entire gang will be caught by to-morrow.

The three worst criminals have not yet been arrested. They are Incarcarletra, who strangled the boy, and Gianduza and Stefano Monfre, who cut the body in pieces.

The news of the recovery of the kidnapped boy's body caused such an excitement in the Italian quarter that a large extra force of policemen was placed there to prevent any demonstration against those who are suspected of connection with the "Black Hand," while on St. Philip street, where the Lamanas live, no one was allowed to pass except by special permit.

There were threats of lynching, but the parish prison authorities took energetic steps to prevent a repetition of the Italian lynching of 1892. Sheriff Long swore in seventy extra deputies armed with rifles, and gave notice that he would sacrifice his life before the prisoners should be taken. At the suggestion of Acting Mayor McRacken, the funeral of the murdered boy was held this afternoon, instead of tomorrow, as intended, as the sight of the dead boy's body in the Lamana home was working the Italian population up to the highest pitch of excitement, and it was deemed advisable to get rid of the corpse as soon as possible.

The funeral at the St. Louis Cathedral was attended by 2,000 persons, mostly Italians. A call for a mass meeting has been made, but the mayor has issued instructions to Chief of Police Boyle to allow no meeting or speeches which propose violence.

An immediate trial of the prisoners is demanded as the only way to quiet the excitement that the crime has aroused. The trial will be in St. Charles Parish, and the chances are that it will take place at once.

5

THE MURDER OF GRACE MAE BROWN

Chester Gillette's brutal murder of his pregnant, nineteen-year-old girlfriend Grace Mae Brown on July 11, 1906, and his subsequent trial created a nationwide sensation. Brown's short and tragic life inspired Theodore Dreiser to create the character of Roberta Alden in his novel An American Tragedy. Gillette murdered Brown, who worked with him at his uncle's skirt factory, while they were sitting in a small boat in South Bay on Big Moose Lake in New York's Adirondack Mountains. He struck her in the head with a tennis racket, whereupon she fell overboard and drowned.

The fact that Gillette was handsome and Brown beautiful and innocent no doubt added to the titillating effect of the story, and its attractiveness to the media. Gillette, age twenty-four, died in the electric chair at the state prison in Auburn, New York, on March 30, 1908.

To this day, some people maintain that the ghost of the murdered Grace Mae Brown haunts the shores of Big Moose Lake, where she met her untimely and violent end. In 1996, the television program Unsolved Mysteries aired an episode about Grace Mae Brown's murder and her alleged restless spirit wandering the shore of South Bay.

PEOPLE v. GILLETTE

No controversy throws the shadow of any doubt or speculation around the primary fact that at about six o'clock in the afternoon of

July 11, 1906, while she was alone with the defendant, Grace Brown met an unnatural death and her body sank to the bottom of Big Moose lake. But the question which is bitterly disputed, and which is of such supreme importance to this defendant, is whether this tragedy was the result of suicidal drowning or of violence inflicted by his hand under such circumstances as constituted deliberate murder. The jury, after a long and arduous trial, have adopted the latter theory, and, therefore, the serious responsibility comes to us of determining whether their conclusion is infected with any such error, either of fact or of law, as requires the judgment based thereon to be reversed and the defendant to be relieved from that sentence to the extreme penalty of the law which now hangs over him.

In pursuing the first branch of our investigation and in the discussion of the evidence for the purpose of making clear and stating our conclusions with reference to its weight and effect, it will not be possible to refer to all of the details which have been developed with such care by counsel on either side in support of his theory of guilt or innocence. All of them have received our painstaking consideration and the omission of reference to many of them is due to those limitations of reasonable length which should be imposed upon this opinion.

At the date of her death Grace Brown was about twenty years of age and the defendant was about three years her senior. The former had been brought up in a country home of an apparently simple and wholesome atmosphere, and, subject only to her relations with the defendant, she seems to have been a girl of pure character and of unusual intelligence and attractiveness. The defendant was possessed of education, of previous good character, and had had considerable experience in the world. They came together as employees in the factory of defendant's uncle in the city of Cortland, New York, and this common employment led to acquaintance and intimacy, and finally to the seduction, and three or four months before her death to the pregnancy of the deceased by the defendant. The defendant largely screened this association from observation, and in public sought the society of young ladies belonging to what would be regarded as a more pretentious social grade than that to which decedent belonged.

In the latter part of June, evidently by pre-arrangement and with the expectation that the defendant soon would join her, the deceased left the factory and went to her father's home not far from Cortland. While there several letters passed from her to him and two or three from him to her. The great body of the former is filled with expressions of affection for defendant and with pathetic references to her physical and still greater mental distress caused by her condition; with references to their coming trip and what manifestly were preparations for marriage; with complaints at defendant's lack of affection and consideration and his pursuit of pleasure elsewhere and his failure to write to her more frequently; with entreaties that he should soon come to her, and doubts whether he would come as he had promised, followed by expressions of contrite sorrow for her distrust of him; and finally with very significant statements that if he did not come to her she would return to him at Cortland.

Finally on the evening of July 8th the defendant went to a neighboring railroad station where the next morning he was joined by the deceased; thence they journeyed to Utica where they stayed that night; thence the next morning to Tupper lake in the Adirondacks where they stayed that night, the next morning retracing their course to Big Moose lake, and thus reaching the spot where was to be enacted the closing scene of their unhappy association. This journey must have been planned with the theory, genuine of course on the part of the woman, that it would lead to marriage. It could have presented no other reasonable or lawful purpose. The time had passed when desire would prompt such a trip as the cover or opportunity for mere illicit enjoyment. A condition existed which only could be relieved in a legitimate way by marriage and the defendant has testified that at that time he loved the deceased and intended to marry her.

Yet every significant step taken by him seems to have led away from this consummation. At all times when he was in the neighborhood or presence of those who knew him he concealed his companionship with the deceased, and at Utica and Tupper lake where he stayed with her as his wife he registered both under assumed names and from fictitious residences, and the final registry made at Big Moose lake which gave correctly the name and residence of the deceased, still utilized a false name and place of residence for himself. And while he was thus carefully suppressing the facts of identity and companionship he was arranging through social engagements with young lady acquaintances and otherwise to be present a few days later at certain pleasure resorts, publicly and undisguised.

From these circumstances, the People argue with much force that at the time when defendant started out on the journey he did not intend to marry the deceased; that he did not purpose during the latter days of the week openly to acknowledge a relationship which he was so carefully concealing during the first days, and that, therefore, already he must have planned to rid himself of its embarrassments. At least it is manifest that during those days when they journeyed back and forth he was unready and unwilling to solve their difficulties by the lawful remedy of marriage.

Shortly after arrival at Big Moose the defendant engaged a row boat and alone with the decedent started out on the lake. Some of the incidents which attended the setting out on this trip are treated as of great importance by the district attorney and we think properly so. While an article of decedent's wearing apparel was left in a conspicuous place in the hotel from which they started, defendant gathered up and took with him all of his property, including an umbrella, an overcoat and a heavy suit case upon which he carried a tennis racket which became an article of much importance on the trial. We do not think that the evidence fairly establishes any legitimate explanation of this latter conduct, and we are forced to the conclusion urged by the People that the defendant was then planning such a termination of the boat ride that he would not desire to return to the hotel and, therefore, was taking with him all of his possessions.

The two people were seen on the lake at various times during the afternoon and finally towards its close were observed going toward a secluded portion of the lake where subsequently the tragedy occurred, the defendant rowing and the decedent sitting in the stern of the boat, and soon after and at about the time when death was happening and from the direction where it was happening a sound was heard which was described as a woman's scream.

After the death the defendant went on shore and taking his possessions with him struck through the woods to a road with which it is claimed he had become familiar and journeyed on foot and by steamboat to another resort of the Adirondacks near that at which as before stated he had planned to be the last of the week. As he went, he carefully hid his tennis racket in the woods. He became a guest of the hotel under his own name and there and in that neighborhood spent the following two days after the manner of an ordinary summer tourist, showing no outward signs of distress and giving no information of what had happened. Upon the following morning he was taken into custody.

The next day after the tragedy the boat was found floating bottom side up and the body of the decedent was recovered from the lake.

Of the facts thus far stated most are undisputed and all are established in our judgment beyond any reasonable doubt whatever. And now with the light which they shed upon it we will revert to the crucial question, What was the cause of Grace Brown's death? and that leads us to an examination of the condition of her body as it was disclosed by the autopsy performed July 14th by five physicians who were sworn as witnesses.

According to their testimony there were found on her head and face many marks of violence, especially there being evidence of a blow near the left eye sufficient to cause blindness and of a blow on the side of the head three inches above the ear of sufficient severity to cause unconsciousness even if not more serious consequences, and it is the theory of the prosecution that these wounds were inflicted by the defendant in the boat with the tennis racket and thereafter the body thrown into the water.

The accuracy and completeness of this autopsy and the candor and truthfulness of these doctors were assailed with unflinching vigor and with much ability on the trial by the learned counsel for the defendant. He sought to minimize the evidence of violence and to make the witnesses admit that there were present all of the prominent signs of drowning, thus combating the People's theory and sustaining the defendant's theory of suicide. We think that he failed of success. It may be admitted that at times on cross-examination the answers of witnesses were unsatisfactory and that in the form in which questions were put they were compelled to admit the presence of signs incident to drowning, this latter evidence many times when occasion offered being modified to the effect that such signs as were actually found in this body might result from death in other ways or from the embalming which had been performed. But aside from this, through the examination of these witnesses as an entirety, there runs constant, consistent and convincing evidence that the decedent bore upon her head the marks of violent blows. In the statement compiled from the notes of the autopsy within sixteen days after the death and before witnesses, even if they were willing, could intelligently prepare for this trial, we find this concluding statement: "From the findings of the autopsy the cause of death was primarily concussion, followed by syncope and then asphyxiation."

This testimony to the presence of marks of violence is no expression of opinion or theory. It deals with actual, visible conditions. The witnesses either saw what they describe or else with wholesale and wicked perjury they are attempting to sacrifice a human life by pretending to describe that which they did not see. We cannot adopt the latter view, and when we reject it and reach the conclusion that the body bore proof of external wounds, we are led directly and irresistibly to the next conclusion as to the authorship of those wounds. No reasonable theory sustains the possibility of their infliction after death, and no reasonable theory accounts for their infliction before death save by the hand of the defendant.

And again, when we reach this second conclusion, we are necessarily driven to the third and last one. If in those final moments whose events were seen by no living eye save that of the defendant himself, he was beating the head of Grace Brown, there is no room for conjecture about the quality and intent of his acts, and it becomes a matter of small consequence whether he thus wounded her to insensibility or worse, or whether he flung her still partly conscious into the water, there for a brief period to maintain a feeble struggle for life and thus produce those signs of drowning whose presence is so earnestly asserted by counsel.

Thus far we have tested the People's case almost entirely by the weight of their own evidence. But limited as we are to a choice between two theories of the decedent's death, the one advanced by the People is strengthened in our minds, if that were necessary, by the improbability and apparent untruthfulness of the one offered by the defendant, and to a consideration of which we now turn.

He testifies that shortly before her death he and the decedent commenced a discussion of their situation, and after a while he said in substance that he would communicate it to her parents; that they could not keep on as they were, and that thereupon she stated, "Well, I will end it here," and jumped into the lake; that after some ineffectual efforts to rescue her, and without any cry for help he went on shore and gathering up his property and without informing any of the cottagers or hotel guests on the lake of the accident, he proceeded to Eagle Bay and Arrowhead, as already stated, where he spent two days in various amusements, still giving no information of what had happened. So that by this evidence, offered by the defendant himself as the only innocent explanation of what transpired, we see him emerging from this catastrophe where he had made no outcry for help, and with apparent composure turning in other directions and to other pursuits while he left the body of the woman, whom he says he loved better than any one else and intended to marry, lying unrecovered and unsought at the bottom of the lake.

And when we have passed beyond the impressive unnaturalness of some of the principal features of this account, we encounter much evidence which still further impeaches its truthfulness. According to the People's witnesses there were several, and, by the admission of the defendant himself, some statements with reference to the tragedy made by him after his apprehension widely at variance with his present testimony. There was no satisfactory explanation of the dry condition of the suit case which he had taken in the boat, or of the condition of his clothes, or of the completely overturned boat with the decedent's cape lying on top of it. And in addition to these inherent deficiencies and improbabilities of his evidence there are repeated contradictions by a large number of witnesses who apparently had no interest in telling anything but the truth.

While incomplete in respect to minor details this summary of the evidence is sufficient for the purposes of this opinion, and as a basis for the statement of our convictions with respect to the merits of the prosecution.

We are mindful at every step that this is a case of circumstantial evidence and that the only eye-witness denies that death was the result of crime. But in obedience to the most exacting requirements of that manner of proof, the counsel for the People, with very unusual thoroughness and ability, has investigated and presented evidence of a great number of circumstances for the purpose of truly solving the question of the defendant's guilt or innocence. We might think that the proof of some of these facts standing by themselves was subject to doubt by reason of unsatisfactory or contradictory evidence and that other occurrences might be so explained or interpreted as to be reconcilable with innocence.

But it is earnestly urged that material errors were committed in respect to, and upon, the trial whereby substantial rights of the accused were so prejudiced that for this reason he should be granted another opportunity to establish his innocence, and we take up the consideration of these arguments.

Independent of the competency secured for decedent's letters by reason of the fact that they were part of a correspondence which included letters from defendant also introduced in evidence, her letters were perfectly proper evidence upon the subject of motive. They forced upon his mind, after he had proposed a termination of their intimacy, a vivid realization of the fact that the decedent, distressed in body and agonized in mind as the result of his acts, was clinging to him and was looking to marriage as the only solution of her difficulties, and that while pleading that he should come to her, she was intimating at the same time in no uncertain terms that if he did not keep faith and come to her she would come to him to accomplish this. They must have suggested with irresistible force that he had arrived at a point where unless he was willing to publicly acknowledge his relations with the decedent as he never had done and permanently cement them by marriage he must escape by another way leading in a different direction and, as the People say, to the tragedy at Big Moose lake.

In conclusion, we think that no error was committed which substantially impaired defendant's rights. We believe that the adverse verdict was not the result of any of those occurrences which are criticised by his counsel and which possibly we could say might better be modified or omitted on another trial. But rather we think that it was based on the substantial features and essential character of the case which was fairly established against him, and that so long as the conduct of an accused is to be tested in such an investigation as this, by the intentions and purposes which ordinarily prompt human acts, and by the consequences which ordinarily follow them, no other result reasonably could have been expected in this case than that which has overtaken the defendant.

Judgment of conviction affirmed.

6

THE MANSFIELD WALWORTH PARRICIDE

Frank Walworth was the eldest child of historian, author, and Daughters of the American Revolution co-founder Ellen Hardin Walworth and her abusive husband, Mansfield. Mansfield apparently routinely beat his wife, even while she was pregnant. After their divorce in 1871, Mansfield continued to threaten his ex-wife, and generally to behave like what today would be considered a stalker. In June 1873, young Frank summoned his father to his New York City hotel room and shot him three times, killing him. The case garnered tremendous publicity. Frank was convicted and sentenced to life imprisonment, but after four years (thanks largely to lobbying on his behalf on the part of his mother) the governor of New York pardoned him on grounds of insanity.

THE WALWORTH PARRICIDE!

A FULL ACCOUNT OF THE ASTOUNDING MURDER BY HIS SON, WITH THE TRIAL AND CONVICTION OF HOMICIDE AND HIS SENTENCE FOR LIFE TO THE STATE PENITENTIARY AT SING SING.

THE PARRICIDE.

On the morning of Tuesday, the third day of June, 1873, the people of New York were startled by the news of one of the most remarkable murders ever perpetrated in that city. Though long accustomed to see, in the papers of almost every morning, the details of some new and unheard-of crime, such tragedies as that which marked the morning of the third of June have been so very rare that it gave rise to a general feeling of amazement, and caused an expression of horror to escape from the lips of almost every resident or sojourner in the city. In many years there has not been, in the United States at least, any very remarkable instance of a murder of a father by his son or daughter. There have been in the city of New York, within the past seven or eight years, some three or four cases of matricide, a score of uxoricides, several fratricides, and hundreds of homicides, but not one parricide — at least none that has been determined to be such.

Since the day of the Fisk murder indeed no such excitement has been seen in the city of New York over any single event. The eminence of the family, the reputation of the murdered man as an author, and the peculiarly horrifying circumstances of a son killing his own father, gave the affair an appearance of sensationalism which was justified by the facts. It was a true sensation, not simply washed, and the startling circumstances no pen could overdraw. Those who read felt that the people of New York were to be edified by another cause celebre, in which the facts were more repletely terrible than any for many years. From mouth to mouth the story passed, and was soon known all over the city. At the various hotels, in the many lobbies, little else was spoken of, and it engaged the deepest attention. In front of the Sturtevant, inquisitive crowds would occasionally collect and gaze into the empty hallway with that singularly idiotic stare which crowds possess.

Of all the crimes that shock the souls of men none has ever been held in greater abhorrence than parricide. To conceive that the offspring should become the slayer of the parent is fearful under any circumstances, but when the offense is committed with intent and knowledge, its enormity is intensified a thousand-fold. It was a crime punished by the ancients with awful rigor and held in the deepest detestation; and, according to mythological record, the culprits were delivered up to the torments of the Furies. (Edipus slew his father Laius as they chanced to meet in the way, while the son was journeying to Phocis, and the aventring Fates followed him thereafter with misfortune, disgrace, remorse, and cruel tortures to his death. Orestes, too, the son of Agamemnon and Clytemnestra, slew his mother to avenge the death of his father at her hands, and to blot, out her adulterous shame, and he likewise was tormented by the Furies, though afterward purified by the people of Argos.

In all ages the offense, considered in proportion to the aggregates of murders, has been comparatively rare, and in the majority of these instances the deed has usually been the result of anger, accident or mental aberration.

The circumstances of the murder of Mansfield Tracy Walworth by his son, Frank II. Walworth, renders this tragedy one of the most remarkable of the present or any past period of our history. At about 3 o'clock, on Monday afternoon of June 2d, a tall and slim young man, with frank and winning large blue eyes, a smooth face, fair complexion, light whiskers and refined features, and dressed in a light tweed suit, and a spring overcoat, applied to Mr. Barrett, the clerk at the Sturtevant House, for a room. He registered his name Frank II Walworth, and was allotted room No. 267 on the second floor. Afterwards he went to the house where his father was boarding, in Fourth avenue, near Fifty-fourth street. His father was not at home, the servant girl informed him, whereupon he left with her the following note:

3 o'clock.

"I want to try and settle some family matters. Call at the Sturtevant House after an hour or two. If I am not there I will leave word at the office. F. H. WALWORTH."

The servant girl promised to give the note to his father. He then left, and went back to his hotel. Later in the evening he spoke with Mr. Barrett, who had had a previous acquaintance with him, and the two young men took supper together. During the meal Walworth appeared cheerful and unconstrained. The two gentlemen conversed on ordinary topics, and both ate heartily. Mr. Walworth retired to his room early.

At a quarter past six on Tuesday morning a tall, robust gentleman, middle aged, erect and fine looking, entered the Sturtevant House and asked that his card, on which was the name Mr. M. T. Walworth, might be sent to the room of Mr. Frank II Walworth. The call boy took up the card, and after knocking twice was answered by Mr. Frank Walworth, who told him to ask the gentleman to wait, as he was not dressed. A few minutes after the call boy had descended with this message the bell of 267 rang. The call boy hastened up stairs, and on knocking at the door was told to enter. He did so, and saw Mr. Frank Walworth fully dressed, with his overcoat on, seated in a chair close by the window.

"Ask the gentleman to come up to my room," he said.

The hall boy departed, and on delivering his message, Mr. M. T. Walworth ascended the stairs accompanied by the boy, to show him the way.

The boy says that he had barely time to get down stairs and look around him when he heard the report of a pistol, followed by another report, and still another.

In a few moments Mr. Frank Walworth came running down stairs, and going to the desk said to the clerk:

"I've just shot and killed my father up stairs in my room."

The clerk was first bewildered and then horror stricken.

"Get a policeman as soon as you can, " said Walworth. "I wish to give myself up."

He then, through the telegraph office at the hotel, at once sent a dispatch to his uncle, C. Walworth, at Albany: "I have shot father; look after mother."

He then went to the Thirtieth-street police station, and advancing to the desk where Sergeant Keating was in charge, said:

"Officer, I've just shot and killed my father at the Sturtevant House."

"I'm sorry to hear it," said the Sergeant, thinking at first that the self-accuser might be insane.

The Sergeant called an officer and told him to take charge of the young man. Another officer was sent to the Sturtevant House to ascertain the truth of the story, and on his return with the dreadful confirmation, the facts were formally entered on the record. The young man delivered to the Sergeant a small Colt's five-shooter, with four of the barrels discharged.

"That," said he, "is the pistol I shot him with."

At half past ten Coroner Young and Dr. Marsh arrived, and Walworth gave the following statement in reply to the Coroner's queries:—

"I reside with my mother in Saratoga, my father having parted from her some years ago. My father is an author, and I have been studying law. I think my father is about forty-one years old, but do not know where he was born. My father has not lived with my mother since we left here three years ago, but he has repeatedly sent us threatening and insulting letters. It is only a short time ago since he threatened to shoot my mother and myself. 1 shot him because of this. Not long ago I met him in the street in Saratoga, and I then told him that if he did not keep away from us, or insulted my mother any more, I would shoot him. I also told him that there were bounds which I would not allow any man to go beyond with impunity, especially when my mother was being insulted. I went to his house yesterday and left a note for him to call on me, which he did this morning. When he came into the room I drew out a revolver and told him to promise me that he would not threaten or insult us any more, which he promised. Shortly afterward we began speaking on family; matters, and he used some very insulting language and put his hand in his pocket as though to draw out a pistol, when I shot him. He then came towards me and I fired three other shots at him. When I fired the last shot He had me by the collar. I only regret this on account of the effect it will have on my family. I would like Judge Barbour to know this, as he was interested in the case before."

When he had answered the Coroner's questions Walworth sent the following dispatch to Chicago:

M. I. Hardin, La Salle street, Chicago:
I Shot father this morning.
F. H. WALWORTH.

A reporter of the New York *Sun* obtained an interview with young Walworth, and gives the following as the conversation which occurred:

Reporter — What led you to this dreadful crime?

Walworth — Family troubles. It's been going on for some time, and the story is a long one.

Reporter — When did you come to the city ?

Walworth — I left Saratoga yesterday, and arrived here at a quarter of three in the afternoon.

Reporter — Excuse my asking the question (here the prisoner looked hard at the reporter and smiled. His smile is very sweet), but did you come here with the intention — why did you come here?

Walworth — I came here to do what I have done.

Reporter — When you arrived here what did you do first?

Walworth — I went straight to my father's boarding-house, on Fourth avenue, near Fifty-second street.

Reporter — You did not find your father in?

Walworth — No; but I had prepared a note, which I left for him.

Reporter — When your father entered your room this morning what passed between you ?

Walworth — I took out my pistol and pointed it at him. I said, "I want you to promise that you will not threaten to shoot, me or my mother any more."

Reporter — What did he answer?

Walworth — He said, "I will promise not to do so."

Reporter — What did you do then?

Walworth — I said, "Will you promise that you won't insult me or my mother any more? In the past you have done it with impunity, but you cannot do it any more."

Reporter — And what was the reply?

Walworth — He said, "I won't trouble you any more." Then I said, "You have broken your promises many times before. I am determined you shall keep them this time. Then I shot him.

Reporter — Did he offer to defend himself?

Walworth — The last shot I fired he was close up to me.

The venerable Judge Barbour was holding a court in the Superior Court, No. 2, when one of the counsel stepped up to him and informed him of the killing of Mansfield Tracy Walworth by his son. Judge Barbour immediately gave way to an emotion he could not control. He leaned his head on the desk for a few moments and then said:

"Gentlemen, we will adjourn the Court for to-day."

He then tottered down the steps, so that he had to be helped out of the court room. He immediately took a coach, and, going in search of ex-District Attorney Garvin, went in his company to the Sturtevant House, where he asked for the "boy." When told that he was a prisoner at the Twenty-ninth precinct station house he asked where it was, and immediately repaired there. He entered the police station at one o'clock, accompanied by ex-District Attorney Garvin.

After a few words with Captain Burden, they were admitted to the prisoner's cell. Judge Barbour merely looked at the prisoner and immediately quitted the cell without speaking. He walked up and down the station while Mr. Garvin was conversing with the prisoner. Mr. Garvin was occupied with the prisoner nearly half an hour.

Mr. William A. Beach, while in Court in the morning, also received a telegram from Saratoga asking him to take the case of Frank H. Walworth in charge, and await the arrival of his mother, Mrs. Ellen Harden Walworth, who was expected to arrive in New York in the evening.

Soon after the interview with Mr. Garvin, Frank Walworth was removed to the Tombs. Officer Malony, who went with him, asked him several questions in regard to the murder, but he refused to say anything. He smoked his segar and spoke about the squares and streets which they passed and his having forgotten most of their names.

"I have seen a great many murderers," the officer told a *Herald* reporter, "But I never saw one who was so cool. He was just as much excited as you are now."

Walworth reached the prison between half past two and three o'clock. He was attired in a suit of light colored spring clothing, and had also a spring overcoat of a light color and texture. He had none of the appearances of a prisoner.

"You might say he came down here himself," said a keeper. "He walked in free and quiet in manner. There was no excitement about him, and I tell you it's a rare thing to see a man come in here as easy and offhanded as he did."

The prisoner was duly registered by the clerk at the desk, and in a minute afterward passed through the grated doors which were to shut him out from the world. He passed with a quick, thoughtless pace through the prison yard, walked into the main prison building and the clanking iron door that leads up to the first iron gallery in the corridor was opened for him. In two minutes more the door of cell No. G7 was opened to him, and he stepped inside without any hesitation, being obliged to stoop as he entered in consequence of the lowness of the doorway. This cell is on the north corner of the corridor, on the rear or Elm street side, and was furnished simply with a cot and stool, the bed being provided with the ordinary prison clothing. The door was then closed on him.

After an interval of about an hour Walworth was removed to cell No. 44, in the southern wing of the corridor, but on the same tier.

This brought him into the neighborhood of the notables who occupy "Murderers' Row," and his fellow residents on the same block of habitations were Sharkey, Scannel, King, and some other subjects of sanguinary fame. In this cell also the furniture was of the same plain description.

When left alone Walworth took off his his light overcoat and sat down on the miserable bed, alone with his thoughts. Up to six o'clock he sat on the bed, thinking deeply, but in no wise depressed in spirits, he made no requests to the prison officials for food or extra pharaphernalia, two candles being the only things furnished him.

Shortly before six o'clock a reporter wrote a series of eight questions to the prisoner, which were conveyed to him by one of the keepers, with a request that, if unobjectionable, he would make either written or verbal reply.

When the keeper presented the questions, together with the reporter's personal card, Walworth was seated on the bed. Without rising he listened to the keeper's explanation of his visit, then took the paper, read the questions and the name on the card, and handed them back to the keeper saying:

"Will you please tell him that I cannot answer any questions, as I am advised by my counsel not to hold any communication with any one."

AT THE STURTEVANT HOUSE.

Immediately after the shooting, the greatest excitement prevailed in the Sturtevant House. The room adjoining that in which the tragedy was enacted was occupied by Mr. Morehead. He was aroused by a shot, instantly followed by a shriek of murder — a shriek so loud and terrific that it chilled and almost paralyzed him. A second shot and a second shriek, not loud but full of appalling agony, rang out and echoed through the corridor. A third shot startled the horrified listeners — for by this time a score of guests stood at their open doors with bleached faces and quaking forms. Then there was a heavy thud and silence!

Soon the door of No. 267 was opened, and a young man, wearing a light overcoat and Alpine hat, stepped into the corridor, closed the door after him, and rushed toward the staircase, down which he disappeared. The alarmed guests re-entered their rooms, and dressed hurriedly.

As soon as the young man reached the clerk's desk and uttered the words, "I've shot and killed my father," the night watchman, the steward, and the bell boy rushed up stairs, entered the chamber, and catching one glimpse of the horrible truth precipitately retired.

The watchman hastened to Mr. Louis Leland's room and aroused him, informing him that a man was shot in 267, but that he still breathed. Mr. Leland told the man to run forthwith for Hrs. Childs and Mulford.

On Mr. Leland's descending he went, accompanied by the watchman, to the fatal room. Mr. Morehead joined them, and pushing open the door, Mr. Leland entered, followed by Mr. Morehead. The two men stood with suppressed breath and whitened lips, gazing first at the awful spectacle at their feet and tlum at each other with mute horror. The watchman grasped the door with his trembling hand, and fastened his distended eyes upon the hideous sight.

There, stretched out upon the floor, with the head against the washstand, lay the lifeless form of a strong, hale, handsome man, in the prime of life. One hand was thrown over his forehead, the other lay by his side.

[An included diagram exhibited the scene of the murder, including the door to room where the murder took place, the location of the hallway, the position of the washstand and hatrack, where Walworth had stood when when the fatal shots were fired, the place where the murdered man fell with his head resting in a pool of blood, and the bed where he was placed immediately after death.]

Blood was on the face, the hands, and hair. The marble top of the washstand was covered with clotted blood, the murdered man having probably leaned upon it while his lifeblood was ebbing away. There was also a quantity of blood which had trickled down the wall. But more singular than this, there was also a quantity of blood on the opposite side of the washstand, about three feet away, where it had apparently spurted, some being congealed on the surface of the marble and a quantity being in a still liquid condition under a glass on the further side of the washstand. The soap dish was half full of blood, as was also the toothbrush dish, which had mingled with the soap into a kind of frothy foam. Where the murdered man lay, there was a large quantity of blood, probably several quarts, which had run through the carpet for a space of about two feet in diameter. A towel also lay on the floor, saturated with blood. Along the carpet over which the dead man was carried to the bed there were spots of blood. A black hat, surrounded with a three-quarter mourning band, was picked up and hung on a peg.

Dr. Mulford and Dr. Childs examined the body simply to satisfy themselves that the man was dead. They found a pistol shot wound in the right breast, another in the left breast near the heart, another in the left arm, and another under the right ear.

One of the doctors who attended on the murdered man said that when he went up stairs to room 207 [sic] he found Mr. Walworth was not yet dead. He was lying on the floor with his head on the carpet and gasping. His pulse gave one or two pulsations when the Doctor took his arm in his hand and then stopped completely. Blood was gushing from the wound in his left breast and from his arm. He died in about a quarter of a minute after the Doctor went into his room. He was shortly after placed upon the bed. The Doctor says that when young Walworth was brought into the room he reported the conversation between him self and father as follows:—

Walworth the Son (standing before his father) — You have again written to my mother threatening both her life and my own. Will you solemnly promise never to make such threats again?

Walworth the Father — I do make that promise.

Walworth the Son — You have also repeated the insult made to my mother. Do you promise to never use insulting language to my mother again?

Walworth the Father — I do make such a promise.

Walworth the Son — (drawing the revolver and pointing it at his father) — You have made that promise before, and I do not believe you. You shall never have the opportunity of doing so again.

And then the firing took place, without a moment's interval of hesitation.

When Coroner Young arrived at the hotel the undertaker was sent for. At about ten o'clock the undertakers' wagon, from Senior & Benedict's, in Carmine street, drove up to the door of the hotel. The large ice coffin was then taken up stairs and the body was speedily placed in it, just as it was. The whole thing did not take more than fifteen minutes, when the box, with its dead freight, was again placed in the

wagon, which rapidly drove away. When in the undertakers' establishment it was disrobed and washed and placed in a preserving coffin.
The face bore, an expression of great suffering; the lips were slightly
parted, and the wound in the forehead plainly showed the terrible
death he had died.

7

LAURA BULLION AND THE WILD BUNCH

Laura Bullion (1876–1961) was a female outlaw of the Old West, best known for her occasional association with members of the Wild Bunch of outlaws and train robbers, whose fame was renewed by the 1969 film Butch Cassidy and the Sundance Kid *starring Paul Newman and Robert Redford. At the time of her November 6, 1901, arrest in St. Louis (partly recounted here) police said she was a prostitute. She also had banknotes in her possession that were part of the loot from the Great Northern Train Robbery of July 3, 1901.*

STOLEN BANK NOTES REPRESENTING $7,000 IN SATCHEL OF BANDIT'S WOMAN COMPANION.

St. Louis Police Are Fast Weaving a Web About the Suspected Montana Train Robber Arrested Tuesday Night—Admissions From Woman Already Point to Guilt of Pair—Complete Confession May Be Secured Leading to Arrest of Others and Recovery of More Plunder.

"BUTCH CASSIDY," THE THIRD MEMBER OF THE GANG, THOUGHT TO HAVE BEEN HERE.

In "John Arnold," the prisoner arrested Tuesday night on suspicion of being implicated in the robbery of the Great Northern express at Wagner, Mont., July 3, Chief of Police Kiely and Chief of Detectives Desmond are confident they have Harvey Logan, alias Harry Longuebaugh [sic], alias Harry Alonzo. The prisoner answers exactly the photograph and description of Logan, sent broadcast immediately after the robbery, for whose arrest a reward of $5,000 has been offered.

Laura Bullion, a companion and possible confederate of Logan, was arrested yesterday morning at the Laclede Hotel, just as she was on the point of taking her departure. She had been living there since last Friday, when she arrived there with a male companion, said by the police to be Logan, who registered the couple as "J. W. Rose and wife, Vicksburg, Miss." "Mrs. Rose" at first made a show of indignation when arrested, but later consented to accompany the officers to the Four Courts. Her baggage, consisting of a trunk and a satchel, was also taken there.

Chief of Police Kiely took "Mrs. Rose" in hand early yesterday morning for examination, and Chief of Detectives Desmond took Logan into his "sweat box." The two Chiefs spent the entire day and evening endeavoring to elicit a confession or, at least, some damaging admissions from the prisoners, but with very unsatisfactory results until a late hour last night, when the woman made admissions, which, the Chief believes, will materially assist them in rounding up the remaining members of the gang and recovering much of the stolen money.

When "Mrs. Rose's" trunk was searched in the Chief's office, nothing of an incriminating nature was found. It contained masculine and feminine apparel, toilet articles, bric-a-brac and odds-and-ends. A pocket dictionary, however, which she said belonged to Logan, contained something which interested the police. On the inside of the cover was pasted a newspaper clipping containing an account of the capture of Sam Ketchum, a train robber, in Wyoming on July 19, 1900. Ketchum had a broken arm, shattered by a ball, and died a month later. On the fly leaf, in pencil was the following memorandum: "45.500, 51,000. H. in W. Wyoming," followed by a series of initials. Chief Desmond believes this memorandum refers to the booty obtained in the Great Northern express robbery, and that "H. in W. Wyoming" means that a portion of the spoils is hid in some Wyoming town.

STOLEN BANKNOTES FOUND IN "MRS. ROSE'S" SATCHEL.

"Mrs. Rose's" satchel contained $7,000 of the stolen banknotes, in denominations of $10 and $20. The notes are unsigned. On her person was found $600 of the same notes, to all of which had been forged the name "J. W. Smith" as president of the bank on which they were issued.

Logan is one of the most uncommunicative prisoners Chief Desmond has ever handled. He is 6 feet tall, weighs 200 pounds, and possesses a powerful frame and the active, alert bearing of an athlete. He is a good-looking chap, though dark, sullen face and his wicked eye, when in surly mood, rob his features of much of their attraction. All together, he is a fair type of what is known as a "dangerous man."

Although the Chief "sweated" him continuously from early morning till midnight and used his most persuasive methods, he elicited little information. Logan was sullen and replied, when at all, mostly in monosyllables. His photograph and Bertillon measurements were taken yesterday morning, and will be sent to the authorities at Wagner and other Western cities.

Logan persisted in declaring that his name was John Arnold, even when confronted with his photograph, taken from the Bertillon bureau, containing a record of scars and blemishes which tallied with those found on his body. He refused to tell anything of his past history, or to give an account of his whereabouts since last July. When asked where he obtained the $483 found upon him, he said he had won it in a gambling game in a town in Mississippi. Later, when confronted with the unsigned banknotes found in the woman's satchel, he acknowledged they were his, but denied having given them to the woman. He said the satchel found with her belonged to him. He said he had known the woman a couple of months, having picked her up in Hot Springs.

WOMAN GETS TANGLED UNDER FIRE OF QUESTIONS.

"Mrs. Rose" made several conflicting statements when first questioned, and later, when detected in them, acknowledged that she had lied. She first said she met Logan in Hot Springs two months ago, and had been with him since, coming to St. Louis via Nashville and Memphis. Later she ad-mitted that this was a lie, and that she had been a companion of the train-robbing gang for years. Her real name, she said, is Laura Bullion, and her former home in Knickerbocker, Tex., where she had lived with her grandparents. Mr. and Mrs. E. B. Fyler. The Fylers, she said, are now living on a ranch near Douglas Post Office, Ariz.

The woman declared that the bank notes found in her purse and in the satchel had been given her by Logan. She said she had forged the name of "J. W. Smith" to the notes found upon her and Logan, purporting to be the name of the president of the Montana bank. Later, when the discrepancy between her own handwriting and that on the bills was shown her, she confessed that Logan had forged the signatures.

When Chief Kiely finished his final examination of the woman at midnight and sent her back to the holdover to steep, he appeared to be in a satisfied frame of mind, indicating that he had succeeded in obtaining some information of value to the department. When asked to give out the result of the woman's statement, he replied: "I can't tell you anything just now. Later on I may do so. I have learned some things which I believe will be of material benefit to the authorities. If it were to make it public, it would be of material benefit only to the rest of the gang, and thus the ends of justice would be defeated."

CHIEF DESMOND GIVES OUT NO INFORMATION.

Chief Desmond was equally reticent in imparting the results of his examination of Logan. It was evident from the Chief's demeanor, however, that he had received information which might assist him in rounding up the other two train robbers.

"How about "Butch" Cassidy?" he was asked. "Isn't it a fact that he was in town with Logan and the woman?"

"We're looking that part of the case up now," was the reply.

"Isn't 'Mrs. Rose' the companion of Cassidy, and not of Logan?"

"I don't think so."

"Didn't she acknowledge as much to-day?"

"Oh, she's been an associate of train robbers for years," was the reply. "You can't believe half of what she says."

Telegrams were sent by Chief Desmond yesterday to the Chief of Police of St. Paul, Pinkerton of Chicago, President J. J. Hill of the Great Northern, Chief of Police of Wagner, Mont., and to the presidents of the National Bank of Bellefouche, S. D., robbed July 26, 1897, and the National Bank of Montana at Helena, notifying them of the arrests, and informing them that Bertillon measurements and pictures would follow.

As soon as the identification is complete the prisoners, or Logan at least, will be taken back to Montana for trial. Train robbery is a capital offense in that state, and if Logan is convicted he may be hanged. If he succeeds in defeating this charge, the United States Government officials will prosecute him for forging the signatures to the bank notes.

One of the most important features which developed in yesterday's examination of the prisoners and their recent movements is the fact, which is almost certainly established, that George Parker, alias "Butch" Cassidy, another of the train robbers, was in the city as late as Tuesday night, and presumably in communication with Logan and the woman. Two of the operatives of a local private detective agency declared yesterday that they are confident they saw "Butch" Cassidy on the downtown streets within less than a week, and one of the chief operatives of the United States Secret Service declares that he saw Cassidy Tuesday night and shadowed him for more than an hour, in and out of the downtown saloons and cafes.

The story related by this Secret Service operative to a *Republic* reporter is an interesting one, and may serve to throw some light on the conflicting statements made to the Chief of Police by the woman yesterday. This operative had in his possession one of the circulars containing photos and descriptions of the robbers. and when he learned Tuesday that a suspect had worked off some of the stolen money on Barnett, he obtained from the latter an accurate description of the man, and then started out to do a little man-hunting on his own responsibility.

CASSIDY AND LOGAN WORE THE SAME DISGUISE.

While making the rounds of the downtown saloons he learned that a stranger had visited many of them, and was spending money freely and changing money freely and changing bills frequently. Within the course of an hour the detective found his man. The suspect tallied accurately with the description given by Barnett as to his clothing and jewelry, but he was a blonde, with light hair and a light, short, stubby mustache, whereas Barnett's customer had black hair and black mustache. Later, the detective learned that the clothing worn by his suspect is the exact counterpart in cut, texture and quality as that worn by Logan, and both affected the same style of rings, tie pin and watch chain.

The fact that the man he was shadowing was a blonde, instead of a brunette, puzzled the detective, and he followed him for an hour without attempting to have him arrested. As he watched him narrowly whenever occasion offered, it suddenly dawned on him that the man was "Butch" Cassidy. Cassidy has a peculiar, vicious face, which the operative said, once seen would not soon be forgotten, and this was the face of the man he was shadowing. The detective supposed Cassidy was out West, but with this proof confronting him, he abandoned his shadowing tactics and went to the Four Courts to apprise the Chief of what he had learned. When he reached there the officers, had just arrived with Logan in custody, and in the ensuing excitement and bustle no action was taken to apprehend "Cassidy."

"I am positive," said the Secret Service man, that Cassidy, Logan and the woman came here together. The police are under the impression that it was Logan who registered at the Laclede with the woman as "J. W. Rose and wife," but I believe they are wrong, for two reasons. Logan was stopping at the Lindell, as the detectives learned Tuesday night. He hired a hack to take him out for a 'time,' and went up to the Tenderloin. Why should he do that when he had this woman at the Laclede? Criminals of his class are usually faithful to the women who share their fortunes. It is my belief that it was Cassidy who lived with the woman at the Laclede, and Logan took a room at the Lindell, so they would not be seen together.

"You remember down in Nashville last October, when some of the stolen bank notes were passed, a woman was arrested and is now in jail there? That was Logan's companion, and he quietly got away when she was arrested. The man who had the desperate fight with the seven policemen down there, in which he made his escape after killing two bloodhounds, was 'Butch Cassidy.' Logan rejoined 'Cassidy' and the woman at some point later, and the three came to this city to get rid of some of the money.

STORY OF THE CAPTURE READS LIKE A STORY BOOK.

The capture is one of the most important made in this city in many years and reflects credit on the men immediately engaged in it. To Detective Al Guion must be awarded the greatest need of praise, since it was largely due to his keenness that the quarry was located and to his coolness, judgment and presence of mind that the capture was a bloodless one. Had it not been for his quick wit the members of the Police Department would, as Detective Brady dryly remarked later, "be now buying floral emblems for some of Bill Desmond's sleuths."

Immediately after the teller of the Mechanics' National Bank had refused to accept the four $20 banknotes tendered by Max Barnett, as related in yesterday's Republic, the teller telephoned to John E. Murphy, United States Secret Service Agent, who lost no time in responding. When he learned that the bills tendered were part of the proceeds of the train robbery, Murphy told the teller he had no jurisdiction in the case, as the Government was not a sufferer. He, however, called on Mr. Hoffman, the Pinkertons' local agent, and informed him of the matter. Hoffman, armed with the pictures of the three train robbers, went to Barnett's pawnshop and showed them to Barnett. Barnett unhesitatingly picked out Logan's picture as that of the man who had given him the bank notes in payment for a watch. He gave also an accurate description of the customer's clothing, jewelry, etc., to the smallest detail.

At Murphy's suggestion Hoffman telephoned to Chief Desmond asking him to send a squad of good men down to his office, as he had a big case on hand requiring immediate attention. Four men were sent down posthaste. The nature of the case was outlined and the accurate description and photograph of the suspect were placed in their possession.

Logan is 36 years old. He was born In Dodson, Mo., and went West at an early age and became a cowboy and "rustler" and, later, one of the most notorious criminals in the Northwest. He is known as a bank robber, train robber, horse and cattle thief, hold-up and murderer. His residence just before the Great Northern express robbery was Landusky, Mont., where he killed Pike Landusky Christmas Day, 1894. He is accused of the robbery of a Union Pacific train at Wilcox, Wy., in June, 1899. When pursued by a posse and overtaken he shot and killed Sheriff Joseph Hazen of Converse County, Wyoming.

Logan's two confederates in the Great Northern express robbery were George Parker, alias "Butch" Cassidy," and O. C. Hanks, alias "Deaf Charley."

On October 3 Logan and a woman known as Annie Williams attempted to pass some of the stolen money in Nashville, Tenn., and the woman was arrested and is still in jail. Logan escaped. On October 27 Cassidy also attempted to pass some of the notes in Nashville, was detected, and after a desperate struggle, in which he fought his way through seven policemen and detectives, made a sensational escape. Nothing has been heard of Hanks since the robbery.

VIGIL IS ESTABLISHED OVER THE TENDERLOIN.

The seasoned thief-takers, knowing the habits of criminals of Logan's class, deduced that the suspect had not purchased the watch for personal adornment. They argued that he had purchased it either to present to some woman who had caught his passing fancy or to dispose of it to another pawnbroker, thus obtaining "safe" money for the dangerous banknotes he had disposed of. Accordingly, their plan of action was quickly mapped out when they reported to Chief Desmond. The regular force of detectives assigned to watch pawnshops and secondhand stores was detailed to make a thorough inspection of every such place in the city, and Detectives Guion, Shevlin, Brady, John McGrath, Jim Burke and George Williams were assigned to keep a close watch on the resorts in the Tenderloin district.

The detectives had been in the Tenderloin only a short while when they learned that a stranger answering the description of Barnett's customer had been changing $20 bills freely during the afternoon, and they re-doubled their watchfulness.

At 11 o'clock Detective Guion, standing at Twenty-first and Chestnut streets, saw a hack drive westward rapidly containing one occupant—a man. As the hack passed under the glare of the electric light the officer got a fair but fleeting look at the man through the glass panels. He tallied closely with the description of the man wanted, and Guion immediately gave chase to the vehicle. His brother officers were scattered up and down Chestnut street from Nineteenth to Jefferson avenue, and he had no time to communicate with them. The hack was soon out of sight in the darkness, but Guion, by making inquiry, learned that it had stopped at a resort near Twenty-third street. When he reached this address he found that his man had left, after changing a banknote, re-entered the hack and driven east. Believing the suspect was making for Union Station, Guion hot-footed down there, but careful inquiry convinced him that the hack had not been there. Then he took the back track, and learned that the hack had stopped at a resort on Twentieth between Locust and Olive. When be reached there his quarry had disappeared, after changing another banknote.

ARNOLD CAPTURED BY A CLEVER RUSE.

Guion worked carefully back to Twenty-first and Chestnut streets, and reached there just as the hack drove up in front of No. 2025. The suspect went into the house, and reappeared a few minutes later. Then he and the driver went into Manley's saloon on the corner and had a drink. Guion sauntered in casually after them and got a good look at the man he had been chasing. That look stifled all his doubts. He knew then that he was on the right trail, as the description furnished by Barnett fitted the man before him perfectly in every detail.

Without betraying a hint of his identity or suspicions. Guion allowed the man to depart unmolested. Then he sent runners out in search of his brother officers, and as soon as the suspect entered his hack he jumped on the seat of another hack across the street and ordered the driver to follow the other. The first hack stopped a few yards down the street, and the occupant entered the house No. 2025. Guion alighted and hid in the shadows across the street, awaiting the arrival of the other detectives. They came, hastening cautiously, a few moments later.

"I've got him, boys," said Guion quietly.

"Where?" was the ejaculated response.

"Over there in No. 2025," was the reply. "Get ready for quick work."

The six filed across the street and were admitted by the negro maid. In answer to a question, she said the suspect and the hack driver were in the rear parlor. Then came a brief whispered parley among the officers in the hall, as to the best method of effecting the capture without letting the man inside, whose desperate nature was well known, get the "drop" on them. The problem was solved by Guion.

CLEVER RUSE PREVENTED FIGHT IN MAKING CAPTURE.

"We'll never get him standing here." he said. "There's only one way to get him—go in after him. Get ready."

With his hand on the knob of the parlor door, his revolver in his coat pocket, Guion was about to push the door open, when the woman of the house appeared from a back room.

"Here," she cried. "You can't go in there; there's a gentleman in there."

Like a flash an inspiration came to Guion. Simulating to the life the manner and speech of a drunken man, he loudly declared, as he opened the door: "What the ---- We're all good fellows—hic—and we've got money to spend."

As he uttered these words in a maudlin drawl and reeled through the doorway he saw the suspect seated in a large easy chair near a window at the further end of the parlor. The hack driver sat near him. The suspect looked up, but made no move as he saw Guion reeling unsteadily toward him, evidently believing the intruder was really out on a drunken lark. An instant later, as he caught sight of the other jive detectives crowding into the room, he scented danger and made a quick movement with both hands to his hip pockets.

Quick as he was, he was too late. Like a flash Guion threw himself upon him, pinioning his right hand with his right and securing his 45-caliber with the left, all in one motion. In another second McGrath grasped his left hand as it rested on the butt of another 45-caliber revolver in the other pocket. Shevlin reached over and drew the revolver out, and the prisoner was helpless. A pair of handcuffs was produced, and within two minutes from the time the officers entered the house their man was ready for the holdover.

SEARCH OF PRISONER REVEALS A WALKING ARSENAL.

During the entire time the suspect never uttered a word—not even an oath escaped him, but his dark eyes spoke volumes as he sat in sullen silence regarding his captors. When the officers sized up the prisoner's

6 feet of brawn and muscle and examined the heavy Colt's revolvers, they breathed a sigh of profound relief as they realised what might have happened had he obtained the slightest inkling of their presence in the house before they were upon him. Twenty-five extra cartridges were found in the pockets of his coat, evidence that he was prepared to make a desperate resistance if a chance was given him.

When taken before Acting Night Chief Boyd at the Four Courts the prisoner said his name was John Arnold, but beyond that little information was secured. He was taken down to the holdover and securely guarded, pending his examination by Chief Desmond in the morning.

*****

LAURA BULLION RELATES HER CAREER AMONG THE OUTLAWS.

Companion of Train Robbers All of Her Life, the Little Woman at the Four Courts Clung to the Man Who Had Made a Promise That He Would Give Her Protection.

BRAVE, THOUGH PRISON BARS RESTRAIN HER FROM LIBERTY.

LAURA BULLION, The woman who has spent many years among outlaws.

Laura Bullion, the companion of John Rose, alias John Arnold, alias Harvey Logan, the train robber who carne to grief at the hands of Chief Desmond's men, is not of the type of woman a person would associate in his mind as the companion of a desperate bandit. There is nothing in her manner, appearance or speech at all suggestive of the "bandit queen" of the wild and wooly regions, whose dash and daring exploits are luridly set forth in sensational dime novel literature.

The first thought that suggests itself to one's mind at first view of this frail, sallow-faced wisp of diminutive femininity sitting half hidden in one of the high-backed chairs in Chief Desmond's office is: "How in the name of common sense did big, brawny, wicked-looking John Rose, crafty and shrewd in his criminal career, come to select this woman as his companion, the sharer of his criminal secrets? And the only answer as yet set forth by the Hawkshaws, who have propounded the query is that it is a natural selection on the basis of the old theory of the affinity of extreme types.

By no stretch of the imagination could any one looking at Laura Bullion conceive of her participating in any wild night ride after a daring raid, or of engaging a posse to cover the retreat or secure the release of her mate, after the accepted manner of bandit queens in well regulated novels. On the contrary. Laura would be much more at home on the steering wear of an Arkansas plow, or piloting a potato digger, or frying flapjacks for the men folks. As for shooting, Laura says that perhaps she could shoot a revolver, but she doesn't know whether the bullet would hit "all of creation." As for her horsemanship, she says, her feats were confined to riding a roan mare to the pump in her Texas home when she was a child.

LAURA BULLION WAS REARED ON A FARM.

In truth and in fact, as gleaned from her own statements and from one of her neighbors who knew her years ago in Texas, Laura is a rather dull, spiritless country girl, a product of Arkansas, reared on a farm and possessing the meager intelligence and education common to that type whose early lives have been spent in and around small isolated villages. She is about 5 feet 2 inches tall and weighs about 90 pounds, and her appearance indicates extreme frailty. Her face is sallow and expressionless, with an entire absence of mobility save when her lips relax ever so slightly in a smile or laugh, exposing a double row of small white, even teeth. Her eyes are of a greenish yellow hue, bright enough, but without any life or expression in them even in moments of excitement. The most prominent features of her face are her prominent cheek bones and aquiline nose, suggesting a trace of Indian blood back among her ancestors. Her whole face is suggestive of dullness of intellect, which is accentuated by her drawling speech. Her voice is low and pleasant.

Such is a description of the woman whom Rose, guilty of almost every crime in the calendar, whose hands are red with the blood of at least three fellowmen, upon whose head three States have set a price, "hooked up with," to use her own vernacular.

Perhaps he was wiser in his selection than appears at first glance, because Laura, plain-featured. uneducated and uncouth, would not he tempted to mingle in society dangerous to both, or arouse suspicion by indulging in luxuries and finery above her station, whereas a handsomer and more worldly-wise companion might indulge her fancies to a point that would attract the attention of the vigilant sleuths of the law.

Although Laura has chummed with outlaws for nearly ten years and was cognizant of many of their secrets, she is not much of a raconteur on this interesting subject, and approaches it with the halting timidity of a victim of a "badger fight" pressed to tell his experience before a company of rounders.

When she was brought into Chief Desmond's office yesterday for an interview she still wore the tan dress and jacket which she had on when arrested. A man's white Fedora hat rested on her hair, the loose ends of which straggled over her brows and around her ears, and down her neck, suggesting that she had not paid much attention to her toilet. She complained of not feeling well, and the lines about her mouth and the droop of her under lip indicated that she was suffering physically. She asked the Chief's permission to change her dress, which was granted. She selected a muslin housewrap from her trunk and retired to an inner room, where she made the change. During the interview she kept the brim of her hat pulled drawn well over her eyes.

SUBMITS TO INTERVIEW WITH THE NEWSPAPER MAN.

"Well," she began, in answer to a question, "I don't know what you-all want to know about me, 'cause I've done told everything 1 know—and a heap more, I guess," she added, with a glance at chief Desmond, and a smile.

"Yes, you know you lied to us," observed chief Desmond; "now I want you to tell us the truth."

"Yes, I lied to you about some things," she said, "but that was when I was excited and didn't know what was the best to do. But I've done told you-all since then everything I know."

"Well, tell us about your connection with this man 'Rose,' and how you first met him and all about yourself," was suggested.

"Well, I'm going to tell you-all on the start," she said, "'cause I take it you're for the newspapers, that they ain't nothing blood-and-thunder about me. How I come to hook up with this man Rose was because I'd been hooked up with Bill Carver. Carver was in the business, too, and when he got shot up down Texas way his pardners kind o' thought I'd feel lonesome without Bill nor nobody to look after me, and take care of me, so Bill Cheney he brings me and Rose together, and we've been together since. That's all they is to it."

"How old are you, Laura, and where were you born?"

"I'm 25 years old, and I was born in Arkansas somewheres. I don't know whereabouts. I don't know as I ever remember my parents. They spilt up when I was a kid. The first place I remember being is down in Tom Greene County, Texas. My grand-folks lived on a ranch in Knickerbocker, Texas. That's where I got to know Bill Carver. Carver was raised on a ranch down there, and so was the Ketchum boys, Sam and Tom. I never got much schooling, 'cept a little now and then in the district school.

"Part of the time I lived out and part time I helped at home, but you-all know how it is in small country places—they ain't much for a girl to do, and when a girl ain't got no parents to look after her and tell her how to do right, she just naturally gets to running wild. I got brushed up a heap agin Bill Carver, and he sort o' took a shine to me, and me and him went to Fort Worth. I expected Bill was fixing to marry me, but nothing ever come of it. I knowed Bill had been train robbing, but he told me he'd reformed, and, as far as I know, he didn't do nothing in that line while I was with him. 'Course, he'd leave me every little while and go away for days, but I never asked him no questions.

"The Ketchum boys, they was raised around there, too, and while I knowed them, I never went with 'em none. They went up Northwest after awhile, and was killed there."

TELLS ABOUT TRAIN ROBBERY BY CARVER BOYS IN TEXAS.
"Carver and some more boys held up a train down Texas way last spring and hid out in the woods. In April Bill and Kilpatrick come out o' hiding in get some provisions and horses, they was both shot up by the Marshal and his posse. Then I was left to do by myself, and I guess some of Bill's pardners kind of felt sorry for me, and so when they got away and went up North they kept looking out for somebody who'd

take care of me. Bill Cheney, he told me so, and so one day when Bill was up to Douglass, Arizona, where my grandfolks moved, he meets this here Ross and the boys told him to bring Rose down and stake me to him. Cheney brought Rose down to Fort Worth and said, 'Laura, this is John Rose. He's a good fellow and he'll take care of you.' So we just hooked up like that, and that's all they was to it."

"Did you know he was a train-robber?"

"Well, he didn't say nothing and I didn't ask no fool questions. I'd read about the Wagner robbery, and when I saw the money Rose had, I had a kind of idea what it was I was getting into. That was about a month ago. He gave me all the money I needed, and treated me right, and I didn't care for no more. We went from there to Hot Springs and from there to Memphis, and then came to St. Louis. We didn't stop at Nashville.

8

HENRIETTA ROBINSON,
THE VEILED MURDERESS

A notorious, mysterious—and infamously unstable and paranoid—woman of means annoyed and frightened her neighbors in Troy, New York. She was known to carry a revolver everywhere, and to brandish it threateningly at a moment's notice, for any real or imagined slight. She claimed to be the victim of an ill-defined dark conspiracy, and was known to be a heavy drinker. She called herself Henrietta Robinson—but this was a pseudonym and she refused to reveal her true identity. Timothy Lanagan, one of her neighbors, ran a neighborhood store that sold groceries, and also operated a bar on the premises, where Henrietta went frequently to drink. On numerous occasions Mr. Lanagan or his wife would ask her to leave after she got into heated arguments with other customers.

On May 25, 1853, Mr. and Mrs. Lanagan and Mr. Lanagan's sister-in-law Catherine Lubee were eating at the store and invited Henrietta to join them. To repay their kindness, she claimed, Henrietta offered to buy beer for all of them. Mrs. Lanagan declined—a decision that probably saved her life. But Mr. Lanagan and Catherine drank the beer, and before long both were dead, poisoned with arsenic. There was little doubt that Henrietta was responsible, and she was soon arrested. A local pharmacist testified that he had sold her arsenic, and more was found in her home.

Throughout her trial, Henrietta insisted upon wearing a black veil, lifting it only briefly so a testifying witness could see her face. Because *there were many months of delays and postponements before the trial begant, many people assumed she had friends in high places.*

~~~~~~

THE VEILED MURDERESS.

Henrietta Robinson, better known by the *soubriquet* of the *"Veiled Murderess"* was born in Canada East, in the year 1827, where her youthful days were spent in the possession of every luxury that wealth and refined taste could furnish. All the pains that affectionate parents and experienced teachers could confer, were bestowed on her education. At the age of sixteen she was sent to a distant institution of learning, where she remained two years. During her residence at this place, she became acquainted with an accomplished and intelligent young gentleman, whom she soon loved with the whole of her ardent and impulsive heart; but he, though wealthy and of good character, was not of so exalted a rank as her parents desired for her future husband. They therefore removed her from school, thinking that absence would be the most effectual remedy for what they called her "love-sick fancy." This separation it seems in no wise lessened her attachment, as we find that a correspondence was for some time maintained by her with her lover, to whom she was so fondly attached, that she attributes her subsequent misconduct and misery to her coerced separation from him.

About one year after her return home, she was married, notwithstanding her reiterated assurances, both to her parents and to her intended husband, that her heart was irrevocably given to another—to a young lieutenant in the British army then stationed in Canada, of an aristocratic family and great wealth, with whom she shortly started for England. Soon after marriage she began to manifest bursts of passionate and undisciplined rage, which ultimately merged into periodical fits of insanity, to which she owes her present degradation. She remained with her husband (to whom she does not attach the least blame) three years, during which period she visited with him a considerable portion of Europe; he thinking that the excitement of travel might restrain her unhappy temper; but nothing could do so. Her dislike to him gradually turned into such disgust, that she determined to leave him and her two children and return to her parents in America. On her arrival at home she was received with such a torrent of reproaches and upbraidings that she left her father's house on the night of her arrival and threw herself, unprotected and almost without means, on the world.

Shortly after her leaving Canada, subsequently to the quarrel with her parents, we find her living in Troy, N. Y., under the assumed name of Henrietta Robinson, and under the (so called) protection of one whose name shall not sully these pages. A year or two passed in this manner, when the memory of her children seems to have induced her to make an effort to break the vicious bands that held her, and to return to her husband in England. Under the influence of this feeling, she left Troy clandestinely, and reached Boston, when her evil genius in the shape of her "protector" overtook her, and fatally for herself, induced her to return with him to her late residence at Troy.

Her fall seemed now to be complete, and her case hopeless to herself. During the next few years of her life, she seems to have set at defiance all outward forms of modesty and respectability, to have become addicted to the use of intoxicating liquors, and to have completely surrendered herself to the impulses of her disposition already verging towards madness. She imagined that a conspiracy was formed to rob her of life and property. The slightest provocation was resented as an insult, and she carried pistols (which she often threatened to use) in her bosom, to protect herself from imaginary assaults. In fact, reason seems at times, to have completely deserted her, for we find her attending a dance at a low grocery kept by an Irishman called Lana-gan—for the poisoning of whom she was subsequently tried—where her conduct was so improper that she was expelled from the place.

Her funds getting low, her "protector" absent, (if he had not deserted her altogether,) her mind distracted by reports that he was about to marry, seems completely to have driven away whatever rea-soning powers she had left, that we find her absolutely wandering about the streets of Troy in her night clothes, associating with drunken rowdies, invoking the aid of the police for imaginary assaults, and act-ing as only a maddened woman would. Rendered desperate and per-fectly reckless by treatment which she did not think was deserved, she now approached the climax of her evil deeds and unrestrained temper. The Troy papers of the 20th May, 1853, contained the following para-graph:—

Horrible double murder by poisoning!—The upper part of the city was thrown into a state of great excitement yesterday, by the startling report that two persons had been poisoned, and that both would probably die from the effects. Before seven o'clock, P.M., the truth was partially realized by the death of one of the victims, and at an early hour this morning by the death of the other. The supposed murderess, a Mrs. Robinson, who undoubtedly nourishes under an alias, was during the eve-ning arrested in the street, near the Mansion House, by officers Sayles and Burns, night policemen, and committed to jail. Cor-oner Boutccou was soon after called, and an inquest held over the man, and after taking some testimony, adjourned until this morning. We were unable to put the evidence before the Cor-oner, as the jury have not, as yet, rendered their verdict. The stomachs of the deceased persons have been taken charge of by him for analyzation. We give the particulars of the affair as near as we have ascertained them. We learn that the supposed murderess, Mrs. Robinson, had been in and out of the store of Mr. Lanagan, the murdered man, a number of times during yesterday, and in the forenoon wanted to borrow some money. She was refused and left, but returned in the afternoon, when she was evidently laboring under the effects of strong drink.

About one o'clock she called at the grocery for the last time, and asked for some beer. Lanagan's wife brought it into the back room, with two tumblers. Mrs. Robinson then asked for some white sugar, which was supplied in a saucer. She took the saucer and walked across the room a number of times, and then poured out the beer into the tumblers, and put the sugar into it. She invited those present to drink. Timothy Lanagan and the murdered girl, Catharine Lubee, both partook of the beverage—Mrs Lanagan refused. The girl remarked immediately after drinking it, that it did not taste good, and asked the woman, Robinson, what she had put into it. "Nothing but what will do you good; do not spit it out." The girl was soon after taken sick, and died at five o'clock this morning. The man died at the hour above mentioned. He left his store to go down street soon after drinking the fatal draught, was taken ill on the way, but managed to get back home, where he soon breathed his last.

Timothy Lanagan kept a grocery store on the corner of River and Rensselaer Streets, was 37 years of age, and has left a wife and four small children. The girl, Catharine Lubee, was unmarried, and aged about 25 years. She resided in Albany, but had been on a visit here some weeks. Her acquaintance with Mrs. Robinson, who pretended to be her friend, had been short. We learn, also, that no quarrel had existed between Mrs. Robinson and Lanagan, except some slight words that had passed on his refusing to give her liquor on a previous occasion. Mrs. Robinson, alias_____, the supposed murderess, lived nearly opposite Lanagan's. in a cottage adjoining the residence of O. Boutwell, Esq., on the North. She is 25 or 30 years of age, good looking, and has a foreign air. She claims to be French, but is undoubtedly English by birth. Her manner of late has attracted the attention of the neighborhood. She has manifested an ungovernable spirit, resisting all efforts to restrain her, and has frequently threatened to use her revolvers, with which she is supplied. Her house was well furnished, and she has been reported as having plenty of money, until within a short time. Since her imprisonment last night, she appears rather excited, and does not seem to realize her situation. She was searched after her arrest, and her pistols taken from her, as it was thought she might commit suicide.

During her long confinement in jail previous to her trial, she did not seem to have comprehended her awful situation. She was continually impressed with the old ideas that she was in danger of violence, and that she was the victim of a political conspiracy. One of her wild notions was, that two persons, a man and a woman, entered her cell in the night, heated a cauldron of water, and gave her the option of getting in herself, or of being put in by violence, and boiled to death. While telling this circumstance with a wild, frightened look, to a friend who was visiting her, she suddenly stopped short and referring to her dress, said, " Don't I look shabbily." She made an unsuccessful effort to destroy herself by taking vitriol, and also played the following trick upon the grand jury. We copy the account of it from the *Times* of April 27th:—

"The Grand Jury sold !—As usual, the grand jury at the close of the sessions to-day, visited the jail, for the purpose of seeing its inmates.

They visited the different departments, and found every thing clean and in good order. Finally, the jailor, Mr. Hegeman, offered to conduct them to the room of Mrs. Robinson, in compliance with their particular request, as each one of them was very anxious to see her. The door was opened, and the grand jury with much dignity walked in. They surrounded a large rocking chair in which she sat closely veiled. Some of them very politely requested her to withdraw it; she made no response whatever, but sat perfectly silent and motionless. Their anxiety was so great, that they requested the jailor to remove the veil, which he respectfully declined to do. Finally, one of the jury stepped up and removed it himself, when to their great surprise, no Mrs. Robinson was there; but on the contrary a silk dress, neatly stuffed, after the latest Parisian fashion! The bird had flown—where? The jailor was asked if she had escaped. Search was instantly made. A slight titter at length was heard proceeding from under the bed. The curtain was raised, and there she lay, so full of laughter that she could hardly contain herself.

Between the time the crime was committed and the day of trial, the newspapers teemed with curious and contradictory stories about her birth and parentage. The absorbing question in every-one's mouth was, "Who is she?" Whole sheets were written, some attempting to prove one thing and some another. Indeed, so much was written and said on the subject, and so long a period has elapsed since, that I prefer leaving the matter as it was; merely adding that whoever are her relatives, we hope that in their day of tribulation they may find a firmer

Friend and greater mercy than any of them have proved to this poor fallen one.

After considerable delay, the day of trial was at length appointed. On Monday, the 22d day of May, 1854, the trial commenced before a full bench and with a great array of counsel on both sides.

The prisoner, most magnificently attired, was brought into court by the Sheriff, and accommodated with a seat near her counsel. After the jury was impannelled, the District Attorney rose and opened the case on the part of the people, with a brief outline of the testimony he proposed to offer.

The wife of the deceased detailed the particulars of the affair, which will be given in her own words.

On the 25th of May, about 6 o'clock in the morning, she came to the grocery for a quart of beer and some crackers. She came again about 8 o'clock. She had sent a man called Ilalev (who was her gardener), to borrow $2 for her, and came to see what detained him. I told her that I had no money in the house, and thought of sending to borrow it. She replied she "was sorry I was so short and would tomorrow lend me $100. She then went away, but returned about 11 o'clock and told me that she had received a telegraphic dispatch informing her that Robinson was hurt on the cars. She went into the kitchen, a lot of men were there. I soon heard her quarrelling with them and went in to advise her to go home.

After a short time she left. I saw her again about 1 o'clock, she came into the kitchen, where myself, Lanagan and Catharine Lubee were at dinner. She took the egg and eat it while I peeled a potato for her. She then said that Catharine and I must have a glass of beer with her. We answered that we did not like beer, when she said she would put some sugar into it to make it good. I took a saucer and fetched from the store some white powdered sugar and then went for the beer, which

I poured into two glasses. When I came back, she was walking about the room with the sugar in her hand. I did not have beer enough to fill both glasses, so Mrs. Robinson sent me for more; when I returned she was putting sugar into the tumblers, and I filled up the glasses with beer. As I sat down to my glass, the other one was placed before Catharine. I noticed a little foam on the surface of the beer, which I thought might be dust from the sugar, so I took a spoon and was going to skim it off, when Mrs. Robinson took the spoon out of my hand and said, "Don't you do so—that is the best of it." At this moment my husband called me, and I went into the grocery, leaving my beer untouched.

Then my husband went into the kitchen and I turned round and saw he was drinking my beer. I don't know that Mrs. Robinson drank any. Boon after this she went away. When she was eating the *egg* I saw a white paper in her hand. A short time elapsed when Catharine asked Lanagan how he felt after taking the beer; he replied he did not feel very comfortable. Mrs. Robinson came again. Catharine was laid on a bed in the kitchen very sick. Mrs. Robinson went to her and asked her how she felt; she said, very poorly; you have put something into the beer and it made me sick. About 3 o'clock my husband came back very sick and could hardly speak; he said " Run for the doctor, I am done for." I turned round to Mrs. Robinson, who was standing near, and said, "What have you done? you have killed the father of my children." She answered, "No, I have done no such thing." She then attempted to speak with him; but I prevented her. Lanagan's mother came in now and assisted me to put her out of doors. She did not come back again, but sent by Haley that I was to go and see her. I refused to go.

During the examination of this witness the prisoner was closely shrouded in her veil so that she could not be easily identified. An attempt was made to induce her to remove her veil, but she would not. Several times during the trial similar scenes occurred, the prisoner firmly resisting all attempts to remove the blue veil, and even when compelled to do so by the court, she contrived by her hands or in some other way, as effectually to screen her face as if the veil were still before it.

The officer who arrested Mrs. Robinson testified that he found two revolvers on her. And on searching the house found some arsenic under a carpet which was tacked down to the floor, and some jewelry, a watch and a locket. On her way to the jail, she joked and laughed, but made no allusion to the murder.

The coroner, who was also a physician, gave an account of the inquest and *post mortem* examination He testified that arsenic was found in the stomachs of both the deceased persons in sufficient quantities to produce death. As to the appearance and manner of the prisoner he added:

There was a strange, wild, unnatural appearance of the eye. She laughed a good deal at times, and her answers to questions were not pertinent. I saw her frequently after this and was always impressed with the idea that she was not sane. Once I charged her with the crime. She seemed to take no notice of what I had said, but chattered on with the same incoherent jumble as before. I do not think she comprehended what I said. On my first visit to Mrs. Robinson in jail, I said, I have come to search you. She elevated her hands so as to facilitate the search. One reason why I believed her to be insane was the wild, unnatural expression of her eyes, and the strange, unnatural expression of her countenance. At our first interview I came to the conclusion that she was irrational. When I told her that she had poisoned these people, I thought it strange it did not affect her in some way. I thought it queer, she did not say something one way or another.

Her counsel at the trial demanded her acquittal on the ground of insanity.

The pleading was begun by *Martin J. Townsend*, Esq., on behalf of the prisoner. He began by paying a compliment to the ability of the opposing counsel, and added, "Not only on this account, but from the fact that the defence of insanity was looked on with suspicion, he felt considerably embarrassed.

On the 8th of December last, I examined with attention the evidence taken before the coroner's jury, and found that no cause of enmity existed between Lanagan and the prisoner, and that Miss Lubee sat at the table during the time Mrs. Robinson was alleged to have put the poison in the sugar. Then I was driven to the irresistible conclusion that the story was absurd. How could she put the arsenic in before the eyes of this girl ? "No gentlemen, I have stated that I should express fearlessly what I had to say, and now I have no hesitation in declaring it to be my deliberate judgment, founded upon her own evidence, that it is far more probable, that Mrs. Lanagan herself poisoned that beer than the prisoner at the bar." If we believe her evidence, she herself consented to take a friendly glass with Mrs. Robinson. Why did she fill only *two* glasses if all were going to drink, when as she asserts three had consented to drink together. She retired from the kitchen, leaving only two glasses there. Her husband happened in then, and what must have been her surprise when she saw him drinking the fatal draught that had been prepared for another. I do not charge Mrs. Lanagan with this crime, but in order to acquit her of all suspicion it is necessary to prove Mrs. Robinson insane."

He then reverted to the point that there was no motive on the part of the prisoner, and went into the question of her insanity, contending that it was real, not feigned. In this poor woman's case, all her hopes were centered in _____. For him she sacrificed her virtue, her honor, her all, and then imagined she was to be cast away a worthless, dishonored thing. Is not this a sufficient cause for insanity? There is not a woman on God's footstool who would not have lost her reason under similar circumstances. After referring to the question of intoxication and some other points, he concluded an address which occupied him five hours in its delivery.

As Mr. Townsend sat down, the prisoner leaned forward and whispered to him the following equivocal compliment, "A very able speech, Mr. Townsend, but you might have said all that was necessary in fifteen minutes. The idea of my insanity is absurd."

Mr. *Van Santvoord* for the people rose and said, he supposed that the plea of insanity would be the only ground of defence; the idea that any one else perpetrated the crime was absurd, for the irresistible evidence was that the prisoner poisoned Lanagan and Lubee. As a motive for the crime he referred to the quarrel at the time of the dance, and the refusal of Mrs. Lanagan to lend her two dollars. This to a woman of her reckless and depraved nature, of violent temper and turbulent disposition, would be a sufficient motive for the crime.

After reviewing the testimony against the prisoner, he said that there was such a thing as a moral certainty as well as a mathematical calculation. The blood of the murdered victims is on the hands of the prisoner, and like the conscience-smitten Lady Macbeth she may exclaim, " Out, damned spot," in vain. The "smell of blood" is there still; "all the perfumes of Arabia cannot sweeten" it; it never can be washed out. To sustain the plea of insanity, he said, the defence ought to have proved her previous life and disposition, to let us see that her behavior lately is at variance with it; but they have not done so. The mystery that has been thrown around the prisoner is still unveiled, and I see no proof of her insanity. Her eccentricities were rather the fruits of intoxication than insanity. Her counsel tell you that she supposed _____ had deserted her; is that circumstance likely to drive a woman who carries pistols in her bosom, drinks bad brandy, and indulges in profane and obscene language, into madness. With regard to what she tells about herself, it only proves that this woman had a mania for lying, and her dancing and frantic laughter are nothing but the strivings of a wicked heart to throw off the painful memories that oppressed it. As to her conduct while in jail, you may attribute it to delirium caused by deprivation of the stimulants she had been used to, and the gnawings of a guilty conscience.

Her counsel made indefatigable efforts to obtain a new trial, which the prisoner as strenuously opposed; in fact, when she heard that the Supreme Court had denied the motion, she celebrated the news with a grand illumination, and walked amidst the blaze, with great glee, listening to the shouts of the mob who were drawn together by the illumination. On the 14th of June, 1855, she was finally called up for sentence. After some preliminary remarks, which were often inter-rupted by the prisoner, Judge Harris said—"The sentence of the Court is, that you, Henrietta Robinson, be detained in the county prison of the county of Rensselaer until the 3d day of August next, and on that day, between the hours of 10 o'clock in the forenoon and two o'clock in the afternoon, you be hanged by the neck until you be dead, and may God, in his infinite mercy, save your soul."

Mrs. Robinson immediately said, "You had better pray for your own soul;" then springing on her feet, denounced in very strong lan-guage both her friends and her supposed foes, and declared with great vehemence that she was the victim of a " political conspiracy." The Court hero said she had better be removed, when pointing her finger at the Judge, said solemnly, "Judge Harris, may the Judge of judges be *your* judge." She was then removed from Court.

Great exertions were made to prevail on the Governor to commute her sentence to imprisonment for life.

On the evening of the 27th of July, it was announced to her that the Governor had commuted her sentence to imprisonment for life in Sing Sing Prison.

When the prisoner obtained this information, she commenced breaking up the furniture, and tearing the bed clothes into strips, and then threw them from her barred window to the people in the street, exclaiming while doing it, "I will not go to State prison. I want to die. Why will they torment me more?"

Notwithstanding the every day intercourse which I have had for ten years with cases similar to Henrietta Robinson's, and notwithstanding I have conducted all her correspondence, and had other official dealings with her, during her three years' confinement in this prison, I am by no means positive as it regards the question of her insanity; but am inclined to the opinion, that she is, at least, a monomaniac, or periodically deranged, and that she was so when she committed the murder. I doubt, in fact, whether she ever had a "well-balanced mind." At any rate the same eccentricities that the testimony on her trial attributed to her are still manifested. She makes the same efforts to hide her countenance from the gaze of strangers now that she made then. She changes from the most innocent and inoffensive looks and language to the most repulsive and vehement, as suddenly now as she is reported to have done then. She assumes the ability to control the political destinies of certain candidates for office as she did then. In a word, here, where for about three years she has had no artificial stimulants whatsoever, (to which the prosecution attributed any appearance of insanity on her part,) she has continued to exhibit, almost daily, the very traits of character upon which her counsel founded a plea of insanity. "Mrs. Robinson," says one of our Inspectors, in a late newspaper article, "still keeps on her airs, and is a high-spirited, head-strong woman. Whenever a stranger enters her presence, she turns her face to the wall with an air which seems to disclose the inner working of the uppermost thought of her heart—that she is some superior" being.

The impressions I have gathered from the ever changing course pursued by this woman since she came here, respecting her sanity, are so well and cogently expressed by a gentleman who had frequent personal interviews with her in Troy jail, besides being familiar with the testimony given at her trial, that I beg leave to close this sketch by quoting his words as then uttered:

If the doomed woman was not insane, it is difficult, indeed, we may add, impossible, to analyze to any degree of satisfaction, her mental or moral character. On any other supposition her deportment is without a parallel, and utterly incomprehensible. That she believes herself a political victim, sacrificed upon the altar of party vengeance, there can be little question. Neither can there be much, if any doubt, that she regarded the suggestion of a commutation of her sentence as a subtle device of her enemies, to accomplish a political end, and to subject her to grievous wrongs and injuries. In her religious moods she was evidently sincere, for the time being. Still in all her acts, so unnatural and inconsistent, there were evidences of hallucination. In one breath she would beg for the salvation of her own soul, and in the next consign the souls of her enemies to perdition. In the midst of her devotions, with hands clasped, and kneeling before the cross, some mirth provoking memory would arrest the solemnity, and as the visitor approached her cell, whether his ears were to be greeted with sounds of prayer, the voice of laughter, or the utterance of bitter malediction, depended on her mood.

9

THE MOUNTAIN MEADOWS MASSACRE

MARK TWAIN

B.G. PARKER

On September 11, 1857, at Mountain Meadows in southern Utah, a
Mormon militia (with some members disguised as local Paiute Native
Americans) slaughtered about 120 men, women, and children of the
Baker-Fancher wagon train, known as "emigrants." Only seventeen
were spared, all children under age seven, whom the assailants assumed
were too young to bear witness to the evil they had experienced. Every-
one else was murdered with guns and knives after being disarmed, and
their bodies hastily buried in shallow graves. The emigrants, headed
for California, were mostly from Arkansas, and camped at Mountain
Meadows on September 7. The killers disguised themselves as Paiutes
and attacked. The emigrants circled their wagons to form makeshift
defenses and fought back. Several were killed, and—running low on
food, water, and ammunition—they surrendered a few days later after
being told, falsely, that the Mormons had worked out a truce to spare
their lives with the attacking "Paiutes." On a signal, the Mormons
attacked and murdered all emigrants but the aforementioned children,
who were taken in by local families. Mormon militia leader John Doyle
Lee (1812–1877), who apparently spun this tale to the emigrants, was
the only person ever convicted in the massacre. He was executed by
firing squad on March 23, 1877, at the site of the massacre he'd helped
perpetrate almost twenty years before.

Famed author Mark Twain wrote the following passage about the
Mountain Meadows Massacre in Appendix B of his travelogue Roughing

It, *published in 1872. B.G. Parker also wrote about the massacre in his book,* Recollections of the Mountain Meadow Massacre, *published in 1901. His account, partially reproduced here, follows Mark Twain's.*

~~~~~~

The persecutions which the Mormons suffered so long—and which they consider they still suffer in not being allowed to govern themselves—they have endeavored and are still endeavoring to repay. The now almost forgotten "Mountain Meadows massacre" was their work. It was very famous in its day. The whole United States rang with its horrors. A few items will refresh the reader's memory. A great emigrant train from Missouri and Arkansas passed through Salt Lake City and a few disaffected Mormons joined it for the sake of the strong protection it afforded for their escape. In that matter lay sufficient cause for hot retaliation by the Mormon chiefs. Besides, these one hundred and forty-five or one hundred and fifty unsuspecting emigrants being in part from Arkansas, where a noted Mormon missionary had lately been killed, and in part from Missouri, a State remembered with execrations as a bitter persecutor of the saints when they were few and poor and friendless, here were substantial additional grounds for lack of love for these wayfarers. And finally, this train was rich, very rich in cattle, horses, mules and other property—and how could the Mormons consistently keep up their coveted resemblance to the Israelitish tribes and not seize the "spoil" of an enemy when the Lord had so manifestly "delivered it into their hand?"

Wherefore, according to Mrs. C. V. Waite's entertaining book, "The Mormon Prophet," it transpired that—

A 'revelation' from Brigham Young, as Great Grand Archee or God, was dispatched to President J. C. Haight, Bishop Higbee and J. D. Lee (adopted son of Brigham), commanding them to raise all the forces they could muster and trust, follow those cursed Gentiles (so read the revelation), attack them disguised as Indians, and with the arrows of the Almighty make a clean sweep of them, and leave none to tell the tale; and if they needed any assistance they were commanded to hire the Indians as their allies, promising them a share of the booty. They were to be neither slothful nor negligent in their duty, and to be punctual in sending the teams back to him before winter set in, for this was the mandate of Almighty God.

The command of the "revelation" was faithfully obeyed. A large party of Mormons, painted and tricked out as Indians, overtook the train of emigrant wagons some three hundred miles south of Salt Lake City, and made an attack. But the emigrants threw up earthworks, made fortresses of their wagons and defended themselves gallantly and successfully for five days! Your Missouri or Arkansas gentleman is not much afraid of the sort of scurvy apologies for "Indians" which the southern part of Utah affords. He would stand up and fight five hundred of them.

At the end of the five days the Mormons tried military strategy. They retired to the upper end of the "Meadows," resumed civilized apparel, washed off their paint, and then, heavily armed, drove down in wagons to the beleaguered emigrants, bearing a flag of truce! When the emigrants saw white men coming they threw down their guns and welcomed them with cheer after cheer! And, all unconscious of the poetry of it, no doubt, they lifted a little child aloft, dressed in white, in answer to the flag of truce!

The leaders of the timely white "deliverers" were President Haight and Bishop John D. Lee, of the Mormon Church. Mr. Cradlebaugh, who served a term as a Federal Judge in Utah and afterward was sent to Congress from Nevada, tells in a speech delivered in Congress how these leaders next proceeded:

They professed to be on good terms with the Indians, and represented them as being very mad. They also proposed to intercede and settle the matter with the Indians. After several hours parley they, having (apparently) visited the Indians, gave the ultimatum of the savages; which was, that the emigrants should march out of their camp, leaving everything behind them, even their guns. It was promised by the Mormon bishops that they would bring a force and guard the emigrants back to the settlements. The terms were agreed to, the emigrants being desirous of saving the lives of their families. The Mormons retired, and subsequently appeared with thirty or forty armed men. The emigrants were marched out, the women and children in front and the men behind, the Mormon guard being in the rear. When they had marched in this way about a mile, at a given signal the slaughter commenced. The men were almost all shot down at the first fire from the guard. Two only escaped, who fled to the desert, and were followed one hundred and fifty miles before they were overtaken and slaughtered. The women and children ran on, two or three hundred yards further, when they were overtaken and with the aid of the Indians they were slaughtered. Seventeen individuals only, of all the emigrant party, were spared, and they were little children, the eldest of them being only seven years old. Thus, on the 10th day of September, 1857, was consummated one of the most cruel, cowardly and bloody murders known in our history.

The number of persons butchered by the Mormons on this occasion was one hundred and twenty.

With unheard-of temerity Judge Cradlebaugh opened his court and proceeded to make Mormondom answer for the massacre. And what a spectacle it must have been to see this grim veteran, solitary and alone in his pride and his pluck, glowering down on his Mormon jury and Mormon auditory, deriding them by turns, and by turns "breathing threatenings and slaughter!"

An editorial in the *Territorial Enterprise* of that day says of him and of the occasion:

> He spoke and acted with the fearlessness and resolution of a Jackson; but the jury failed to indict, or even report on the charges, while threats of violence were heard in every quarter, and an attack on the U.S. troops intimated, if he persisted in his course.
>
> Finding that nothing could be done with the juries, they were discharged with a scathing rebuke from the judge. And then, sitting as a committing magistrate, he commenced his task alone. He examined witnesses, made arrests in every quarter, and created a consternation in the camps of the saints greater than any they had ever witnessed before, since Mormondom was born. At last accounts terrified elders and bishops were decamping to save their necks; and developments of the most starling character were being made, implicating the highest Church dignitaries in the many murders and robberies committed upon the Gentiles during the past eight years.

Had Harney been Governor, Cradlebaugh would have been supported in his work, and the absolute proofs adduced by him of

Mormon guilt in this massacre and in a number of previous murders, would have conferred gratuitous coffins upon certain citizens, together with occasion to use them. But Cumming was the Federal Governor, and he, under a curious pretense of impartiality, sought to screen the Mormons from the demands of justice. On one occasion he even went so far as to publish his protest against the use of the U.S. troops in aid of Cradlebaugh's proceedings.

B.G. PARKER'S ACCOUNT:

Monday morning, just as daylight began to appear, the emigrants were getting up and beginning to prepare for cooking breakfast, when suddenly they were fired on by a band of Mormons and Indians in ambush.

At this first murderous assault, coming without warning and totally unexpected, about twenty of the emigrants were killed or wounded and for a few minutes the confusion and consternation rendered them helpless, but their situation soon recalled them to the fact that immediate action was needed. They soon saw they were attacked and nearly surrounded by an enemy of perhaps ten times as many as themselves, and their assailants concealed in the brush. Then as soon as it was light enough they saw that all their stock, except a few favorits [sic] that were staked near the wagons, had been run off.

Just think of the anguish and despair of those mothers and little children, wives and sweethearts. Consider, what must have been the thoughts of the survivors as they realized that twenty of their comrads [sic] and friends were dead or dying, and expecting every moment to receive the same fate themselves! They were alone, one small band of humans, far from their home and kindred. They were surrounded by a horde of human fiends who thirsted for their lifes blood. And yet, desponding as their thoughts were, little could they realize the hideous end of their long, toilsome journey.

They were in a desperate plight and as soon as possible corralled the wagons and commenced throwing up intrenchments so as to get what protection they could, and for a time doubtless felt that they could make a brave fight for their lives, as the intrenchments rendered some protection, but they were soon made aware that untold agony was before them. For they were cut off from the water, and although the spring was within sight, yet it was certain death to attempt to go to it.

The emigrants fired whenever an Indian or a Mormon appeared in sight, but this was seldom as the besiegers were very careful to keep out of sight, while, with the exception of the wagons the emigrants were on open ground.

By Monday evening this ill-fated train began to suffer for want of water, especially the little children and the wounded persons.

For four days and nights the emigrants were kept within their camp, as to leave it meant certain death. On the evening of the fourth day, what appeared to be a ray of hope came toward them. But it was destined to be the most base betrayal of human confidence, ever, perhaps. encountered in the history of any part of the civilized world.

THE EMIGRANTS SURRENDER. THEIR BETRAYAL. THE FRIGHTFUL BUTCHERY.

I have described the journey of the Baker train from its start until they were camped at Mountain Meadows, and had been besieged for four days and nights.

The Mormons found it a hard task to capture those people without exposing themselves and this, such cowardly fiends would not do.

At last John D. Lee, Jaws Hamblin and two other Mormons named Higby and Haight, procured three wagons and came driving down the road leading from Salt Lake toward the fortified camp of the emigrants. This sight filled the suffering camp with wonder, and a hope of deliverance cheered their souls.

What did it mean! Was it a messenger of relief or destruction? They dressed a little girl in white and sent her out with a flag of truce; the Mormons in the wagons waved a flag in return, then Captain Francher, one of the leading men of the emigrants, went out to meet the Mormons.

They told him that the Indians were very hostile, and the Mormons were afraid to pass by them, because the Indians accused the emigrants of putting poison in some dead cattle and giving it to the Indians to eat, thus causing the death of two chiefs. Nothing but the blood of the emigrants and the possession of the outfit would appease the Indians.

The Mormons also added that "the Indians now have possession of most of your stock and are living off them, and we are powerless to get the stock back from them, however, we want to compromise with them and save the lives of you emigrants. We think that if you will give up your firearms to our Mormon soldiers, that the Indians will understand you do not care to fight any more, and will allow you to go in peace. We will guard you out about two miles to Mr. Hamblin's tonight, and from there on to Cedar City we will see that you have protection. Then, if you wish, you can go on to California, or back to the home you left, just at you wish."

Francher asked them to drive into camp and give the terms; the Mormons did so, then the emigrants began talking among themselves as what was best to do. To stay as they were meant sure death; to continue on to California without teams or fire arms was out of the question; "What shall we do?" they asked each other. They were still in doubt when a Mormon rode up in a great hurry, and cried out:

For God's sake decide at once. I cannot keep the Indians quiet any longer."

The emigrants then said, "Tell them that we surrender to the Mormons, and give up all our fire arms, and ask for mercy.

The fire arms were then all put into one of the Mormon's wagons, and the wounded and sick emigrants into another, and some of the smaller children into the third wagon.

The women marched in front, and the men in the rear with the wagons between. The men were guarded by Mormon soldiers who were kept in ambush for that purpose.

The march then began.

There had been but little firing that day, the Mormons waiting to see if they could not betray the suffering camp, and now their plans were so well carried out the result will be described in the next chapter.

THE HORRIBLE MASSACRE. SEVENTEEN CHILDREN SAVED. A BABE'S EXPERIENCE. BURIAL OF THE DEAD.

The emigrants were ordered to march single file, but they had not advanced more than some sixty or eighty rods until they had entered a thicket of sage brush and dwarf oaks. In hiding here were the Indians and Mormons.

Suddenly one of the Mormon leaders fired off a pistol and shouted, "Do your duty." At this signal nearly five hundred Indians bounded from the brush, in among the unarmed emigrants, and with guns, pistols, knives and clubs began their deadly work, all the time keeping up the most horrible war-cries, yells and fiendish laughter, as they brained their helpless victims and cut the throats of innocent babies.

Think of the terror of those helpless men, women and children! Driven like rabbits into a corral for slaughter! I can almost imagine I hear the wild shrieks of agony and despair as the victims were being butchered. Think of those women and their children, the men powerless to protect them; they had no one to look to but their God. Not over thirty minutes was taken to complete the frightful deed.

Then what an awful sight appeared. More than one hundred mutilated bodies were piled in heaps just as they fell, here and there, in and out through the sage brush; left to be devoured by wolves or birds of prey.

It is said that three men escaped at the time of the massacre, but were hunted down and killed. My informant, however, said that while none escaped from the massacre, two young had escaped before the surrender. They had crawled out one dark night, and made their way to Muddy River, some eighty miles away, but were overtaken by some Mormons and decoyed back until they met some Indians, by whom they were killed. The Mormons and Indians then rode back together.

In the big massacre, the most heartrending scene was that through which the little children had to pass; trampled under foot, splashed with human blood, deafened with the cries of the murderers and the shrieks and groans of their friends or parents, and so frightened the knew not what to do or where to go. Two girls who had been captured by an Indian chief were brought to John D. Lee. The Indian asked what should be done with them, and Lee replied "You know what your orders are."

"They are too pretty to kill," said the chief.

"They know too much," answered Lee.

The chief then shot one of the girls, while Lee deliberately cut the other one's throat and threw the quivering body from him.

A young lady was brought before Maj. Higby and she fell upon her knees begging for mercy for him to spare her life, She would work for him! She would be his slave! Anything if he would only save her. When the dead were gathered up this girl's body was found with the skull crushed in.

Two Mormon teamsters, named Shultz and Tullis, the latter being a son-in-law of Hamblin were ordered to kill the sick and wounded who still lay in the wagon; the two men were heard to exclaim, as they proceeded to their ghastly work: "O Lord receive their spirits, it is for the good of the Kingdom of Heaven that we do this deed." And then they killed the helpless prisoners, one by one.

The little children who remained alive, were then gathered up. One of the little Dunlap girls, now Mrs. Evans, wrote me not long since all she knew of the terrible time. She was between five and six years old at that time and remembers a little about it. In writing she says:

"While the massacre was going on, myself and one younger sister hid among the sagebrush

"After it was all over, it then being dark, I heard my little baby sister crying. I listened and could not hear any Indians around so we ventured out of the brush and went to my baby sister. I found her with one arm around our dead mother's neck, the other poor little arm was nearly shot off. I saw a man collecting up the children and putting them in a wagon. I ran to him and begged him to save my two little sisters and self. He put us in the wagon and took us all to his house."

There were seventeen little children gathered up by the Mormons; they were all frightened nearly out of their sences [sic], hungry, covered with blood, clothing all torn, amid cruel strangers, no beds, no comforts and above all no kind words to soothe them in their grief.

The next morning John D. Lee started to Cedar City with all the children except Jesse Dunlap's baby girl—the one whose arm was broken—who he intended to leave with Mrs. Hamblin, but the affection of the three sisters was so great that the Mormon's wife persuaded Lee to let all three of them remain.

He then took the others to Cedar City to distribute among other Mormon families. Just as they were entering the city a little girl who was riding behind Lee, on his horse, pointed to some of the stock they were driving, and said: "That is my mamma's cow." Lee reached around and seizing her by the hair, dragged her around in front of him, and said, "You know too much," then cut her throat, and threw the body in the street in Cedar City.

A band of men was then sent out to gather up the bodies of the emigrants, and throw them into a deep ravine or washout. It was done with the aid of horses, and long ropes to drag the bodies to the ravine. One report said that no dirt was thrown over them, but my informant told me that just enough dirt was thrown over them to hide the bodies, but the wolves and vultures dug them up.

The bodies were stripped of all valuables and even the clothing, but what became of these is hard to tell. The Indians afterward complained that they did not receive half what was promised them. My informant told me that there was about four hundred head of nice American beef cattle sold at some place on the Jordan River, to our Government soldiers, the following winter. It is generally understood that the Mormons got most of the booty, and these cattle were supposed to have been the emigrants'.

The statements made in this book were told me as true facts, while I was in Utah and near Mountain Meadows in 1877, but I was put tinder the most solemn pledge not to repeat it for twenty years. As the time is up I want the public to know the truth, for I feel sure from all I have read or heard, that this is the most correct history of the affair ever published.

10

RACHEL WALL, PIRATE AND ROBBER (1789)

Born in Pennsylvania and hanged in Boston on October 8, 1789 (giving her the dubious distinction of being the last woman ever hanged in Massachusetts), Rachel Wall was one of only a few women to practice piracy. After marrying George Wall, she moved to Boston. After a brief stint as fishermen, George and several male friends and their female companions decided piracy would be a more lucrative occupation. Rachel agreed. Setting up shop in 1781 on a borrowed schooner in the Isles of Shoals off the coasts of New Hampshire and Maine, they waited for storms to pass, then set their trap, pretending the schooner was in distress. Rachel was the gang's decoy, standing on the deck and screaming loudly for help. When passing ships and boats came to offer assistance, the pirates murdered everyone aboard and stole everything of value. In just a few years' time they murdered at least two dozen people. George and his fellow cutthroats were lost at sea, and Rachel continued her thieving ways in Boston until her arrest.

LIFE, LAST WORDS AND DYING CONFESSION, OF RACHEL WALL, WHO, WITH WILLIAM SMITH AND WILLIAM DUNOGAN, WERE EXECUTED AT BOSTON, ON THURSDAY, OCTOBER 8, 1789, FOR HIGH-WAY ROBBERY.

BOSTON-GAOL, WEDNESDAY EVENING, October 7, 1789.

I RACHEL WALL, was born in the town of Carlisle, in the state of Pennsylvania, in the year 1760, of honest and reputable parents, who were alive and in good health not long since: They gave me a good education, and instructed me in the fundamental principles of the Christian Religion, and taught me the fear of God; and if I had followed their good advice should never have come to this untimely fate. When I left home I had three brothers and two sisters alive and well.

Without doubt the ever-curious Public, (but more especially those of a serious turn of mind) will be anxious to know every particular circumstance of the Life and Character of a person in my unhappy situation, but in a peculiar manner those relative to my birth and parentage.

With regard to my Parents, I have only room in this short Narrative to observe, that my father was a Farmer, who was in good circumstances when I left him. [*She then professed to being of a devout and well bought-up family, both her parents*] being of the Presbyterian, or rather Congregational Persuasion, I was educated in the same way. . . .

I left my parents without their consent when I was very young, and returning again was received by them, but could not be contented; therefore I tarried with them but two years, before I left them again, and have never seen them since.

I came away with one George Wall, to whom I was lawfully married: If I had never seen him I should not have left my parents. I went with him to Philadelphia; we tarried there some time, but left that place and went to New-York, where we staid about three months.—From thence we came to Boston, where he tarried with me some time, and then went off, leaving me an entire stranger: Upon which I went to service and lived very contented, and should have remained so, had it not been for my husband; for, as soon as he came back, he enticed me to leave my service and take to bad company, from which I may date my ruin. I hope my unhappy fate will be a solemn warning to him. He went off again and left me, and where he is now I know not. . . .

I hope my awful and untimely fate will be a solemn warning and caution to every one, but more particularly to the youth, especially those of my own sex.

I acknowledge myself to have been guilty of a great many crimes, such as Sabbath-breaking, stealing, lying, disobedience to parents, and almost every other sin a person could commit, except murder; and have not lived in the fear of God, nor regarded the kind admonitions and counsels of man.

In short, the many small crimes I have committed, are too numerous to mention in this sheet, and therefore a particular narrative of them here would serve to extend a work of this kind to too great a length; which crimes I most sincerely desire to confess . . .

But as I could heartily wish that the innocent may not suffer with the guilty, I shall, in some degree, deviate from my first intention, by relating the particulars of some material transactions of my life, which, perhaps, may serve as a solemn warning to the living, of my sex at least; especially to those whom they may more immediately concern: They are as follow, viz.

In one of my nocturnal excursions, when the bright goddess Venus shined conspicuous, and was the predominant Planet among the heavenly bodies, sometime in the spring of 1787, not being able to ascertain the exact time, I happened to go on board a ship, lying at the Long-Wharf, in Boston;—the Captain's name I cannot recollect, but think he was a Frenchman: On my entering the cabin, the door of which not being fastened, and finding the Captain and Mate asleep in their beds, I hunted about for plunder, and discovered, under the Captain's head, a black silk handkerchief containing upwards of thirty pounds, in gold, crowns, and small change, on which I immediately seized the booty and decamped therewith as quick as possible; which money I spent freely in company as [word missing] and wicked as myself, fully proving the old adage, "Light come light go."

At another time, I think it was about the year 1788, I broke into a sloop, on board of which I was acquainted, lying at Doane's Wharf, in this town, and finding the Captain and every hand on board asleep in the cabin and steerage, I looked round to see what I could help myself to, when I espied a silver watch hanging over the Captain's head, which I pocketed. I also took a pair of silver buckles out of the Captain's shoes: I likewise made free with a parcel of small change for pocket-money, to make myself merry among my evil companions and made my escape without being discovered.

I would beg the patience of the public for only a few minutes, while I relate another adventure that happened in the course of my life, which, were it not for the novelty thereof, might be thought too trifling to mention in this sheet; but with a view of gratifying the curiosity of some particular friends, who have been very kind to me under sentence. I have consented to give it to the publisher for insertion, which is as follows:

Sometime about the year 1785, my husband being confined in the Goal in this place for these, I had a mind to try an expedient to extricate him from his imprisonment, which was to have a brick-loaf baked, in which I contrived to enclose a number of tools, such as a saw, file, &c. in order to assist him to make his escape, which was handed to him by the goaler in person, who little suspected such a trick was playing with him; however, it like to have had the desired effect the crafty contriver intended; for, by means of this stratagem, the poor culprit, Wall, had busily employed himself with the implements that his kind help-mate had in this curious manner conveyed to him, and had nearly effected his design before it was discovered.

[*The prisoner then declared*] Miss Dorothy Horn, a crippled person in Boston Alms-House, to be entirely innocent of the theft at Mr. Vaughn's in Essex-Street, tho' she suffered a long imprisonment, was set on the gallows one hour, and whipped five stripes therefor.

As to the crime of Robbery, for which I am in a few hours to suffer an ignominious death. I am entirely innocent to the truth of this declaration I appeal to that God before whom I must shortly appear, to give an account of every transaction of my life.

With regard to the above Robbery, I would beg permission to relate a few particulars, which are, that I had been at work all the preceding day, and was on my way home in the evening, without design to injure any person: in my way I [words missing] in the street; what it was I knew not, until I was taken up; I never saw Miss Bendar (the person I was charged with robbing that evening) and was quite surprised when the crime was laid to my charge. The witnesses who swore against me are certainly mistaken; but as a dying person I freely forgive them.

Rachel then thanked her judges and other presiding officials, and committed her soul to God. Her confession, "taken from the prisoner's mouth, a few hours before her execution," was then signed by "Rachel Wall, Joseph Otis, Deputy-Goaler, [and] Wm. Crombie, Assistant." Rachel and her male companions in crime were then hanged on Boston Common, ultimately on order of Governor John Hancock.

In their Proceedings, published 1905 and excerpted here, the Massachusetts Historical Society detailed the crime for which she gave up her life—seeming mundane by comparison with her prior exploits—and the ever-evolving laws and criminal punishments that took her there:

HANGED FOR STEALING A HAT.

Just at the spot, nearly opposite Mason Street, where preparations have been made for an entrance to the subway on the Common, in which the tracks for south-bound cars are to be deflected westerly before intersecting the Boylston street branch in order to resume the parallel at Tremont street, is the point which may be said to have witnessed the most unaccountable execution on record in this State.

"Is it true that Governor John Hancock ordered a woman to be hanged on the Common for snatching a bonnet?" was asked by a Bostonian as he passed this spot where the subway operations are the centre of curiosity.

There is at the State House a document with the bold autograph that headed the signatures of the Declaration of Independence. Governor John Hancock, under date of Oct. 8, 1789, and in language identical with that addressed to Sheriff O'Brien in connection with the hanging of Gilbert, with the appropriate variation of time and place, ordered Joseph Henderson, "sheriff of our county of Suffolk," to hang Rachel Wall, on Boston Common, on the 20th of that month.

To find the specific cause, the record of the court that convicted her was searched. It said that Rachel Wall, on the 18th of March, 1789, at Boston, on the public highway, assailed Margaret Bender, and with "bodily force" seized and put on the bonnet of said Bender, "of the value of seven shillings." "This," says the record, "did she carry away against the public peace of this Commonwealth." In the document "sundry other thefts" were referred to, but in point of fact the tradition in the case as generally believed is that the offence was one involving a quarrel between two women, one of whom snatched the bonnet of the other. The sentence of execution was duly carried out, under the rule of the first Governor of our Commonwealth, and within four days of the time when the first President of the United States was welcomed on these streets. . . .

An examination of the court records proved that the story, with some slight inaccuracies, was true. . . . No evidence in the case has been preserved, and of the original papers there remain only the indictments and a bill of costs [indicating] a trial of considerable length. . . .

The Boston newspapers of the time give some few facts and furnish some additional particulars.

The occurrence seems to have excited but little comment, and the accounts in their brevity and quietness are in striking contrast with the flaming headlines and the multitudinous details of the journals of to-day. It was taken for granted that laws were made to be enforced,—and enforced without evasion or compromises,—and that the Executive was bound to see to their exact execution without faltering or shrinking from the obligation of his oath and the faithful performance of his official duty.

Extracts from two journals give the account of the offence and the ending of the affair.

From the "Independent Chronicle and the Universal Advertiser," published in Boston, April 2, 1789:—

A singular kind of robbery, for this part of the world, took place on Friday evening last: As a woman was walking alone, she was met by another woman, who seized hold of her and stopped her mouth with her handkerchief, and tore from her head her bonnet and cushion, after which she flung her down, took her shoes and buckles, and then fled. She was soon after overtaken, and committed to jail.

From the same paper of September 10, 1789:—

Last Tuesday afternoon, Sentence of Death was pronounced against William Dennifee, William Smith and Rachel Wall, who were severally convicted of High Way Robbery at the Supreme

Judicial Court, holden in this town; the sentence was pronounced by Chief Justice Cushing. . . .

From the same paper of October 8, 1789:—

This day, between the hours of 12 and 4, William Dennofee, William Smith, and Rachel Wall, are to be executed, pursuant to their sentence, for the crime of highway robbery.

The law as it stood at the time was rigorously enforced. No doubt or hesitation seems to have arisen. A question may perhaps reasonably suggest itself whether, though the offence fell technically within the language of the law, it was within its spirit and intent. The point, however, seems not to have been taken, no question to have been raised, and no attempt to secure a stay or commutation of the sentence. The prisoner was an old offender, the crime fully proved, and that seems to have been considered enough. Evidently the weak commiseration for a convicted criminal now so common found little favor then.

The case itself naturally suggested an inquiry as to how Massachusetts had dealt with the crime of highway robbery in its several periods of colony, province, and commonwealth.

The first law touching the crime of highway robbery was in 1642. The colonists brought with them the general principles of the common law and the habits of legal practice which they had acquired as Englishmen. The courts established were required to proceed " to heare and determine all causes according to the lawes nowe established, & where there is noe lawe, then as neere the lawe of God as they can." . . .

The earliest legislation came at "The Generall Court of Elections, the 18th Day of y 3d Month, 1642. This law was of the utmost flexibility, and left everything to the discretion and determination of the judges.

Between 1630 and 1644 no case of highway robbery appears upon the records of the Court of Assistants, but there are several trials and sentences for stealing. The penalty imposed is fine, restitution, whipping, and occasionally branding, according to the gravity of the offence.

In 1642 a woman "for hir many theftes and lyes was censured to bee severely whipt, & condemned to Slavery, till shee have recompenced double for all hir theftes."

In 1635, in the case of "a knowen theife, who since his comeing hither bath committed dyvers fellonyes &c. as appeareth by his examinacon, It is therefore ordered that the said Scarlett shalbe severely whipt & branded in the forehead with a T & after sent to his said Maister whome the Court enioynes to send the said Scarlett out of this Iurisdiccion" &c. . . . .

And in the records from 1673 to 1692 no case of simple highway robbery is found. There are cases of burglary and piracy, where robbery is charged as an incident and the punishment varies with the offence. In one in 1681 the sentence is "to be branded in the forhead wth the letter B. and be severely whipt wtth thirty stripes paying treble damages . . . dischardging fees of Court & ye prison standing Comitted till Sentence be performed."

And in another, in 1685, " to be branded wth the letter B on ye forhead & have his Right eare Cutt of dischardging ye charge of ye witnesses tryall & fees & then make Restitution to the party Injuried & in deflect thereof to be sold to any of the English plantations. And for another burglary tried at the same time "to be againe Branded . . . & have his left eare cutt of," etc. as before. The offenders seem most frequently to have been bond-servants. . . .

The Province passed away, the Commonwealth succeeded, and there came new legislation. Acts of 1784, ch. 52. [January Session.] Be it enacted by the Senate and House of Representatives, in General Court assembled, and by the authority of the same, That every person who shall feloniously assault, rob and take from the person of another, any money, goods, chattels or other property that may be the subject of theft, and shall be thereof convicted, shall be adjudged guilty of felony, and shall suffer the pains of death. March 9. 1785. For assault with intent, the punishment is:—

fine not exceeding 1000 pounds, imprisonment, setting in the pillory, whipping, setting on the gallows with a rope about his neck [and the other end thereof thrown over the gallows,] confinement to hard labor, not exceeding three years, or either of these punishments, according to the degree and aggravation of offence.

It was under this Act of 1784 that Rachel Wall was tried and convicted and executed. It held in force for twenty years.

11

MADAME DELPHINE LALAURIE, NEW ORLEANS MONSTER

Of all the obvious horrors of slavery in America, few can match the terrifying story of Delphine Lalaurie (ca. 1780–1849), who was found to have cruelly abused and tortured her slaves in New Orleans, Louisiana. In April 1834, a female slave who was a cook set a fire in the kitchen of Lalaurie's French Quarter mansion, apparently hoping either to commit suicide or to otherwise escape the terrible, cruel situation. The flames soon spread throughout the structure. Firefighters and volunteers found several slaves, chained and clearly mistreated over a long period of time. Not long thereafter, an angry mob formed and destroyed what was left of the house. Lalaurie and her husband apparently fled the city (barely escaping the angry rabble) and traveled to Paris, France, where she lived the rest of her life, never facing punishment for her crimes.

The infamous Lalaurie mansion was eventually restored and used for other purposes, including as a home for young criminals and as a school. Some claim the mansion is haunted. Actor Nicolas Cage owned the building for about two years, from 2007 to 2009.

A TALE OF SLAVERY TIMES.

It was on the morning of the 10th of April, 1834, that from the corner of Royal and Hospital streets, crepitating flames were seen to burst forth, threatening the entire destruction of a spacious brick mansion that adorned that locality. It was an imposing family residence, three stories in height, and the resort of the best society of New Orleans. Within its walls, European notabilities, including the Marquis of Lafayette, had been housed and entertained with that munificence, easy grace and cheerful hospitality peculiar to a Creole generation, now so rapidly disappearing. Its furniture and appointments—exquisite and costly gems of Parisian workmanship—were cited as *"chefs-d'oeuvres"* in a city where objects of *"vertu"* and princely elegance were by no means rare. (It is a mistake to say that the Orleans princes were ever guests in that residence, as their visit to our city had occurred long before its construction. The Marignys were their hosts.)

Around this house were congregated a dense and excited throng, apparently feasting their eyes on the lambent and circling streams of fire that with forked tongues were rapidly enveloping the upper portions of the aristocratic abode. Their frowning brows and fiercely glistening eyes bespoke the terrible passions that raged within their breasts, for, that house, according to common tradition, was a hot-bed of cruelty and crime, and bore upon its frontispiece the curse of God.

The entire width of Hospital street was literally wedged in by a compact, surging tide, overflowing even adjacent thoroughfares. The pent-up blaze had burst forth from the kitchen above the basement, and from thence was rapidly ascending the story occupied by the family. The firemen, with their inadequate hand engines and equipments, were manning their brakes with might and main against the devouring element with only partial success, and were finally compelled to cut their way through the roof. On penetrating into the attic, and while ranging through the apartments, their blood curdled by the horrid spectacle which struck their view—seven slaves, more or less mutilated, slowly perishing from hunger, deep lacerations and festering wounds.

In describing this appalling sight, Jerome Bayou, the proprietor of the New Orleans *"Bee,"* wrote: "We saw where the collar and manacles had cut their way into their quivering flesh. For several months they had been confined in those dismal dungeons, with no other nutriment than a handful of gruel and an insufficient quantity of water, suffering the tortures of the damned and longingly awaiting death, as a relief to their sufferings. We saw Judge Canonge, Mr. Montreuil and others, making for some time fruit-less efforts to rescue those poor unfortunates, whom the infamous woman, Lalaurie, had doomed to certain death and hoping that the devouring element might thus obliterate the last traces of her nefarious deeds."

When every door had been forced open, the victims were carried off and escorted by an immense crowd to the Mayor's office, where their irons were immediately struck off. Among those piteous blacks, was an octogenarian whose tottering limbs barely supported his emaciated frame. Among them, a woman confessed to the Mayor that she had purposely set fire to the house, as the only means of putting an end to her sufferings and those of her fellow captives. From nine o'clock in the morning until six in the evening, the jail yard was a scene of unusual commotion. Two thousand persons, at least, convinced themselves during that eventful day by ocular inspection of the martyrdom to which those poor, degraded people had been subjected, while the ravenous appetite with which they devoured the food placed before them fully attested their sufferings from hunger. None of them, however, died from surfeit, as it has been erroneously alleged. Numberless instruments of torture, not the least noticeable of which were iron collars, with sharp cutting edges, were spread out upon a long deal table, as evidences of guilt.

While these prison scenes were being enacted, supplying aliment to public curiosity, the excitement around the doomed building was increasing in intensity. As soon as the fact became generally known that Mrs. Lalaurie, with the connivance of the Mayor, had eluded arrest and effected her escape to a secure place of concealment, the howling mob, composed of every class, became ungovernable. They demanded justice in no uncertain tones, and had the hated woman fallen into their hands at that particular moment, it is impossible to say what would have been her fate. Actaeon-like, she in all probability would have been torn to pieces, not by a pack of ravenous hounds, but by men whom rage had converted into tigers. During the whole of that exciting period, the populace awaited with anxiety, but without violence, the action of the authorities. It was the lull that precedes the coming storm. It was said that Etienne Mazureau, the Attorney General, had expressed his determination to wreak upon the guilty parties the extreme vengeance of the law. But when the shadows of night fell upon the city, and it was ascertained beyond a doubt that no steps in that direction had been taken and that powerful influences were at work to shield the culprits, their fury then knew no bounds and assumed at once an active form. At eight o'clock that night, the multitude having swollen to immense dimensions, a systematic attack upon the building was organized and begun. Their first act was the demolition of one of her carriages, which happened to be standing in front of Hospital street, and the same, it was said, that had borne her away. The sidewalk was literally strewn with its "débris." Next came the onslaught on the main entrance on Royal street, the portals of which had been previously barred and fastened and seemed to bid defiance to the shower of stones and rocks hurled against it. Abandoning this attempt, they obtained axes and battered down the window shutters, through which a wild horde of humanity poured in. No earthly power at that moment could have restrained the phrenzy of the mob—people resolved on exercising their reserved rights. Their work was no child's play. Everything was demolished; nothing respected. Antique and rare furniture, valued at more than ten thousand dollars, was mercilessly shivered to atoms. The cellars were emptied of their precious contents, and wines of choicest vintage flowed in copious streams, even into the gutters. Gilt panels, carved wainscots, floorings, carpets, oil paintings, objects of statuary, exquisite moldings, staircases with their mahogany banisters and even the iron balconies were detached from their fastenings and hurled upon the pavements. As crash succeeded crash, yells of delight rent the air. When Royal and Hospital streets became obstructed with the accumulating wrecks, the latter were heaped together in monticules and set on fire, which, together with the glare of the blazing torches, offered a sad and weird-like appearance. This first outburst of popular retribution, notwithstanding the efforts of our local magistrates, continued not only during the entire night—"noche triste"—but long after sunrise on the following morning. Then came a calm, a deceitful calm. The fire had only partially destroyed the building, and to obliterate the last vestiges of this infamous haunt became now the object of the rabble. The work of demolition lasted four days, and only the charred partition walls remained standing, as a solemn memorial of a people's anger. Tacitus says: "Solitudinem faciunt, pacem vocant." In the instant case, the work of destruction only ceased when there was nothing more to destroy. The story that human bones, and among others those of a child who had committed self-destruction to escape the merciless lash, had been found in a well, is not correct, for the papers of the day report that, acting under that belief, the mob had made diligent search, even to the extent of excavating the whole yard, and had found nothing. When, on the subsidence of this unwonted spirit of effervescence, reason had had time to resume her sway, the local troops, with U. S. Regulars to support them, were called out, headed by Sheriff John Holland, who proceeded to the scene of disturbance and read the "riot act" to the crowd of curiosity mongers who were loitering in the neighborhood. Slowly and peaceably the people dispersed. Their anger was allayed and their verdict carried into effect. They now determined to wait and see what the constituted officers would do in furtherance of public justice.

In the meantime, thousands had been repairing to the police station to witness the condition of the slaves, and as the sickening sight only excited and increased their resentment, our denizens were not slow in expressing their contempt at the apathy and inaction of their municipal worthies. Judge Canonge, a man of strict integrity, and sound judgment, had not escaped the insults of the enraged populace on the night of the first attack, and while in the act of expostulating with them upon the impropriety of their course several pistols had been leveled at his head. Much, therefore, was yet to be feared from the general discontent, as it was reported that bodies of men had banded together for the purpose of looting several residences, where similar barbarities were said to have been commonly practiced. In fact, this report proved no idle rumor, for a gentleman's house in close proximity to Mrs. Lalaurie's was partially sacked, for which act the city subsequently was mulcted in damages.

To repeat what I have previously mentioned, nearly the entire edifice was demolished, the bare walls only standing to indicate the spot where the God accursed habitation had stood—walls upon which had been placarded inscriptions in different languages, conveying anathemas in words more forcible than elegant. The loss of property was estimated at nearly forty-thousand dollars. Says a contemporary:

This is the first act of the kind that our people have ever engaged in, and although the provocation pleads much in favor of the excesses committed, yet we dread the consequences of the precedent. To say the least, it may be excused, but can't be justified. Summary punishment, the result of popular excitement in a government of laws, can never admit of justification, let the circumstances be ever so aggravated.

At last the wheels of justice were set in motion and Judge Canonge proceeded to the office of Gallien Préval, a justice of the peace, and furnished under oath the following information. The facts therein stated may, therefore, be relied upon as strictly true, and furnish data of a reliable character, of which some future historian of Louisiana may avail himself."

Deponent (J. F. Canonge) declares that on the 10th inst. a fire having broken out at the residence of Mrs. Lalaurie, he repaired thither, as a citizen, to afford assistance. When he reached the place, he was informed that a number of manacled slaves were in the building and liable to perish in the flames. At first he felt disinclined to speak to Mr. Lalaurie on the subject and contented himself with imparting the fact only to several friends of the family. But when he became aware that this act of barbarity was becoming a subject of general comment, he made up his mind to speak himself to Mr. and Mrs. Lalaurie, who flatly answered that the charge was a base calumny. Thereupon, deponent asked the aid of the bystanders to make a thorough search and ascertain with certainty the truth or falsity of the rumor. As Messrs. Montreuil and Fernandez happened to be near him, he requested those gentlemen to climb to the garret and see for themselves, adding, that having attempted to do so himself, he had been almost blinded and smothered by the smoke. These gentlemen returned after a while and reported that they had looked around diligently and had failed to discover anything. A few moments after, some one, whom he thinks to be Mr. Felix Lefebvre, came to inform him that, having broken a pane of glass in a window of one of the rooms, he had perceived some slaves and could show the place. Deponent hurried on, in company with several others. Having found the door locked, he caused it to be forced open and entered with the citizens who had followed him. He found two negro women, whom he ordered to be taken out of the room.

Then some one cried out that there were others in the kitchen. He went there, but found no one. One of the above negresses was wearing an iron collar, extremely wide and heavy, besides weighty chains attached to her feet. She walked only with the greatest difficulty; the other, he had no time to see, as she was standing behind some one whom he believes to be Mr. Guillotte. This latter person told him he could point out a place where another one could be found. Together they went into another apartment, at the moment when some one was raising a mosquito bar. Stretched out upon a bed, he perceived an old negro woman who had received a very deep wound on the head. She seemed too weak to be able to walk. Deponent begged the bystanders to lift her up with her mattress and to carry her in that position to the Mayor's office, whither the other women had been already conveyed. At the time that he asked Mr. Lalaurie if it were true that he had some slaves in his garret, the latter replied in an insolent manner that some people had better stay at home rather than come to others' houses to dictate laws and meddle with other people's business."

In support of the above statement, which is merely the recital of the discoveries made by the Judge personally and does not purport to include the result of the investigations of others, the names of Messrs. Gottschalk and Fouché were appended as witnesses.

What was the final issue of the affair? the reader will naturally ask. Nothing, absolutely nothing. From the 10th to the 15th of April, the day on which the riot was finaly [sic] quelled by the intervention of the Sheriff, the inactivity of the government officials had been glaring. The criminals, wife and husband, had been deftly smuggled through the unsuspecting throng, driven up Chartres street in a closed carriage which I saw speeding at a furious gait and, after remaining in concealment some time hurriedly departed for New York. From that point they had continued their flight to Paris, which they made their permanent residence. There I shall not follow them, nor relate the effects of the ban under which refined society placed them, nor of the hissing and hooting with which the "parterre" assailed her once at the theatre when their misdeeds became known. The woman, it was currently reported in New Orleans circles, finding every door closed against her, had subsequently adopted a strictly pious life and, spending her time in works of practical charity, was fast relieving her character from the odium that attached to it. A characteristic trait in this singular woman's history is, I am positively assured by persons who lived in her intimacy, that, at the very time when she was engaged in those atrocious acts, her religious duties, in external forms at least, were never neglected and her purse was ever open to the hungry, the afflicted and the sick. Like Doctor Jekyl's [sic], her nature was duplex, her heart at one time softening to excess at the sight of human suffering, while at another it turned obdurate and hard as adamant. In manners, language and ideas, she was refined—a thorough society woman. Her reunions were recherché affairs, and during the lifetime of her former husband, Mr. Jean Blanque, who figures so conspicuously in Louisiana's legislative history, and whose important services to the State during a long series of years should be gratefully remembered, her home was the re-sort of every dignitary in the infancy of our state. There the politicians of the period met on neutral ground, eschewing for the notice their petty jealousies, cabals and intrigues, to join in scenes of enjoyment and refinement;

among whom I may cite Claiborne, the Governor; Wilkinson, the military commander; Trudeau, the Surveyor General; Bosque, Marigny, Destréhan, Sauvé, Derbigny, Macarty, de la Ronde, Villeré and others, all representatives of the "ancien régime;" Daniel Clarke, our first delegate to Congress; Judge Hall, Gravier, Girod, Milne and McDonough, destined to become millionaires, and hundreds of others whose names now escape my memory.

But "revenons à nos moutons." There is a class of females, few in numbers it is true, the idiosyncrasies of whose natures are at times so strange and illogical as to defy the test of close analyzation, and to that class Mrs. Lalaurie, with her sudden contrasts of levity and sternness, melting love and ferocity, formed no exception. Whence proceeded this morbid spirit of cruelty? we ask ourselves. Was it a general detestation of the African race? No, for, of her large retinue of familiar servants, many were devotedly attached to her, and the affection seems to have been as warmly returned. All the theories, therefore, that have been built upon this particular case, from which deductions have been drawn ascribing exclusively the wrongs which I have just narrated to the baneful and pernicious influence of the institution of slavery, as some writers will have it, rest upon no better foundation than mere speculation. Slavery was a social device, replete, it is true, with inherent defects, but by no means conducive to crime. The system was patriarchal in its character, not essentially tyrannical. The master was not unlike the "pater familias" of the Roman Commonwealth, but more restricted in power and dominion. Hence, it is more rational to suppose, and such is the belief of many, that looking into the nature or "indoles," as the Latins had it, of the woman from its different points of view, she was undoubtedly insane upon one peculiar subject—a morbid, insatiate thirst for revenge on those who had incurred her enmity. Our lunatic asylums, it is said, are filled with similar cases, all traceable to similar causes.

Upon the site of the old building, a fine structure, entirely new, was erected, noticeable in its design and architectural proportions. A belvedere was added to it. It has been named by some the "Haunted House." There is no reason for the appellation, and if several of its occupants, with whom I have often conversed, are to be believed, there is nothing therein to haunt its inhabitants save ghastly memories of a by-gone generation. No spirits wander through its wide halls and open corridors, but in lieu thereof there rests a curse—a malediction—that follows every one who has ever attempted to make it a permanent habitation. As a school house for young ladies; as a private boarding house; as a private residence; as a factory; as a commercial house and place of traffic, all these have been tried, but every venture has proved a ruinous failure. A year or two ago, it was the receptacle of the scum of Sicilian immigrants, and the fumes of the malodorous filth which emanated from its interior proclaimed it what it really is, a house accursed.

12

THE BEADLE FAMILY
MURDER-SUICIDE

William Beadle (ca. 1730–1782) was born in England, and had become a wealthy merchant in Wethersfield, Connecticut by the time of the American Revolution. He moved easily in the most elite social circles of his day, collected costly furniture and works of art, and lived in a splendid home in Wethersfield with his wife Lydia, son Ansel, and daughters Elizabeth, Lydia, and Mary. But the Revolution brought trouble for Beadle's business, and his fortunes waned. He accepted the Revolutionary government's Continental currency in payment for the goods he sold, but as the war dragged on the currency's value fell, and Beadle did not raise the prices he charged. (It was illegal to do so, but many other merchants ignored the law.) Beadle went from being a man of great wealth to one of only "middling" (his term) riches, and this prospect apparently horrified him. He fell into despair, and began to plot the destruction of his family and himself. Finally, on the morning of December 11, 1782, using an ax and a knife, he murdered his thirty-two-year-old wife and his children, who ranged in age from twelve to six years. Then, tracking his family's blood through the house, he made his way downstairs to his favorite Windsor chair, where he put two pistols to either side of his head and fired both simultaneously.

A LETTER from a Gentleman in Wethersfield, to his Friend, containing a Narrative of the Life of William Beadle (so far as it is known) and the particulars of the Massacre of himself and Family.

SIR,

'TIS not strange that reports various and contradictory should have circulated on so interesting and terrible a subject as that of a man's consigning to the grave himself and family in a moment of apparent ease and tranquility. The agitation of mind which must be the consequence of being near such a scene of horror, will sufficiently apologize for not answering your request for the particulars e'er this. Our ignorance of the history of this man at first precluded a possibility of giving you satisfaction on this head. Perhaps no one in this town had more favorable opportunities of obtaining the particulars of his history: yet, could never induce him to mention a single syllable relating to his age, parentage, or early occupation. To have asked him directly would have been rude when he evidently meant to be silent on these subjects. My conjecture was, that he was the natural son of some gentleman in England, and that he had been brought up in or near London, and had been about the Court. Since his decease I have been able to learn from undoubted authority, that he was born in the county of Essex, in a village not very far from London. As to his business in youth I am still left in the dark, but find he has once mentioned to a gentleman, some little incidents which happened to him while in company with his father, and that he very early became acquainted with a club in London who were Deists, where 'tis probable he received the first rudiments in those principles. While in England, where he left a mother and sister, he had a fair character for integrity and honesty. In the year 1755 he went out to the island of Barbadoes, in the family of Charles Pinfold, Esq, Governor of that island, where he tarried six years, then returned to England, purchased some merchandize, and from thence came to New-York in the year 1762, and immediately removed to Stratford in this State, from thence to Derby, and then to Fairfield, where he married and dwelt some years.—By this time he had acquired about twelve hundred pounds property, with which he removed to this town, about ten years since, where he resided until his death. His business was that of retailing, he formerly credited his goods, but since his residence in this town he has refused to give any credit, intending to keep his property within his own reach, believing it always secure while his eye was upon it. While here he added considerable to his stock, none of which he ever vested in real estate; the Continental currency taught him that wealth could take to itself wings and fly away: Notwithstanding all his vigilance.

When the war commenced he had on hand a very handsome assortment of Goods for a country store, which he sold for the currency of the country, without any advance in the price the money he laid by, waiting and expecting the time would soon arrive when he might therewith replace his goods, resolving not to part with it until it should be in as good demand as when received by him. His expectations from this quarter daily lessening, finally lost all hope, and was thrown into a state little better than dispair, as appears from his writing ; he adopted a plan of the most rigid family economy, but still kept up the outward appearance of his former affluence, and ever to the last entertained his friend with his usual decent hospitality, although nothing appeared in his outward deportment, which evinced the uncommon pride of his heart; his writings show clearly that he was determined not to bear the mortification of being thought by his friends poor and dependent. On this subject he expresses himself in the following extraordinary manner: "If a man, who has once lived well, meant well and done well, falls by unavoidable accident into poverty, and then submits to be laughed at, despised and trampled on, by a set of mean wretches as far below him as the moon is below the sun; I say, if such a man submits, he must become meaner than meanness itself, and I sincerely wish he might have ten years added to his natural life to punish him for his folly."

He fixed upon the night succeeding the 18th of November for the execution of his nefarious purpose, and procured a supper of oysters, of which the family eat very plentifully; that evening he writes as follows: "I have prepared a noble supper of oysters, that my flock and I may eat and drink together, thank God and die." After supper he sent the maid with a studied errand to a friend's house at some distance, directing her to stay until she obtained an answer to an insignificant letter he wrote his friend intending she should not return that evening—she did however return, perhaps her return disconcerted him and prevented him for that time. The next day he carried his pistols to a smith for repair; it may be, the ill condition of his pistols might be an additional reason for the delay.

On the evening of the 10th of December some persons were with him at his house, to whom he appeared as chearful and serene as usual; he attended to the little affairs of his family as if nothing uncommon was in contemplation. The company left him about nine o'clock in the evening, when he was urgent as usual for their stay; whether he slept that night is uncertain, but it is believed he went to bed. The children and maid slept in one chamber; in the grey of the morning of the 11th of December he went to their bed chamber, awaked the maid and ordered her to arise gently without disturbing the children; when she came down stairs he gave her a line to the family physician, who lived at the distance of a quarter of a mile, ordered her to carry it immediately, at the same time declaring that Mrs. Beadle had been ill all night, and directing her to stay until the physician should come with her; this he repeated sundry times with a degree of ardor. There is much reason to believe he had murdered Mrs. Beadle before he awaked the maid. Upon the maid's leaving the house he immediately proceeded to execute his purpose on the children and himself. It appears he had for some time before, carried to his bed side every night an ax and a carving knife; he smote his wife and each of the children with the ax on the side of the head as they lay sleeping in their beds; the woman had two wounds in the head, the scull of each of them was fractured; he then with the carving knife cut their throats from ear to ear; the woman and little boy were drawn partly over the side of their beds, as if to prevent the bedding from being besmeared with blood; the three daughters were taken from the bed and laid upon the floor side by side, like three lambs, before their throats were cut; they were covered with a blanket, and the woman's face with an handkerchief. He then proceeded to the lower floor of the house, leaving marks of his footsteps in blood on the stairs, carrying with him the ax and knife, the latter he laid upon the table in the room where he was found, reeking with the blood of his family. Perhaps he had thoughts he might use it against himself if his pistols should fail; it appears he then seated himself in a Windsor chair, with his arms supported by the arms of the chair; he fixed the muzles of the pistols into his two ears and fired them at the same instant: the balls went through the head in transverse directions. Although the neighbours were very near and some of them awake, none heard the report of the pistols. The capital facts of the massacre you have seen in the public papers; a minute detail was too horrible to be given at first, until the mind (especially of the relatives of the unhappy woman) had been prepared for it by a summary narrative, and even now 'tis enough to give feelings to apathy itself to relate the horrid tale.

The line to the physician obscurely announced the intentions of the man; the house was soon opened, but alas too late! The bodies were pale and motionless, swimming in their blood, their faces white as mountain snow, yet life seemed to tremble on their lips; description can do no more than saintly ape and trifle with the real figure.

Such a tragical scene filled every mind with the deepest distress; nature recoiled and was on the rack with distorting passions; the most poignant sorrow and tender pity for the lady and her innocent babes, who were the hapless victims of the brutal, studied cruelty of a husband and father, in whose embraces they expected to find security, melted every heart. Shocking effects of pride and false notions about religion.

To paint the first transports this affecting scene produced, when the house was opened, is beyond my reach.—Multitudes of all ages and sexes were drawn together by the sad tale.—The very inmost souls of the beholders were wounded at the sight, and torn by contending passions: Silent grief, with marks of astonishment, were succeeded by furious indignation against the author of the affecting spectacle, which vented itself in incoherent exclamations. Some old soldiers accidentally passing thro' the town that morning, on their way from camp to visit their friends, led by curiosity turned in, to view the sad remains; on sight of the woman and her tender offspring, notwithstanding all their firmness, the tender sympathetic tear stealing gently down their furrowed cheeks, betrayed the anguish of their hearts; on being shewed the body of the sacrificer they paused a moment, then muttering forth an oath or two of execration, with their eyes fixed on the ground in silent sorrow, they slowly went their way. So awful and terrible a disaster wrought wonderfully on the minds of the neighbourhood; nature itself seemed rustled, and refused the kindly aid of balmy sleep for a time.

Near the close of the day on the 12th of December, the bodies being still unburied, the people, who had collected in great numbers, grew almost frantic with rage, and in a manner demanded the body of the murderer; the law being silent on the subject, it was difficult to determine where decency required the body should be placed, many proposed it should be in an ignominious manner where four roads met, without any coffin or insignia of respect, and perforated by a stake. Upon which a question arose, where that place could be found which might be unexceptionable to the neighbourhood—but no one would consent it should be near his house or land. After some consultation it was thought best to place it on the bank of the river between high and low water mark; the body was handed out of the window and bound with cords on a sled, with the clothes on as it was found, and the bloody knife tied on his breast, without coffin or box, and the horse he usually rode was made fast to the sled—the horse, unaccumstomed to the draught, proceeded with great unsteadiness, sometimes running full speed, then stopping, followed by a multitude, until arriving at the water's edge, the body was tumbled into a hole dug for the purpose, like the carcase of a beast. Not many days after there appeared an uneasiness in sundry persons at placing the body so near a ferry much frequented; some threatnings were given out that the body should be taken up and a second time exposed to view. It was thought prudent it should be removed, and secretly deposited in some obscure spot, it was accordingly removed with the utmost secrecy; notwithstanding which some children accidentally discovered the place, and the early freshets partly washed up the body, and it has had a second remove to a place where it is hoped mankind will have no further vexation with it.

On the 13th of December the bodies of the murdered were intered in a manner much unlike that of the unnatural murderer.—The remains of the children were borne by a suitable number of equal age, attended with a sad procession of youths of the town, all bathed in tears; side by side the hapless woman's corpse was carried in solemn procession to the parish church yard, followed by a great concourse, who with affectionate concern and every token of respect were anxious to express their heart-felt sorrow in performing the last mournful duties.

The person of Mr. Beadle was small, his features striking and full of expression, with the aspect of fierceness and determination; his mind was contemplative, when once he had formed an opinion, was remarkably tenacious; as a merchant or trader, he was esteemed a man of strict honor and integrity, and would not descend to any low or mean artifice to advance his fortune. He was turned of 52 years of age when he died.

Mrs. Beadle was born at Plymouth, in Massachusetts, of reputable parents—a comely person, of good address, well bred, unusually serene, sincere, unaffected and sensible; died in the middle of life, aged 32 years.

The children (the eldest of which was a son, aged 12 years, the other three, daughters, the youngest aged 6 years) were such as cheared the hearts of their parents, who were uncommonly fond of displaying their little virtues and excellencies, and seemed to anticipate a continuance of growing parental satisfaction; alas, like early tender buds nipped by untimely frosts, they did but begin to live!

It is more than probable, this man had for months past desired that some or all of his children might be taken out of the world by accident; he removed all means of security from a well near his house, which he was careful heretofore to keep covered. His little boy he often sent to swim in the river, and has been heard to chide the child for not venturing further into deep water than his fears would suffer him. He has at times declared it would give him no pain or uneasiness to follow his children to the grave—his acquaintance knew these expressions could not arise from want of affection or tenderness for his children, but rather imagined him speaking rashly in jest. He ever spoke lightly of death as a bugbear the world causlessly feared. It appears from his writings, he at first had doubts whether it was just and reasonable for him to deprive his wife of life, and offers against it, only this reason, that he had no hand in bringing her into existence, and consequently had no power over her life.—She set out about the first of November on a journey to Fairfield, which he thought was by direction of Heaven to clear him of his doubts and remove her out of the way, at the time the business was to be done; and his intention was to have executed his design on himself and children in her absence. She proceeded no further than New-Haven, and by reason of some disappointment, returned ten days earlier than expected; he appeared chagrin'd at her early return, and soon began to invent some justifying reasons for depriving her of life also. He finally concludes it would be unmerciful to leave her behind to languish out a life in misery and wretchedness, which must be the consequence of the surprizing death of the rest of the family, and that since they had shared the frowns and smiles of fortune together, it would be cruelty to her, to be divided from them in death.

'Tis very natural for you to ask, whether it was possible a man could be transformed from an affectionate husband and an indulgent parent to a secret murderer, without some previous alteration, which must have been noticed by the family or acquaintance? Yet this was the case in this instance, there was no visible alteration in his conduct. It appears by his writings that he thought he had a right to deprive himself of life and intended to exercise that right if ever he should think himself unfortunate, the extension of this right to his children, was very easy. 'Tis probable, the principle had grown up gradually to the last stage. Since his death I have seen a letter he wrote to a friend as early as 1777, in which he has an expression like this—"I believe I and my family shall not live to see the end of the war."—It was then understood to mean nothing more than his expectation, the war would continue a long time, his late conduct has explained it very differently—Whether Mrs. Beadle had any fears of his evil intentions or not, is uncertain, that she had fears some great calamity would befall the family is evident, both from what she said, and what he has left in writing.—He writes on the 18th of November, that on the morning of the 17th she told him, "She dreamed he had wrote many papers, and was earnestly concerned for her, and that those papers were spotted with blood; and that she also saw a man wound himself past recovery and blood guggle (as she expressed it) from different parts of his body."—In another letter, of a later date, he writes as follows, viz. "I mentioned before that my wife had a dream concerning this affair, she has since had two more, one of them. That she was suddenly seized and liable to great punishment, that it created great confusion, but she afterwards got free and was happy; from her excellence of heart, I have no doubt but this will be the case with her.—On the thanksgiving night she dreamed, that her three daughters all lay dead, and that they even froze in that situation; and even yet I am little affected".

The afternoon before this terrible execution, Mrs. Beadle walked abroad to visit an acquaintance, and it was observed by the lady, she was uncommonly pensive; she asked the reason, Mrs. Beadle with much concern told her, "She had for months been troubled with frightful and uncommon dreams, and that very morning she dreamed violence had been offered her family and her children destroyed; she said those dreams wrought on her mind to a very great degree, to divert her thoughts from them she had walk'd abroad that afternoon; and that she verily believed Providence had judgments in store for their family, which he was about to inflict on them by some sweeping sickness, or in some other awful manner."—Mr. Beadle, who, as appears by his writings, was alone privy to his malevolent intentions, put a very different construction upon her dreams. He doubtless considered them as premonitions from Heaven, and convincing proof to him that his purpose was right, of which he says he had sundry intimations he really thought from God himself, which he does not describe.

From whence those dreams originated it is impossible to determine; whether 'the weapons he carried to his bed side gave her uneasiness and excited a jealousy in her mind of his intentions, or whether any of his conduct which fell under her observation might be alarming to her, which might trouble her sleep, no one can tell. She has lately mentioned sundry dreams of a similar nature, which she had near six months since. Some great and good characters have thought such intimations were at times given from on high, to convince mankind of the reality of the invisible world—to hazard such a conjecture in these modern days would perhaps be thought by the learned world a great mark of fanatacism—every man must think for himself, no one can pronounce with satisfactory certainty with respect to the origin and cause of such thoughts in sleep, which so nearly correspond with the true state of facts. Her last dream penned by him was nearly literally verified. Although the weather was serene and pleasant on the 10th, and near full moon: neither the sun or moon were visible from the time this horrid deed was done, until the body of this man was laid beneath the clods, which redoubled the horror: when suddenly the wind blew from the northwest, dispelled the vapours and discovered a cloudless sky. The air grew cold, and the faces of the other five being opened to view in their coffins, in the front of the meeting-house, the concourse was so great that much time was spent to give opportunity for all to take a view; the cold still increasing, the bodies in all probability were stiffened with frost.

Mr. Beadle left sundry letters directed to his acquaintance, and one laboured treatise in justification of his conduct; they contain many inconsistencies. He professes himself a Deist, but reprobates Atheism. While in life and prosperity he claim'd to be a Christian, and offered two of his children in baptism. Much has been said in favour of publishing his writings by those who have not seen them; those who have perused them have doubted the propriety of such a measure; not because his reasonings against revelation were in any degree unanswerable, but lest they might have some effect on weak and melancholy minds. He attempts to attack all rulers in Church and State, treats the Christian religion with a great degree of bitterness and bigotry; and yet absurdly concludes by saying, "if it is true he shall be saved by it."—He is very unsettled, wavering and inconsistent in his own beloved system of Deism. He flatters his pride by believing it was the height of heroism to dare to die by his own hands, and that the Deity would not willingly punish one, who was impatient to visit his God and learn his will from his own mouth, face to face in some future world, or worlds (which he thinks may be many) and seems to think there is as great probability of succeeding advantageously, in removing from one world to another as from one country, or calling to another; and seeing all men must be jugged off at last (as he expresses it) he was determined to make the experiment voluntarily which all must do through necessity. As he was much out of temper with the world, he was unwilling any of his family should stay behind to encounter its troubles, and since 'tis a father's duty to provide for his flock, he chose to consign them over to better hands.

'Tis doubtful whether any history of modern times can afford an instance of similar barbarity, even in the extreme distress of war. The ancients encouraged by numbers and example, did in hours of despair destroy themselves and families, to avoid the shame of becoming captives to be led in triumph, and the cruelty commonly exercised in those barbarous ages.

By this time your curiosity itself will be pleased to find me subscribing myself,

Your very humble Servant.

Wethersfield, February, 1783.

According to the Reverend Marsh's sermon, delivered at the funeral for Beadle's slain family (and which was later published along with the above text, in 1783, in what became known as the "Beadle Narrative"):

Had he [Beadle] left no written account of his intentions and views respecting the destruction of himself and family we should have been ready to consider it as the effect of a sudden and most vehement frenzy. But by his writings he appears to have had it in contemplation for three years.

The time he first fixed upon for carrying into execution his horrid and detestable purpose was the 18th of Nov. 1782. Not long before this he writes thus: "I mean to close the eyes of six persons thro' perfect humanity, and the most endearing fondness and friendship; for mortal father never felt more of these tender ties than myself.—How I shall really perform the task I have undertaken I know not 'till the moment arrives; but I believe I shall perform it as deliberately, and as steadily as I would go to supper, or to bed."

In one of the last letters he wrote, there is the following passage: "Any man that undertakes any great affair, and at the same time thinks, ought to be very deliberate indeed; and think and reflect again and again. On the morning of the sixth of December I rose before the sun, felt calm, and left my wife between sleep and wake, went into the room where my infants lay, found them all sound asleep; the means of death were with me, but I had not before determined whether to strike or not, but yet tho't it a good opportunity. I stood over them and asked my God whether it was right or not, now to strike; but no answer came, nor I believe ever does to man while on earth. I then examined myself, there was neither fear, trembling nor horror about me. I then went into a chamber next to that, to look at myself in the glass; but I could discover no alteration in my countenance or feelings: this is true as God reigns, but for further trial I yet postponed it." And when the fatal morning was come it does not appear by any one circumstance, but that he set himself about and went thro' the abominable work of murdering his wife, four children and himself, with as much steadiness, composure and firmness as he supposed he should.

13

THE ANTOINE PROBST AX MURDERS (1866)

The notorious and brutal Antoine Probst (1843–1866) was a German-born immigrant to the United States. He took a job as a farmhand with the Dearing family of Philadelphia. On April 7, 1866, thinking the Dearings had money in their farmhouse, he used an ax to murder Mr. and Mrs. Dearing; four of their children (aged eight years to fourteen months); another farmhand (seventeen-year-old Cornelius Cary); and twenty-five-year-old Elizabeth Dolan, a cousin who was visiting the family. He then ransacked the house, but netted less than $20. Probst was arrested and charged with eight counts of first-degree murder, and the jury convicted him after deliberating less than fifteen minutes. After he was hanged, his body was used for medical experiments.

CONFESSION OF EIGHT MURDERS.

The confession of Antoine Probst, the murderer of the Dearing family at Philadelphia, has again revived the absorbing public interest felt in all parts of the country in that terrible tragedy. The mystery which has so long hung over it has been dispelled by this confession, and the manner in which Probst managed to murder eight persons and to successfully conceal the crime is at length explained. Probst says he was excited by the hopes of gain, and supposed that Mr. Dearing had money in the house. He says he would have confessed his great crimes during the trial, but was deterred by the fear that the multitude of people who crowded all the avenues of approach to the court would tear him to pieces. It will be remembered that he murdered eight persons, Mr. Dearing, his wife, and four children, Miss Dolan, a young lady visitor at the house, and Cornelius Carey, a hired boy. They lived in the suburbs of the city upon a small grazing farm, and Probst was their hired man. After the murders he concealed all the bodies in a small stable, where they were discovered the days afterwards. Probst committed the murders on April 7, when Mr. Dearing was absent in the city, whither he had gone to bring Miss Dolan from a steamboat landing where she was expected to arrive that morning.

Probst says he premeditated the murders for several days, and supposed this was a good time to put his plans into execution. He determined to begin with Carey, a hired boy, and for that purpose started away from the house in company with the boy, who was driving a horse and cart. Probst had an axe, and when they were some 200 yards from the house, and concealed from view by a haystack, he went behind Carey and struck him on the head with the axe. He says his heart failed him before he struck the blow, and he drew back the axe four times before he was courageous enough to do it; but when he had done it he felt like a demon, and could have killed a hundred people. Striking Carey two or three times, and cutting his throat with the edge of the axe, he concealed the body under the haystack, and went towards the house to continue the bloody work. He quickly laid his plan, which was to entice the family singly into the stable and then kill them. First, he asked the oldest boy John to come to the stable and help him with some work, and, the boy cheerfully obeying, Probst struck and killed him with the axe which he had previously placed behind the door so as to be convenient. Cutting his throat, and covering the body with hay, he went out and called Mrs. Dearing, telling her to come and help him, as something was the matter with one of the horses. She came quickly, and as soon as she entered he struck her, killing her instantly. Her throat be cut too, and covered the body with hay. He then went to the house for the other children, and told the second son, Thomas, that his mother wanted him at the stable. The boy ran to the door and Probst after him, and two blows quickly despatched him. The murderer, who seems to have had a mania for cutting throats, cut this little boy's throat also, and laid his body with the others. But two children were now left, a little girl three years old, and a babe of 14 months. his cruelty to these helpless beings he thus tells:—

I left the axe in the same place and went to the home and took Annie and told her her mother wanted to see her. At the same time I took the baby on my arm and Annie walked alongside of me to the stable. I put the baby on the floor on the hay and took Annie inside. Annie looked around for her mother. [A question was here asked—'Did she ask for her mother?' and the murderer, smiling, continued- 'I was too much in a hurry to notice.'] I knocked her down and cut her throat, and then I took the baby and cut it; then I took the axe and put it on the bench under the porch, where it was always kept: then I went to the house and took the horse from the cart and put him in the stable, and then went back to the house and stayed there waiting for Mr. Dearing.

This completed six of the murders, and shortly after noon Mr. Dearing and Miss Dolan in a waggon reached the house. Probst had laid his plan, and whilst Miss Dolan took off her bonnet and shawl told Mr. Dearing that a steer was sick in the stable, and all the family were there. Without removing even his gloves, Mr. Dearing quickly walked to the stable. Probst followed him with the axe, striking him as soon as he entered the stable, knocking him down, and killing him by giving two more blows and cutting his throat. Putting a little hay over his body, Probst came out after Miss Dolan. She called to him to take the horse out of Mr. Dearing's waggon. He, in reply, said Mr. Dearing wished to see her in the stable, and that all the family were there. She walked to the stable and he struck her with a hammer. She fell on Mr. Dearing's body, and Probst, to make the tragedy complete, cut her throat too.

This completed the terrible series of murders, and of the family but one person was left —a little boy 10 years of ago—who was absent on a visit in another part of Philadelphia. Probst, not in the least unnerved, says he took the horse out of the waggon, fed him, fed all the cattle and the poultry, fastened the stable doors, and then, going to the house, changed his clothes for a suit of Mr. Dearing's. He shaved himself with Mr. Dearing's razor, and then searched the house. He thought he would obtain great plunder, but his hopes were doomed to disappointment. He pro-cured two pistols, a watch, and in money about $13. For this paltry sum he had committed eight murders. He says he felt bad and ate some bread and butter, and towards evening, fastening the doors he left. For five days he wandered about the city, spending his money in dissipation, and when arrested had about 30 cents. left. He sold the watch and revolvers in his necessity.

Here, another published account (The Life, Confession, and Atrocious Crimes of Antoine Probst) fills in more of the grim details of his maneuvers after the crimes:

Probst, with his dearly purchased plunder, left the house and took his way to the city. A flight we have called it, but it was rather a march of triumph, for he at once went to spend his gains in the worst haunts of dissipation. Saturday night he spent in a brothel, near Front and Moore streets. Sunday he passed in Eckfeldt's [sic] lager beer saloon, in New Market street, near Willow. In the evening he left his valise in the charge of the landlord, and stayed all night at a house near Front and Brown streets.

On Monday he again went to Leckfeldt's, and remained there till Tuesday. In the morning he left without paying for his lodging and meals, and Mrs. Leckfeldt took possession of the valise, intending to keep it as a security for the payment of the bill. Tuesday night he again spent with a prostitute. From Wednesday till Thursday he passed at Front and Brown, and in the morning returned to the lager beer saloon. There, as he sat at a table, a man began to read to the others, who were drinking beer, an account of the discovery of the murder, published in a German paper. Probst listened without betraying any emotion, nor did he blench when he heard the expressions of horror and rage around him. He was even appealed to by one of the company, who said: "What do you think ? Isn't it a d—d shame, that a German should have done this and disgraced his countrymen ?" Probst made no reply, and pretended to be asleep, with his hat drawn over his eyes. But immediately afterward a German who knew him entered, and proposed a game of cards. Probst consented at once, and in the intervals of shuffling and dealing had the hardihood to read the account of his own crime, no doubt criticising the errors made in the general ignorance of the facts. He played cards for an hour, and then remained sullenly in his chair, while the very officers of justice entered the room and spoke to him about the murder. After he had supper, at seven o'clock, he rose and left the saloon. A short time afterward he was arrested near Twenty-third and Market streets.

Strange, indeed, must be the nature of the man who could meditate and execute this crime.

The same account described him as:

. . . a strange being, with a small head, and scarcely any reasoning faculties. He feels some light pangs of remorse, but sleeps soundly and ease breathes heartily. He has been found guilty of murder, . . . The sensation throughout the country caused by this series of murder was very great, and it has been revived by this confession, which was publicly made to the High Sheriff and spiritual adviser of the criminal.

Premeditated it certainly was, for . . . no drunken man could suddenly have planned so shrewdly the destruction of an entire family. For weeks the unsuspecting Deerings [*sic*] had been the companions of a relentless foe, whose lynx eyes, unknown to them, followed every movement; . . .

An account of Probst's arrest given by James Dorsey, formerly of the Pennsylvania Infantry and then appointed to the police force by the mayor, had the following to report:

On the night of the twelfth of April, at about twenty minutes before nine, I was standing at the corner of Twenty-third and Market streets with two brother officers. It was a dark, gloomy night and a drizzling rain was falling. While we were talking a man passed us going toward the bridge. He was slouching along close to the buildings, and one of my companions pointed him out and said: There goes an Irishman, Dorsey, follow him up and arrest him. It may be Probst in disguise.' "I'll see who he is, anyway,' was my reply, and I followed on after him. "My partners laughed derisively and crossed the street to an oyster saloon. I overtook the suspicious stranger just before he reached the bridge, and tapping him on the shoulder, said: "'Good evening!' "How do?' he muttered, and hung his head. "I pulled off his cap and looked him squarely in the face. "'You're a Dutchman!' said I. "No, me Frenchman!" he answered. "Anyway, I want you,' said I, and I took him by the shoulder and led him back to the station-house. When he stood up in front of the rail I noticed that his right thumb was missing, and I knew that it was Probst. The next morning Mrs. Dolan positively recognized him as Probst. Acting under orders from the lieutenant I took him before Mayor McMichael, and in his presence and mine Probst confessed that he murdered the boy Carey who worked for the Deerings [sic]. He denied killing the others, however, claiming that they were murdered by his accomplice, Frederick Genther. Afterwards he admitted murdering the whole family, and he was hanged for the crime."

Probst was hanged on June 8, 1866. His published "Confession" offers insight into the execution process as it was then:

The body was placed in the hands of Dr. B. Howard Rand, who, with five assistants, proceeded to make a number of scientific experiments. The first of those consisted in the examination of the eye, with the aid of a powerful electric light, for the purpose of detecting an image remaining upon the retina.

The right eye was afterward taken out, to allow of more careful examination, as there is a modern scientific theory that events occurring immediately before death remain impressed upon the retina.

The galvanic battery was then applied, one pole being placed in the mouth, and the other to the temple. A powerful current was then passed through the wires, producing a fearful contortion of the frame. The jaws worked convulsively, and the chest heaved as with a strong respiration. This action was, of course, purely mechanical, as the neck had been broken by the fall, and life was entirely extinct.

14

SLOBBERY JIM & THE DAYBREAK GANG (1850s)

Slobbery Jim (his real name is unknown) was a New York City gangster, robber, pirate, and murderer whose cohorts, known as the Daybreak Gang, were mostly Irish teenagers from the slums of the Five Points. Mostly they robbed ships on the East River, typically murdering anyone they perceived as being in their way. Jim is reputed to have murdered one of his confederates in a brutal fight to the death over the disputed ownership of twelve cents.

RIVER THIEVES—THE BIRDS OF PREY WHO PROWL NIGHTLY ALONG THE RIVER FRONT OF NEW YORK—HOW THEY OPERATE—THE SHADOWY SKIFF PROPELLED BY MUFFLED OARS—THE DARK-LANTERN OF THE RIVER POLICE—REVOLVER PRACTICE, "MY GOD! I'M SHOT."—THE HOWLETT AND SAUL CASE—THE DOUBLE EXECUTION—HAUNTS AND HABITS OF THE RIVER-GANG—THEIR DEEDS—TRAGIC END OF " SOCCO THE BRACER."

Many of them are not early risers at the brightest of times, being birds of the night who roost when the sun is high and are wide awake and keen for prey when the stars are out.

—*Dickens, in* Bleak House

To those who nightly cross and recross the rivers on either side of the metropolis, the singularities which strike others so forcibly are of no effect. Familiarity has bred contempt; and where a visitor to the great city would naturally and necessarily be stricken with awe and wonder, the *habitué* is nonchalant and unmoved. In the gloaming, when the variegated lights of the ferry-boats flash like a kaleidoscope of precious stones, more brilliant in their relief against the inky darkness of the river and adjacent shores, the boat of the river-thief shoots out from its concealment like an evil spirit on the night. The shadowy ghostliness of the ships' rigging nor the sad sobbing of the waves has any romantic interest for the thief. To him it is as much a matter of practicality and convenience as is the honest merchant's broad daylight. With all the risk he knows he must encounter, the river-thief is complaisant, and as happy as a criminal can be, when darkness and storm combine to aid him in his nefarious excursions. Shrouded by the murkiness of the night, the boat shoots out into mid-stream, and the muffled oars are plied by strong and skilful arms. There are three men in the boat, and from their unwavering course it is evident that their business has been well planned. No haphazard seeking after stray trifles: the river-thief is too thoroughly a professional. He has previously been instructed by the captain of the gang of the work expected of him. His only is it to find the means, and his long experience renders this an easy matter. The occupants of the boat in mid-stream have made a survey, and seeing no hindrances, they pull rapidly in-shore and listen for the sound of the spy on the dock to tell them whether or not the police boat is in waiting for them. The signal is favorable, and, under the shadows of the docks and ferry-houses, the light skiff is impelled swiftly and silently to its destination. A brig lies in the river, and alongside her the boat pulls and is made fast to her chains. Stealthily one of the crew of the boat climbs to the deck of the vessel, and carefully appropriates whatever loose pieces of chain and rope lie about, but while doing this he does not neglect to note the presence or absence, drowsiness or watchfulness of the guard, for it may be that the booty is rich, and lies in the cabin. If this be the case, four men have been sent, and they are desperate, resolute pugilists, who, if death be necessary to the success of the venture, will not hesitate to take life or sacrifice their own. The men who are lying in the Tombs at this writing, under a sentence of twenty years' imprisonment, were of the character described. Boarding a ship lying in the bay, one knocked the mate on the head, another shot the captain, and the twain then kept the crew at a safe distance while the cabin was ransacked for the plunder they knew to be concealed there; and not content to have secured this, the wife of the captain was held down while a pair of valuable ornaments were taken from her ears. They escaped, but were captured, and are paying the penalty of their misdeeds.

It sometimes happens that as the river-thieves are seeking a haven of safety after a robbery, and as their boat glides quietly along in the dark, that another is seen, and shooting out from behind some wharf or from the shade of some vessel, she makes rapidly for the thieves. They see their enemy and know it for the police-boat. Now comes the race. The police-boat has more men and gaining rapidly on her prey, the latter is called on to surrender. The answer is a laugh of derision as the men lay aside their oars and drawing weapons, prepare to defend them selves to the last. One shot fired at the police-boat brings a dozen in return, and the fusilade is fast and furious for a minute. A cry. "My God, I'm shot," comes from the boat of the thieves, and when the police pull alongside, they find all the men wounded and faint, but one, and he has passed over the river to the Thither Shore.

The tales which these men, criminal as they are, could tell of life at the water-side, would form a page which might be read for the edification of those who seek to know the dark side of life. For as the river-thief, like Rogue Riderhood, pulls up and down in search of plunder, or, in the thieves' vernacular, "swag," he not infrequently hears the splash in the water that tells him of "Another Unfortunate" who has ended a world of trouble and sorrow in that one leap from life to death. He has seen them when they first stood gazing moodily into the water below, and knew from his own experience of life that they, contemplating in bitter agony the past of sorrow and wondering how in the future they may escape the judgment they have been taught to believe is in store for them; he has seen the last leap that told of the first embrace of death; he has noted the rising bubbles that tell of the spirit departed, and the prow of his boat has pushed aside from its course the floating body. And yet none of these things have moved him to reflection, or to such reflection as brings repentance and reformation. And when his trip is performed and he has come safely away with his plunder, he resorts to the vilest drinking saloons of the riverside, and there in the company of his "pals" he forgets the dangers he has passed and sinks deeper and deeper into crime in the exchange of ideas and experiences to be put into practice at the first opportunity.

The Double Execution.—Howlett and Saul.

Twenty years ago, river-thieves were more numerous, if not more daring, than they are to-day. The execution together of Howlett and Saul, which took place in the Tombs on the 28th of January, 1853, struck terror to the hearts of the entire fraternity, and for a brief period their depredations almost ceased.

One murky night in the fall of 1852, a trio of river pirates quietly pulled alongside of the ship *William Watson*, then lying between James slip and Oliver street. They stealthily climbed over the ship's side to her deck. Entering the cabin, they were detected in the act by private watchman Charles Baxter. But one shot was fired, and the watchman fell to the deck dead, the ball having passed through his neck, but the report of the pistol had been heard by a vigilant policeman, and the result was that the murderers were arrested. They proved to be Nicholas Howlett, William Saul, and one Johnson, well-known river-thieves. The three were tried and found guilty of murder in the first degree, and sentenced to be hanged January 28th, 1853. The night previous to the execution, the condemned men appeared in excellent spirits, and laughed and conversed as if their hours on earth were not numbered. They retired about midnight, and both dreamt of being hung. Early on the day of execution, they expressed a desire to see the gallows. When Howlett ascertained that there was a weight to be used, he remarked, "We will go up, instead of going down." Saul answered, "If the spirit went up, it did not matter as to the body." Howlett accompanied the priests to the chapel, where mass was celebrated, while Saul, who was a Protestant, was visited by several eminent clergymen. In the yard surrounding the gallows were about three hundred persons, many of whom had known the condemned men from boyhood. Johnson, whose sentence had been commuted, the day previous, to imprisonment for life, took an affectionate farewell of the men who were to soon suffer the extreme penalty. Sheriff Orser appeared and notified the doomed men that the hour had arrived for their execution, and with little ceremony they were prepared for the gallows. On reaching the foot of the scaffold, Saul expressed a desire to meet several persons, and a number came forward and shook hands with him; among whom were Tom Hyer and Bill Poole, the noted pugilists. Saul uttered a heartfelt prayer for Howlett and himself, and committed his soul to God. The Sheriff, who was much affected, kissed each of the men, and then gave the signal. The axe fell, the rope was severed, and they were jerked six feet from the ground and into eternity.

A Backward Glimpse at the River Pirates.

Not having the inclination, nor the opportunity, in the preparation of this work, to delve into the "flash" memoirs of the river-thieves of New York and Brooklyn, for the purpose of producing a panoramic history of their *personnel* and operations, we gladly avail ourselves of the subjoined article from the *Brooklyn Eagle*. It has evidently been collected by a careful hand, and is a miniature painting of the daring exploits, for years back, of these reckless men. It scarcely needs any comment, as it adorns its own tale and points its own moral.

"Ever since the days of Saul and Howlett, organized bands of pirates and river-thieves have infested both shores of the East River. This fact has been long and well known to the police of New York and Brooklyn, who have not alone become familiar with the members of the different gangs, but have learned their resorts, their 'molls,' their 'pals' and their 'fences,' and yet have failed to make any organized attempt to break up river piracy. The Harbor Police of New York freely admit their inability to suppress stealing on the river, and claim that too much duty is required of too few men, while the Brooklyn Police urge as an excuse the fact that they have no Harbor Police. That there is some truth in these explanations none can deny, for with the many miles of water front possessed by both cities and the inducements held out by the junkmen, the wonder is that more depredations are not committed.

"River-thieves as a class are more reckless of human life than either burglars or highwaymen. They believe in the doctrine that 'dead men tell no tales,' they always go well armed, and never hesitate to sacrifice life rather than jeopardize their own liberty. They are like wharf-rats, as much at home in the water as on shore, and when once they have committed a robbery or a murder, if too closely chased, they are prepared to jump overboard, dive under a pier, and thus escape arrest or even detection, as has often been done. Probably within a day or two afterward the vessel they have robbed and the friends of the man they have murdered will have gone to sea. Thus the circumstances will soon die out of the recollection of the detectives, who, not stimulated by the hope of a reward, will, of course, fail to make any efforts to discover the perpetrators of what the newspapers will style, 'Another River Outrage.'

"The river- thieves of New York and Brooklyn are divided into two classes, namely, those who steal from the docks in the day-time, and those who board and rob vessels by night. In this city the former class abound. Though troublesome, they are not considered dangerous. New York is the haven of the more desperate class; men born on the river who have graduated in crime, and who, after serving several terms in reformatories, jails, and penitentiaries, come forth full-fledged pirates, ready to scuttle a ship, rob a cabin, cut a throat, or throw a watchman overboard. This class belongs to the peculiar institutions of New York city, while our own dock thieves, less known, cruise from Hudson avenue to the Atlantic Dock, paying occasional visits to the Wallabout, back of the Navy Yard Dock, and sometimes inside the Cob Dock of the Navy Yard, thence to that still sparsely settled region between the built-up portion of Williamsburgh and Brooklyn proper. If closely pressed they leave their boats and their 'swag,' and soon find refuge in the classic regions of Irishtown.

"Twenty years ago river pirates were more numerous, if not more daring, than they are to-day. There were 'Sow' Madden, 'Slobbery Jim,' 'Bill Lowrie,' and 'One-armed Charley,' the pals of Saul and Howlett. As they met their fate, younger men took their places. 'Old Tom Flaherty,' 'Tommy Shay,' 'Bum' Mahoney, 'Cow-legged Sam,' 'Socco,' 'Denny' Brady, and others then became the chief of the river-thieves, and more recently there has been 'Scotchy Lavelle,' 'Tom the Mick,'

'Larry Nevins,' Martin Broderick, Dongan, Carroll, Preslin, Coffee, Merricks, the Commodore, and the gangs so well known about the Hook, the Navy Yard, and the shores of Brooklyn, New York, Jersey City, Hoboken, and Staten Island.

"The exploits of these river-thieves make a perfect romance of crime. Devoid of sensationalism, it is a chapter in the criminal history of New York and Brooklyn as thrilling and interesting as it is true.

"Many old citizens will recollect the excitement caused by the murder of a watchman on board the ship William Watson, lying between James slip and Oliver street, nearly twenty-one years ago. Three river-thieves boarded the vessel at night for the purpose of committing a robbery. They were discovered by the watchman while in the act of rifling the cabin, and thinking to escape detection by murder a shot was fired. The watchman fell dead, shot through the neck, but the pistol-shot had been heard by a vigilant policeman, and the result was that the murderers were arrested. They proved to be Saul, Howlett, and one Johnson, all well-known river-thieves. Justice was then more swift than it is now. Johnson turned State's evidence, and Saul and Howlett expiated their crime on the gallows. What became of Johnson is a mystery to the present day, but it has been hinted that he was killed by 'Bill' Lowrie and others of the Saul and Howlett gang for having 'given them away.' At any rate, Lowrie and 'Slobbery Jim' became the leaders of the gang, with their headquarters at Slaughter-House Point, a low gin-mill at the corner of Water street and James slip, kept by Pete Williams, formerly of New Orleans. After seven murders had been committed there, the place was closed by Captain (now Inspector) Thorne, of the Fourth Ward Police. Then 'Bill' Lowrie and his reputed wife, 'Moll' Maher, opened a grogshop in Water street, near Oliver, next door to 'Bilker's Hall.' It was called 'The Rising States,' and for many years was the headquarters of the river-thieves. About this time Charley Monnell, *alias* 'One-armed Charley,' became a recognized power among the thieves and murderers in the Fourth Ward. He opened a place in Dover street, which he called the 'Hole in the Wall,' and with Kate Flannery and 'Gallus Mag' as Lieutenants, soon made his den attractive to his kindred spirits. It was there that 'Slobbery Jim' stabbed and killed 'Patsey the Barber;' it was there that thieves and junkmen would meet to 'put up jobs;' it was there that men were drugged and robbed and women beaten under 'One-armed Charley's' directions; it was there that young thieves became graduates in crime.

"In 1858 the pirates were stronger, more numerous and better organized than they had been since Saul and Howlett were hanged. The police of the Fourth Ward had nightly encounters with the river-thieves, and Roundsman Blair and Officers Spratt and Gilbert were making themselves notorious by shooting a round dozen of the pirates within a year. 'Slobbery Jim' had meanwhile made his escape, and never more was heard of until he turned up as captain of a company of rebels during the late war; Bill Lowrie had been sent to State Prison for fifteen years; Sam McCarthy, alias 'Cow-legged Sam,' had given up the river and become a burglar, and the rest of the mob had moved up town toward the Hook, or to the neighborhood of the Brooklyn Navy Yard. And thus the old Saul and Howlett gang dropped out of existence, and to a great extent out of the recollection of almost everybody. About this time business began to increase in the Seventh Ward, New York. Junkmen, who, as a class, are not inquisitive and buy anything from anybody without asking any questions about where it came from, began moving from the Fourth to the Seventh Ward. They seemed to do a thriving business, thanks to such thieves as Bill Murray, George Williams, John Watson, Socco, Jim Coffee, Valentine, Billy Woods, Tom the Mick, Larry Nevins, Scotchy Lavelle, Martin Broderick, Abe Cokeley, Denny Brady, George *alias* Pat *alias* Sow Madden,

Piggy, Beeny, Nigger and a score of others. This mob did their work very quietly for several years, and were really being forgotten except by the junkmen, when Perry, the junkman, shot and killed ex-Police Officer Thomas Hayes at the Harbeck Stores, Furman street. Perry, the junkman, was one of the New York mob, and Hayes was employed as a private detective at Harbeck Stores. It was found necessary to kill Hayes in order to commit a particular robbery, and his life was sacrificed. With a bullet in his breast, his life's blood flowing out in torrents, poor Hayes jumped on a passing horse-car, and as he fell into a seat, he said to the astonished passengers, 'My name is Thomas Hayes. I am a private watchman at Harbeck Stores. Ned Perry shot me'—and died. The murderer escaped hanging and is now serving out a life sentence in State Prison.

"Four years of comparative quiet again elapsed and the scenes of these midnight murders and robberies had again been transferred, this time to the neighborhood of the Battery. Vigilance on the part of the police soon drove them away, however, and the old ground was visited again. The old river-thieves had all been 'settled,' and the young ones were ambitious. This was the condition of affairs when on the night of May 29, 1873, Joseph Gayles, alias 'Socco the Bracer,' 'Bum' Mahoney, a first-class river-thief, and 'Billy' Woods, formerly a stone-cutter but now a murderer and expert river-thief, stole a boat from the foot of Jackson street, and with muffled oars pulled down stream to Pier 27, East River. They boarded the Brig Margaret, of New Orleans, and while ransacking the captain's trunk awakened the captain and mate. A scuffle ensued which resulted in the thieves leaving the brig and taking to their boat. An alarm brought officers Musgrave and Kelly to the scene of the attempted robbery. It was three o'clock in the morning, the sky was over cast, and not a star was to be seen. As Musgrave flashed his dark lantern under the pier, he saw a boat starting out. Throwing the rays of his lantern full upon it, three men stood up, revolvers in hand, and the firing began. Musgrave's first shot gave 'Socco' his death wound.

"The officers continued firing until they had emptied their pistols, but the thieves escaped in the darkness, and pulled over toward the Long Island shore. 'Socco the Bracer' fainted from loss of blood, and his companions, thinking he was dead, threw him overboard to lighten the boat. The water revived him and he begged piteously to be taken in the boat again. This was done, after much trouble, but as soon as he touched the thwart he gasped and died. The boat was again stopped mid-stream and the lifeless body of 'Socco the Bracer,' with the tell-tale bullet hole through the breast, was thrown to the waters, but four days afterward it came to the surface at the foot of Stanton street, within sight from the residence of the dead river-thief. Secrecy was no longer possible, and now the thieves themselves admit that their pal was killed by Officer Musgrave, of the Fourth Precinct Police.

"Socco's just fate did not prevent the commission of other robberies.

"Less than three months ago the brig Mattano, Captain Conning-ton, was boarded off the Battery by a gang of masked and armed men. The captain and his wife were subjected to many indignities and then robbed of everything of value they had on board the vessel. For this crime two well-known river-thieves, Dougan and Carroll, were arrested, tried, convicted, and sentenced to twenty years' imprisonment in State Prison. They confessed they had been river-thieves all their lives, but denied all knowledge of the crime with which they were charged. Despite their prayers, protestations and oaths, they were convicted, but it has recently been made known to the authorities that the robbery was committed by 'Denny' Brady, 'Larry' Griffin and 'Patsy' Conroy. These three men belong to the gang of masked burglars who have lately been committing such terrible depredations in the suburban villages. Brady is now confined in jail at Catskill, charged with the robbery of Mr. Post's house, and Griffin and Conroy are in the White Plains jail, awaiting trial for the robbery of Mr. Emmett's residence. Brady is a man well known to sports who travel down the Coney Island road; a medium-sized man, with broad shoulders and powerful build. A sentence of, at least, twenty years in State Prison awaits each of them, and the probabilities are that Dougan and Carroll will be pardoned—and arrested again at some not distant day, for a crime they will actually commit. In quick succession several other daring robberies were perpetrated, during the month of December. First came the robbery of the bark 'Zonma,' at Pier 22, East River. Louis Engleman, a Fourth Ward river-thief, who lived at No. 57 Rose street, New York, is the convicted thief. He was captured by Sergeant Blair, of the Second Precinct, after a chase of three hours, during which he jumped overboard and while hanging on to the rudder of a three-masted schooner, at Pier 27, was thrown a rope by a policeman. 'Go to h—l with your rope,' he exclaimed, rejecting it. 'You shan't take me alive.'

"He dove under vessels and docks, and for a long time defied half a dozen officers in boats, but he was at length captured, and is now doing the State some service. The following night an attempt was made to steal some bales of cotton-duck from Pier 8, North River. The watchman gave the alarm, which brought Officer Mulrooney and Captain Lowrie to the scene. The thieves, as they pulled away in their boat, opened fire upon the officers, which the latter returned, apparently with good effect, as one man was heard to exclaim: 'Oh, I'm shot,' but no trace of a dead or wounded river-thief has since been found.

"The 'Hook Gang' of river-thieves is probably composed of the remnant of the successors of Saul and Howlett. Its chief spirits are Merricks, a desperate and bold thief, capable of committing any crime, Jaraes Coffee, who has served one term in State Prison, and has his likeness in the Rogues' Album, Le Strange and Lewis, highwaymen, burglars, river-thieves, or pick pockets, as occasion may require; Preslin, a daring thief, Riley, who has just been sent to Sing Sing, and his three pale, McCracken, Gallagher and Bonner, who 'fell' on another racket. This choice crowd holds forth at the foot of Stanton street, across the ferry, and operates anywhere between Fourteenth street and the Battery. The week before Christmas they planned the robbery of a vessel lying at the Atlantic Dock, but for some unknown reason the job failed, and they had to look about for smaller game nearer home. The canal-boat Thomas H. Brick was lying off the foot of Fourteenth street, and shortly after midnight, on the morning of December 20, she was boarded by Sam McCracken, John Gallagher and Tommy Bonner. With pistols in their hands they confronted the captain, who succeeded in giving the alarm before he was bound and gagged. The battle was short and decisive. Officer Booz and Captain M. J. Murphy arrested them, and they are now doing three and a half 'stretches,' each, in Auburn State Prison. They are all very desperate characters, though Bonner, 21 years of age, is probably the most dangerous. Gallagher is only 19, and has served several times in the Penitentiary, and McCracken, 20 years of age, has been an inmate of Crow Hill Castle. Beyond a few petty dock-thieves who infest the First Ward, New York, and are kept in subjection by Captain Van Dusen and his officers, and the scoundrels who prowl along the Brooklyn piers, and whose histories are not different from those of other sneak-thieves, there is no other regular organized mob worthy of extended notice, except the Seventh Ward gang of New York, of which each man has his individual history. Of course, originally, the 'mob' was composed of more expert and daring thieves than it is at present. 'Bum' Mahoney is now the acknowledged leader, but as he is well known to the Brooklyn and New York detectives, his career on the river is gradually drawing to an end. When he and Big Dennis Brady 'worked' together, they were a powerful and dangerous combination.

"Brady, though only thirty-one years of age, has been connected with nearly every daring, prominent robbery in this country. It was Brady who organized the gang of masked robbers. He is one of the three men who, about two years ago, went into the Kensington Bank, of Philadelphia, tied up the two watchmen and robbed the safe of $100,000. Brady, on that occasion, was dressed in the uniform of a police officer, and for his share in the robbery received $12,000. Shortly afterward he gave out that he had 'squared it,' married a respectable young woman and opened a lager-beer saloon in Bayard street, but before six weeks had expired the money was all gone. Brady was ejected for non-payment of rent, and the reformed burglar became a greater thief than ever.

"'Bum,' or Denny Mahoney, is about twenty-four years of age, very dark complexioned, about five feet five in height, and weighs 140 pounds. He is smart, brave as a lion, and as daring a little fellow as ever lived. No river-thief is better known than 'Bum' Mahoney. Every policeman in the Seventh Ward and every detective in New York and Brooklyn knows him as a river-thief, and yet he has never been to State Prison. He has served two terms in the Penitentiary for dock-stealing, has his photograph in the Rogues' Album, and claims an intimate acquaintance with the notorious Jack Perry of Water street. Perry, from being a notorious thief, has become a notorious liquor-dealer. His saloon is the resort for nearly all the Water street thieves and prostitutes, to whom he likes to tell the story of his stealing Josh Ward's champion rowing belt, how he was captured by Sergeant Slater, convicted, sentenced to State Prison for fourteen years and six months, and escaped serving a full term on account of his political friends and his good looks. 'Bum' Mahoney may be found there often, particularly when about to 'operate' on the Long Island or North River shore. That is to protect himself in case of arrest, by proving an alibi. Nearly two years ago, 'Bum' was caught one night by Detectives Jarboe and Shalvey in the act of robbing a schooner at Pier 50, East River. Jarboe threw himself on his prisoner to pinion his hands, when Mahoney tried to throw him overboard. In the scuffle Mahoney made his escape, jumped into a small boat, and then he and the officers exchanged several shots from their revolvers. Two days afterward Mahoney was arrested at his home in Water street, by the same detectives, but meanwhile the schooner had gone to sea, and 'Bum' was there upon released, as there was no complaint against him.

"The true leader of the Seventh Ward gang of river-thieves is not 'Bum' Mahoney, but 'Tommy' Shay or Shea. He is a notorious villain. His likeness adorns the Rogues' Gallery, and his pedigree is well known to the State Prison authorities. Shay is 36 years of age, 5 feet 9 inches in height, weight 150 pounds, is dark complexioned, and of a sullen temper. Ten years ago, as now, he was a notorious river-thief, and was implicated in killing the mate of a vessel off Bikers Island, with 'Patsy' Conroy and 'Larry' Griffin. He has served one term in Sing Sing, and is looked upon by young thieves as their beau-ideal of a murderous river-thief.

"Probably the most remarkable man of the Seventh Ward gang is 'Jimmy' Whalen. He is 28 years of age, 5 feet 8 inches high, dark complexioned, and weighs 160 pounds. Mr. Whalen is well known to the Brooklyn Police, and when he finds business dull in New York, may easily be found within a short distance of the Navy Yard gate. He returned from a twelve months' sojourn in the Penitentiary only a few weeks ago, having served a term for a most remarkable crime. In company with 'Charley' Davis, he stole a ship's cable, weighing eight thousand pounds. Unaided, these two men piled that immense weight of iron in a boat, and brought it from Pier 50, East River, on the New York side, to a vacant lot in Van Brunt Street, Brooklyn, near Red Hook Point. The men were arrested by detectives Shalvey and Jarboe, and the chain was recovered, and although it could not be taken to court as evidence against them, Whalen pleaded guilty and was sent to the Penitentiary for one year, which he served. Davis pleaded not guilty, was tried, convicted, and sentenced to State Prison for five years. Whalen wields a large amount of political influence, and although he had been arrested a score of times, it had always been found impossible to convict him until he stole the ship's cable. That was found to be too heavy a load for his friends to carry, and now he knows how it is himself.

"Bob Taylor, *alias* 'Shipsey,' is properly one of the Seventh Ward gang, although he is now hiding in this city of churches, when he could and ought to be arrested, as well as his pal, John Kane, *alias* 'Beeny,' who is with him. 'Shipsey' was sentenced to five years in State Prison for river piracy at the foot of Pike street, New York, where he robbed a schooner and shot at the captain. He made his escape at Sing Sing, nearly three months ago, since which time he has made his headquarters near the Navy Yard. 'Beeny,' his pal, is also wanted nearer home, and well he knows it. He is a smooth-looking scoundrel, light complexioned, about 5 feet 6 1/2 inches in height, and weighs nearly 160 pounds. He has a round, full, rather good-looking face, and is continually preaching about his honesty. He has served in the Penitentiary, and having been unfortunate in a wheat speculation, he bids fair to reach that institution again within a very few days.

"James Wallace, alias 'Nigger,' is another one of this select crowd. He is about five feet ten inches, weighs 175 pounds, and is called 'Nigger' on account of his dark, swarthy complexion. He is a fresh arrival from Sing Sing, where he did the State five years' good work for a very clever river job. He sticks closely to the pier at the foot of Jackson street, New York, where he can be found with 'Johnny' Kirby, a young river-thief, twenty-four years of age, five feet eight inches in height, very light complexioned, and weighs about 130 pounds. Occasionally these two gentlemen, representing the blonde and brunette styles of beauty, make a tour of the watering places, as they call them. No. 275 Water street, kept by George Christopher and 'Long Mary,' is their Saratoga, 'Ann Sauk's' dance house is their Newport, 'Kate Carroll's' is their Long Branch, 'Gallus Mag's' is their Coney Island, and the 'Flag of our Union' and 'Liverpool Mary Ann's' are respectively Jerome Park and Fleetwood. They are first-class beats when not in funds, and take great delight in being considered lady-killers and cheek-charmers.

"Excepting 'Tony' Gillespie, who is 'wanted' for a job, the rest of the gang are where they can do but little harm. Tony is a lively young fellow, who has served one term in State Prison and two in the Penitentiary. His particular pal was Michael Noles, *alias* 'Piggy.'

"'Piggy' is now in the Penitentiary for stealing a boat and its contents. Though a nice young man, 'Piggy' has visited the Penitentiary four times in all, and his 'Moll' thinks it's 'a great shame, and he such a pivoter.'

"One of the 'best men' of the gang is one of the most unfortunate. Edward Sullivan, an accomplished river-thief and burglar, the bosom friend of 'Bum' Mahoney and 'Tommy' Shay, has again been torn away from the family circle. Sullivan is 26 years of age. Six years ago he was a terror, but one night he fell into the hands of a 'flatty cop' and was given 'five stretches' for a very badly executed river job. He served every day of his time, and returned to his old associates a short time ago, determined hereafter to do his work ashore and not afloat. In other words, he changed from a river-thief to a burglar. While practising he again fell, and last week he was sentenced to two years at his old quarters.

"Kings County Penitentiary contains only two of these choice spirits from the Seventh Ward of New York. They are 'Old Tom' Flaherty and James Smith. Smith is an ordinary river-thief and sneak, but 'Old' Flaherty belongs to a fine family. The old man has lived half a century, while Smith has yet to celebrate his twenty-second birthday. They would steal a boat from the New York side and then make for South Brooklyn; then they would work up stream, robbing farm-houses, hen-roosts, canal-boats, or anything else that came in their way.

"At length they fell into the hands of the Brooklyn Police, and were sentenced to the Penitentiary for five years. Flaherty's family has recently become somewhat divided. His wife, a notorious thief and shop-lifter, has been in the State Prison, and is now in the Penitentiary, Blackwell's Island. Their eldest son is serving a ten years' sentence in the Illinois State Prison for burglary, and their youngest son is in Sing Sing, where he was Bent for highway robbery and garroting. He will be fifteen years older when he next visits his friends."

15

ABRAHAM LINCOLN'S REMARKABLE CASE (1841)

Abraham Lincoln (1809–1865) was an attorney long before he was a Congressman from Illinois and then president of the United States. He was also an excellent writer, and penned this fascinating account of a case of suspected murder.

A REMARKABLE CASE OF ARREST FOR MURDER

Abraham Lincoln

In the year 1841, there resided, at different points in the State of Illinois, three brothers by the name of Trailor. Their Christian names were William, Henry and Archibald. Archibald resided at Springfield, then as now the Seat of Government of the State. He was a sober, retiring and industrious man, of about thirty years of age; a carpenter by trade, and a bachelor, boarding with his partner in business— a Mr. Myers. Henry, a year or two older, was a man of like retiring and industrious habits; had a family and resided with it on a farm at Clary's Grove, about twenty miles distant from Springfield in a Northwesterly direction. William, still older, and with similar habits, resided on a farm in Warren county, distant from Springfield something more than a hundred miles in the same Northwesterly direction. He was a widower, with several children.

In the neighborhood of William's residence, there was, and had been for several years, a man by the name of Fisher, who was somewhat above the age of fifty; had no family, and no settled home; but who boarded and lodged a while here, and a while there, with the persons for whom he did little jobs of work. His habits were remarkably economical, so that an impression got about that he had accumulated a considerable amount of money.

In the latter part of May in the year mentioned, William formed the purpose of visiting his brothers at Clary's Grove, and Springfield; and Fisher, at the time having his temporary residence at his house, resolved to accompany him. They set out together in a buggy with a single horse. On Sunday Evening they reached Henry's residence, and staid over night.

On Monday Morning, being the first Monday of June, they started on to Springfield, Henry accompanying them on horse back. They reached town about noon, met Archibald, went with him to his boarding house, and there took up their lodgings for the time they should remain. After dinner, the three Trailors and Fisher left the boarding house in company, for the avowed purpose of spending the evening together in looking about the town.

At supper, the Trailors had all returned, but Fisher was missing, and some inquiry was made about him. After supper, the Trailors went out professedly in search of him.

One by one they returned, the last coming in after late tea time, and each stating that he had been unable to discover any thing of Fisher. The next day, both before and after breakfast, they went professedly in search again, and returned at noon, still unsuccessful. Dinner again being had, William and Henry expressed a determination to give up the search and start for their homes. This was remonstrated against by some of the boarders about the house, on the ground that Fisher was somewhere in the vicinity, and would be left without any conveyance, as he and William had come in the same buggy. The remonstrance was disregarded, and they departed for their homes respectively. Up to this time, the knowledge of Fisher's mysterious disappearance, had spread very little beyond the few boarders at Myers', and excited no considerable interest.

After the lapse of three or four days, Henry returned to Springfield, for the ostensible purpose of making further search for Fisher. Procuring some of the boarders, he, together with them and Archibald, spent another day in ineffectual search, when it was again abandoned, and he returned home. No general interest was yet excited. On the Friday, week after Fisher's disappearance, the Postmaster at Springfield received a letter from the Postmaster nearest William's residence in Warren county, stating that William had returned home without Fisher, and was saying, rather boastfully, that Fisher was dead, and had willed him his money, and that he had got about fifteen hundred dollars by it.

The letter further stated that William's story and conduct seemed strange; and desired the Postmaster at Springfield to ascertain and write what was the truth in the matter. The Postmaster at Springfield made the letter public, and at once, excitement became universal and intense. Springfield, at that time had a population of about 3500, with a city organization. The Attorney General of the State resided there. A purpose was forthwith formed to ferret out the mystery, in putting which into execution, the Mayor of the city, and the Attorney General took the lead. To make search for, and, if possible, find the body of the man supposed to be murdered, was resolved on as the first step. In pursuance of this, men were formed into large parties, and marched abreast, in all directions, so as to let no inch of ground in the vicinity, remain unsearched. Examinations were made of cellars, wells, and pits of all descriptions, where it was thought possible the body might be concealed. All the fresh, or tolerably fresh graves at the grave-yard were pried into, and dead horses and dead dogs were disinterred, where, in some instances, they had been buried by their partial masters.

This search, as has appeared, commenced on Friday. It continued until Saturday afternoon without success, when it was determined to dispatch officers to arrest William and Henry at their residences respectively. The officers started on Sunday Morning, meanwhile, the search for the body was continued, and rumors got afloat of the Trailors having passed, at different times and places, several gold pieces, which were readily supposed to have belonged to Fisher. On Monday, the officers sent for Henry, having arrested him, arrived with him. The Mayor and Attorney Gen'l took charge of him, and set their wits to work to elicit a discovery from him. He denied, and denied, and persisted in denying. They still plied him in every conceivable way, till Wednesday, when, protesting his own innocence, he stated that his brothers, William and Archibald had murdered Fisher; that they had killed him, without his (Henry's) knowledge at the time, and made a temporary concealment of his body; that immediately preceding his and William's departure from Springfield for home, on Tuesday, the day after Fisher's disappearance, William and Archibald communicated the fact to him, and engaged his assistance in making a permanent concealment of the body; that at the time he and William left professedly for home, they did not take the road directly, but meandering their way through the streets, entered the woods at the North West of the city, two or three hundred yards to the right of where the road where they should have travelled entered them; that penetrating the woods some few hundred yards, they halted and Archibald came a somewhat different route, on foot, and joined them; that William and Archibald then stationed him (Henry) on an old and disused road that ran near by, as a sentinel, to give warning of the approach of any intruder; that William and Archibald then removed the buggy to the edge of a dense brush thicket, about forty yards distant from his (Henry's) position, where, leaving the buggy, they entered the thicket, and in a few minutes returned with the body and placed it in the buggy; that from his station, he could and did distinctly see that the object placed in the buggy was a dead man, of the general appearance and size of Fisher; that William and Archibald then moved off with the buggy in the direction of Hickox's mill pond, and after an absence of half an hour returned, saying they had put him in a safe place; that Archibald then left for town, and he and William found their way to the road, and made for their homes. At this disclosure, all lingering credulity was broken down, and excitement rose to an almost inconceivable height.

Up to this time, the well known character of Archibald had repelled and put down all suspicions as to him. Till then, those who were ready to swear that a murder had been committed, were almost as confident that Archibald had had no part in it. But now, he was seized and thrown into jail; and, indeed, his personal security rendered it by no means objectionable to him. And now came the search for the brush thicket, and the search of the mill pond. The thicket was found, and the buggy tracks at the point indicated. At a point within the thicket the signs of a struggle were discovered, and a trail from thence to the buggy track was traced. In attempting to follow the track of the buggy from the thicket, it was found to proceed in the direction of the mill pond, but could not be traced all the way. At the pond, however, it was found that a buggy had been backed down to, and partially into the water's edge.

Search was now to be made in the pond; and it was made in every imaginable way. Hundreds and hundreds were engaged in raking, fishing, and draining. After much fruitless effort in this way, on Thursday Morning, the mill dam was cut down, and the water of the pond partially drawn off, and the same processes of search again gone through with. About noon of this day, the officer sent for William, returned having him in custody; and a man calling himself Dr. Gilmore, came in company with them. It seems that the officer arrested William at his own house early in the day on Tuesday, and started to Springfield with him; that after dark awhile, they reached Lewiston in Fulton county, where they stopped for the night; that late in the night this Dr. Gilmore arrived, stating that Fisher was alive at his house; and that he had followed on to give the information, so that William might be released without further trouble; that the officer, distrusting Dr. Gilmore, refused to release William, but brought him on to Springfield, and the Dr. accompanied them. On reaching Springfield, the Dr. reasserted that Fisher was alive, and at his house. At this the multitude for a time, were utterly confounded. Gilmore's story was communicated to Henry Trailor, who, without faltering, reaffirmed his own story about Fisher's murder. Henry's adherence to his own story was communicated to the crowd, and at once the idea started, and became nearly, if not quite universal that Gilmore was a confederate of the Trailors, and had invented the tale he was telling, to secure their release and escape. Excitement was again at its zenith.

About 3 o'clock, the same evening, Myers, Archibald's partner, started with a two horse carriage, for the purpose of ascertaining whether Fisher was alive, as stated by Gilmore, and if so, of bringing him back to Springfield with him. On Friday a legal examination was gone into before two Justices, on the charge of murder against William and Archibald. Henry was introduced as a witness by the prosecution, and on oath, reaffirmed his statements, as heretofore detailed; and, at the end of which, he bore a thorough and rigid cross-examination without faltering or exposure. The prosecution also proved by a respectable lady, that on the Monday evening of Fisher's disappearance, she saw Archibald whom she well knew, and another man whom she did not then know, but whom she believed at the time of testifying to be William, (then present;) and still another, answering the description of Fisher, all enter the timber at the North West of town, (the point indicated by Henry,) and after one or two hours, saw William and Archibald return without Fisher. Several other witnesses testified, that on Tuesday, at the time William and Henry professedly gave up the search for Fisher's body and started for home, they did not take the road directly, but did go into the woods as stated by Henry. By others also, it was proved, that since Fisher's disappearance, William and Archibald had passed rather an unusual number of gold pieces. The statements heretofore made about the thicket, the signs of a struggle, the buggy tracks, &c., were fully proven by numerous witnesses. At this the prosecution rested.

Dr. Gilmore was then introduced by the defendants. He stated that he resided in Warren county about seven miles distant from William's residence; that on the morning of William's arrest, he was out from home and heard of the arrest, and of its being on a charge of the murder of Fisher; that on returning to his own house, he found Fisher there; that Fisher was in very feeble health, and could give no rational account as to where he had been during his absence; that he (Gilmore) then started in pursuit of the officer as before stated, and that he should have taken Fisher with him only that the state of his health did not permit. Gilmore also stated that he had known Fisher for several years, and that he had understood he was subject to temporary derangement of mind, owing to an injury about his head received in early life. There was about Dr. Gilmore so much of the air and manner of truth, that his statement prevailed in the minds of the audience and of the court, and the Trailors were discharged; although they attempted no explanation of the circumstances proven by the other witnesses.

On the next Monday, Myers arrived in Springfield, bringing with him the now famed Fisher, in full life and proper person. Thus ended this strange affair; and while it is readily conceived that a writer of novels could bring a story to a more perfect climax, it may well be doubted, whether a stranger affair ever really occurred. Much of the matter remains in mystery to this day. The going into the woods with Fisher, and returning without him, by the Trailors; their going into the woods at the same place the next day, after they professed to have given up the search; the signs of a struggle in the thicket, the buggy tracks at the edge of it; and the location of the thicket and the signs about it, corresponding precisely with Henry's story, are circumstances that have never been explained.

William and Archibald have both died since—William in less than a year, and Archibald in about two years after the supposed murder. Henry is still living, but never speaks of the subject.

It is not the object of the writer of this, to enter into the many curious speculations that might be indulged upon the facts of this narrative; yet he can scarcely forbear a remark upon what would, almost certainly have been the fate of William and Archibald, had Fisher not been found alive. It seems he had wandered away in mental derangement, and, had he died in this condition, and his body been found in the vicinity, it is difficult to conceive what could have saved the Trailors from the consequence of having murdered him. Or, if he had died, and his body never found, the case against them, would have been quite as bad, for, although it is a principle of law that a conviction for murder shall not be had, unless the body of the deceased be discovered, it is to be remembered, that Henry testified he saw Fisher's dead body.

16

HARRY T. HAYWARD, THE "MINNEAPOLIS SVENGALI" (1895)

Harry T. Hayward (executed in 1895) was likely a classic sociopath and serial killer in Minneapolis, Minnesota. Like the typical serial killers all too well known today, he was said to have been brutal toward others even as a boy, and to have tortured animals. He was renowned for his superficial charm and ability to manipulate people. Convicted in 1895 of the 1894 murder of Catherine Ging, he was hanged in 1895. Aside from the killing of Ging, he is nowadays thought to have been responsible for other murders. In a confession before he was hanged, Hayward confessed to three more killings.

Harry Hayward. Life, Crimes, Dying Confession and Execution of the Celebrated Minneapolis Criminal; other Interesting Chapters on the Greatest Psychological Problem of the Century.

The author has endeavored to treat his interesting subject in a dignified manner. If any justification were needed for the publication of this volume it might be found in the undisputed fact that Harry Hayward is the most interesting psychological study of the age.

The preceding page bears a facsimile of Hayward's last hand writing. The card was penned exactly two hours before the execution. The condemned man was reminded that the world would scrutinize this specimen of his chirography, with the idea of determining whether he was nervous over his impending fate. After finishing the card Hayward said: "I guess people can tell from that I am not nervous, even if I am so near death."

Catherine Ging's Murder.

A woman's face, lying pale and still in a pool of blood, her inanimate form limp and distorted in the sand—this is what the dim starlight revealed to William Erhart on the night of December 3, as he was wending his lonely way homeward along the old Excelsior road, in the outskirts of Minneapolis. Erhart paused only a moment. She was plainly dead. A moment before he had met a horse and buggy plunging at a reckless rate through the darkness, with no driver visible. It was evident to him that the woman was the victim of a runaway accident. Erhart ran to his home, a few rods away, and summoned his brothers, then hurried to the nearest drug store and telephoned to police headquarters. Half an hour later the body was lying at the county morgue, where the patrol wagon had hastily carried it.

In searching the woman's clothing the word "Ging" was found sewn in a garment, and the body was thus identified as that of Catherine M. Ging, a well-known dressmaker with large patronage among people of wealth and fashion. Not until 11 o'clock, or two hours and a half after Erhart's gruesome discovery, did a doctor's hand grate against a bullet, lodged almost at the surface of the left eye. Soon a bullet hole was found at the base of the brain, and it was at once apparent that what had been supposed an accident was in reality an atrocious murder. The police at once commenced an active investigation, and detectives were sent to the Ozark flats, the home of the murdered woman. About the same time word was received from Goosman's livery stable that their "buckskin mare" had returned to the stable driverless about

9 o'clock, while the buggy floor and seat were soaked and bespattered with blood. This was evidently the rig which Erhart had met just before finding the body. It was a slender clue, and availed very little, for Erhart had seen no one in the buggy, and Catherine Ging herself had taken the rig for the drive, meeting the driver at the West hotel.

Next morning Minneapolis was electrified at the news. Conjecture was rife, but there was still no one on whom the crime could be fastened. But certain of the police officers had put two and two together, and had fastened suspicion on Harry T. Hayward, the manager of the Ozark flats. Hayward was very much in evidence on the evening of the murder. As soon as he heard of Catherine Ging's death, and before the doctors discovered the bullet, he exclaimed to a group of friends and newspaper men,

"She has been murdered, and murdered for her money.

It was not her money," he went on to explain, "but money that I let her have. My $2,000 is gone to h__l!" He told the police officers that he had loaned her $7,000, and taken in return a $10,000 policy on her life. She had been trying with some one else to "do him up," and now the other man had killed her and defrauded him. The insurance policy aroused suspicion, and at 10 o'clock the morning after the murder Hayward was taken in hand by Mayor Eustis and subjected to a close examination, lasting till 2 o'clock the next morning, when he was permitted to pass the night on a couch in the office of the chief of police.

It was evident that Hayward himself could not have committed the murder, for at the time when Erhart found the body in the road he was at the Grand Opera House witnessing the play, "A Trip to Chinatown." His station in life tended to avert suspicion. The son of an old and respected family, he had moved in the best society, where his handsome presence and debonnair manner made him to a certain' extent popular, though there were rumors that he was rather "fast." But in the excitement following the murder, it quickly developed from a hundred sources that Harry had been for years a "high roller" among the gambling fraternity, and an inveterate faro bank fiend. Letters came to light showing that for some time Miss Ging had been a sort of a partner in Hayward's gambling transactions, and had furnished him money to play big games at Chicago during the summer previous.

In all this there was nothing to fasten the crime on the suspected man, and the morning after his long term in the "sweat-box" he was released and allowed to go home. That afternoon he attended the funeral of Catherine Ging and that night he slept at home for the last time.

Meanwhile, the authorities had received new light in the case from L. M. Stewart, the Hayward family lawyer, familiarly known as "Elder" Sterwart. He wrote a note to A. H. Hall, assistant county attorney, telling him of a conversation he had a few days previous with Adry Hayward. Adry had often expressed to him misgivings about Harry, but on this occasion he came with fear and trembling and told a horrible story of a plot to kill Miss Ging, devised by Harry, and to be executed by Claus Blixt, a janitor at the Ozark Flats. Mr. Stewart pooh-hoohed the story, and persuaded Adry that his brother would not be fool enough to commit such a deed.

Now, the whole thing came back to him, and he wrote the letter as in duty bound, informing the officers of the law of this important clue. Next day, Thursday, Harry and Adry were placed under arrest; and they spent that night at the Central Police Station, with the charge of murder opposite their names. Adry maintained a firm front and claimed utter ignorance of the whole affair, but the next evening he was taken by the officers to the office of Elder Stewart, and confronted with his old friend; he broke down utterly and confessed the details of the crime, as far as he knew them. That night Blixt was placed under arrest, with one Ole Erickson, who had been in his company and was supposed to have taken care of the bloody clothing. Blixt's wife was also placed in detention. Blixt and his wife were put through the "sweat-box" process, and on Sunday Blixt broke down and confessed.

His first story, which made Hayward the actual murderer, and himself only a sort of accessory, was so plainly untrue that his inquisitors turned again to their work, and Blixt made a second and complete confession of the crime. The story which Blixt outlined on that night to Mayor Eustis, A. H. Hall and the detectives, is in all substantial points the same as told by Hayward in his accompanying confession. The Ozark janitor was the tool of Hayward.

By threats and promises of money Hayward brought him to the point of committing the deed, and nerved him to it with whisky. Catherine Ging was decoyed into taking the fatal ride by a story about some "green goods" men, whom they were to meet at the outskirts of the town for a "deal." She drove out alone from the West Hotel to the corner of Lyndale avenue and Kenwood boulevard, where she was met by Hayward and Blixt. Promising to "bring the others" and meet her at a lonely outof- town spot, Hayward put Blixt in the buggy and left the victim to her fate, hurrying down bye streets to keep his theater appointment. Blixt drove until he reached the lonely place on the Excelsior road. There he fired the fatal shot "where Harry told him to," and rolled the lifeless body from the wagon. Crouching back in the seat as he met Erhart, he drove till near the street car line, where he turned horse and buggy adrift, and took the car for down town. The course of justice was plain from this point on. The grand jury indicted Harry Hayward and Blixt on Dec. 13; they were arraigned and their trial set for Jan. 21. Erickson was exonerated. Adry was released from jail after a time, but at his own request was accompanied night and day by Deputy Sheriff Maish until after the conclusion of the trial.

A Famous Trial.

However public opinion may vary as to the wisdom of the punishment inflicted on Harry Hayward, there can be no doubt that the judicial inquiry into the murder of Catherine Ging was a most notable and gratifying illustration of the triumph of right over wrong.

When, less than two months after his victim's death, the prisoner was brought to face an indictment for murder in the first degree, the conditions were almost ideal for a trial that should be of national interest. The prisoner, supplied with large financial resources, had the ablest and most distinguished criminal advocate in the Northwest, W. W. Erwin, to conduct his defense, whileto assist in the search for and preparation of evidence were such well known counsel as John Day Smith, A. T. Sweetser, and Walter Shumaker, together with numerous detectives of experience. The prisoner had the additional advantage that he had submitted without apparent reluctance to a most searching inquisition by the city and county officials and without making any admission of itself incriminating. The most suspicious saying that was traceable to him was the impulsive exclamation when informed that Miss Ging had been hurt in a runaway: "They've done me up. She has been murdered for her money."

These were but negative, however. The defense had one serious weakness, no basis either of fact or plausibility. The state on the other hand not only had the confession of the actual murderer implicating Hayward, but this, insufficient in itself, was so corroborated by circumstantial and direct evidence that the jury, like the general public, could not refuse to believe in the truthfulness of the trembling wretch who writhed for parts of three days under the merciless inquisition by Attorney Erwin. With the "tall pine" as the defendant's counsel, and County Attorney Frank Nye, assisted by Albert Hall, as the public prosecutors, the presentation of evidence was in most experienced and thorough practitioners, while the presence on the bench of Judge Seagrave Smith, the senior judge of the court, proved, as the record of the trial submitted to the supreme court shows, a guarantee of a trial, not only true to the ends of justice, but faithful to the principles of modern law.

Ten days elapsed before the jury was filled; the utmost care being taken on both sides, and 13 jurors were sworn, before the trial proper commended, the first juror accepted, Ira Newell, being discharged afterwards because of his conscientious scruples against capital punishment.

Then one by one the state called its five score witnesses, each seeming to bring something of weight to bear on the case until they completed a chain of evidence so convincing that discredit was impossible. Following the preliminary testimony, of the finding of the body of the murdered girl, by witnesses who were most thoroughly cross-examined by the defense with the apparent purpose of finding even one weak point in the state's case, how ever trivial it might seem, came the surgeons who officiated at the post mortem examination, and here came the first hard fight, the counsel for the defense spending nearly a day in an effort to show that the terrible crushing of the skull could not have been caused by a fall from the buggy, as it was known that Blixt would testify.

Then followed Blixt, and for parts of three days, the unlettered engineer held at bay one of the most ingenious of cross-examiners, but clinging to his story, evidently true in the main in every detail, to the last. Shocking as was the narration of his dreadful deed, the murderer was listened to by some of the largest crowds that attended the trial, illustrating to a high degree the morbid curiosity which sways a large portion of the community.

Dramatically following this came the betrayer of the crime, Adry A. Hayward, against whose testimony came another vigorous contention that he was insane, and should not be allowed to testify. Judge Smith, however, ruled continually against the broad claim, sometimes with such emphasis on the delay it was causing that led to exciting scenes in court, but without error, evidently.

Then the insurance agents and bankers with whom Hayward had talked about insurable interest, death by violence, and other matters of a suspicious nature, were called in and as the list of witnesses was almost finished the state stumbled upon a hack driver to whom Hayward had talked about driving his rig over a precipice into a lake, and about the power of his conscience, if he had committed a murder.

Last of all came what seemed like a voice from the dead, the testimony of Mrs. Lillian Hazelton, since deceased, to the effect that on the afternoon of Dec. 3d, Catherine Ging had told her she was going out that evening with "Harry."

The defense first exploited the presence of the defendant at the opera house in order to prove an alibi as to the actual murder, and also a number of witnesses to show the whereabouts of Hayward during the afternoon and early evening of the same day to show that Blixt's statements were untrue. However, it was a case where a few minutes' variation did not disprove anything, and Blixt's story in the main was not directly contradicted. But in the midst of its own case, the defense was misled into placing on the stand M. D. Wilson, a liveryman, who had been reported as saying that a rig containing a couple talking loudly had followed him for a mile or thereabouts on Kenwood parkway. His testimony, however, was that the rig only turned into that street from Lyndale as he passed, and in his best judgment the man in the buggy was Harry Hayward. The defense could not impeach the truthfulness of its own witness and from [then] on the fight was against fearful odds.

George A. Grindall, a familiar figure around Minneapolis courts for years, told an implausible story about seeing a man with gray whiskers get into a buggy with a lady on First avenue north just about the time that Miss Ging was known to have left the West Hotel, and Maggie Wachtler, a stenographer formerly employed by R. R. Odell, the attorney for Blixt, testified that in Blixt's' confession, which she took as stenographer, he had said that Adry told him to kill the girl. Both these stories were generally doubted, and indictments for perjury were threatened but never prosecuted.

The defense had distinguished experts on nervous affections to testify that Adry appeared to be insane, but the character of the testimony which they were allowed to give was so general in its character that it affected the case but little.

As a dramatic close to the case of the defense came the testimony of the defendant himself, an ingenious explanation of his tell-tale conversations with the insurance men, which he did not deny, and a graphic history of his gambling exploits much resembling that given in his antemortem confession but without any reference to the crimes therein mentioned. The state's rebuttal was chiefly occupied with the impeachment of the testimony of Grindall and Miss Wachtler, but it did include one new and startling element, the very positive identification of Hayward by Geo. W. Jenks as a man he had seen runnig up Hennepin avenue from the direction of Superior avenue on the night of the murder, a short time after 7 o'clock.

In vain the defense sought to exclude it on the ground that it was too late for them to investigate the incident, and on the heels of this dramatic incident, the closing arguments were begun.

County Attorney Nye, scarcely recovered from an illness that had kept him from the trial during so important a part as the cross-examination of Hayward, made an eloquent argument for the protection of society by the punishment of such an offender.

Then the senior counsel for the defense closed the case of the defense in an address that occupied eleven hours in actual delivery, parts of three court days. All that ingenuity could devise to explain the suspicious conduct of the defendant, and the most eloquent periods of an advocate known throughout the world by causes he had championed, proved unavailing, however, to save the life of the man who had wronged society so grievously, and after a confinement of seven weeks, the jury on the 7th of March arrived at a verdict of guilty within two hours after leaving the court room.

Lessons From the Ging Murder.

I cannot believe any one is born absolutely depraved—wholly destitute of soul. It may seem to be entirely absent, under some conditions of birth and education, so that to all outward appearances the man is soulless and conscienceless. Harry T. Hayward was a most phenomenal example of this class of beings. To all appearances he was without a soul. It was at least latent. It did not speak—did not manifest itself. He knew not love, that universal language of the soul. All humane, sympathetic and tender sensibilities seemed to be absent from his nature. He appeared to be born under a cloud of moral darkness, and his career demonstrated that he loved darkness rather than light. It is impossible to say whether as a criminal he was indebted most to birth or training—whether his depravity was native or acquired. It was doubtless both.

Certain it is that the habits and environments of a life time will do much to transform virtue into vice or vice into virtue. The great lesson of this case is, that man is not man except he have a soul—that the cultivation of this divine attribute in man is not only the duty and high privilege of the individual, but of society as well. It is fortunate for humanity that this case attracted such wide and general attention. The eye of a continent, almost of the world, has been upon it, and the character of Hayward may well enlist the study and contemplation of every thinking mind. Indeed, society is in a measure responsible for such Characters. They are in some degree at least the fruit of our civilization. They are the product of a money-loving and money-worshiping age—an age which feeds the intellect and starves the soul—idolizes mind and assassinates conscience. "The love of money is the root of all evil."

Born of wealthy parents, reared in fashionable society, of smooth and polished exterior, having the appearance of refinement, he moved in the best circles, outwardly a gentleman, inwardly a fiend—a moral monstrosity. He was intellectually acute, cunning and active, original and daring in schemes of wickedness. A genius in crime. A romancer in the realm of wickedness. He loved darkness rather than light. He was a moral owl. His vision, which was purely intellectual, loved the night. The sunlight blinded him.

He was a born gambler and cultivated this native talent, until a dollar became more valuable in his eye than a human life. He took others' money for nothing, till it was easy to take others' lives for money. I have not the slightest doubt he had committed numerous murders before he planned and consummated the cruel and fiendish murder of Catherine Ging. He was a precocious child of crime and his native talent had multiplied and increased in that school of darkness into which he readily entered with great natural advantages and from which he graduated with distinguished ability and complete thoroughness.

After weeks of preparation for the murder of this poor, trusting girl, after he had practiced the most cruel and monstrous deceptions upon her, with professions of love and affection, after he had obtained the insurance policies and after he had placed Blixt in the carriage with her and sent them to the scene of death, he goes to the theater for amusement. He chooses that hour of bloody assassination for pleasure and recreation. In the midst of the multitude, with a thousand eyes to prove his alibi, he watches the shifting scenes upon the stage and cheers and applauds the play. On the morning succeeding the homicide he feigns grief in the presence of her lifeless form, and later brings flowers to the casket and indulges in the hollow and hellish mockery of mourning. In his last confession he says that on his return from the theater, learning in a confused way of the report of the injury, he feared she had not been killed, and that something had intervened to prevent the consummation of his scheme, and that the plot would be at once disclosed; that he was greatly relieved when he learned there had been no failure. These circumstances but illustrate the prodigiously criminal character of the man. The crime and the circumstances of it correspond with the man. The crime fits the criminal. His conduct was not altogether simulated. It was in a large degree natural. His actions were but a part of the man himself. The criminal and his crime were the growth and development of years. The act was not a freak or paroxysm of crime but the inate and natural product of a soulless, conscienceless demon, fully grown and matured.

If such a darkened and depraved condition in a human being is insanity, Hayward was insane. It certainly was not legal insanity, because no one will claim he could not distinguish between right and wrong, or that he did not comprehend the nature and consequence of his acts. It may be, and no doubt is, a condition of moral insanity. "Whoever reasons towards crime reasons wrong," says a learned judge. Wrong reasoning argues an unhealthy mind. Philosophically speaking, therefore, wrong reasoning and wrong conduct are indicative of moral insanity. This kind of theorizing, however, affords no guide for the practical administration of justice or the wholesome preservation of law and order. Law is a practical science, having for its object the general well being of society. Its safe and salutary edict is that which commends what is right and prohibits what is wrong.

Hayward was clearly responsible, under the law, for his acts. His guilt must be wholly unquestioned. It stands prevent to a moral, almost a mathematical, certainty. The law decreed his death. He met it with a disgusting bravado, which the vulgar mind confuses with heroism. He died for no principle. He did not pretend to be sustained in that final and awful hour by any consciousness or claim of innocence. He had been assured that the execution would be attended with very little physical pain. His mind (not his soul) was fully prepared for what was to come, and he died as callous and as conscienceless as he had lived.

This may seem harsh, but it is more charitable than his own estimate of himself. He expressed no regrets at the last hour, but boldly and flippantly flaunted his iniquity before the world and gloried in his unique and colossal career of crime. Unregenerate, defiant and desperate, this unfortunate, misguided and wicked child of earth, dropped into that final and dark abyss, which only the sunlight of God's mercy can penetrate.

Here I might close; but I 1have it in my heart to add a further thought. This child of sin was a child of our race—a brother in the great fallible family to which we all belong. He who beholds the end from the beginning and whose infinite intelligence and love may reach the darkest caverns of hell itself, He who knows how imperfectly and unjustly we often judge our fellow men, grants mercy which in our darkness and hatred we refuse.

There may be circumstances of birth and habit surrounding the character and life of Harry Hayward which it is not in our power to comprehend. We are ever incompetent and unjust judges of our fellow men.

We are our brother's keeper. We cannot absolve ourselves from the strong and God-made ties which bind us together in one common, universal family. God is love and His law is the law of love. As society advances to the supremacy of soul, and its splendid evolution of thought, and stands in the warm and all-pervading light of this great law, fetters will fall from its chafed and wounded limbs and it will move on with new freedom to higher destinies. Justice and mercy, twin angels of heaven, will dispel the darkness. Oppression, cruelty, torture, rack, dungeon and scaffold will disappear under the perfect reign of Him whose seamless robe of love envelopes the globe and, warms and comforts the poorest outcast child in all the universe of God.

FRANK M. NYE.

HAYWARD'S MORAL DELUSIONS.

Harry Hayward's case presents an interesting study for the moralist. It is indeed rare that a man convicted of such a heinous crime as the one for which Hayward was executed and of which he admitted his guilt, goes upon the scaffold apparently so utterly indifferent to his wretched fate, and so unconcerned about the future. Men who have led notoriously wicked lives and who seemed to have been steepd in crime, usually manifest some regret for their misspent life, and some symptom of horror for the dark deeds that have doomed them to the felon's sad fate. Hayward exhibited an indifference not only phenomenal, but apalling. He showed no sign of sorrow for his offenses against all divine and human law, and he gave no evidence of regret that he had brought such grief and shame to his heart-broken parents' declining years.

Yet Hayward was not insane, he rejected with disgust and indignation the theory of his insanity, or that he had not been fully responsible at all times for his conduct. In fact he was particularly vain of the acuteness of his mind, and his adroit reasoning. But this was not the vanity common among men mentally diseased, who often fancy themselves to be the wisest of philosophers.

His was an egotistical conceit, natural, perhaps, to the young man, but which had become stronger as he met, with what seemed to him, flattering success in "fooling the world."

An idiosyncrasy of his character was that he claimed it always gave him special gratification to deceive, and he had reduced lying to a cultivated art. He possessed a certain amount of low, natural cunning, which he skillfully cultivated also, for many years, and which became fully developed in his chosen profession of gambling. Like all egotists, however, he finally over-readied himself and discovered that he had been playing a most hazardous game in attempting to "fool all the people all the time," but he comforted himself with his gambler's philosophy that he had played his stake and lost, had had his day, had reached his limit, and should "die game." Yet Hayward, colossal fool though he was, had formulated a philosophy of his own, that seemed to give some satisfaction to his reason.

No one will be surprised to learn that his was a revolting philosophy, and yet there was some consistency about it, providing his premises were right. Of course his premises were all wrong, and the result of his delusive reasoning was all wrong, but from his standpoint he could not see the disaster before him; and had he been able to see it, he knew no means to employ to avoid it. In his early youth, at least so he asserted, he received no positive religious instruction. Of course he had been taught the difference between right and wrong and had been encouraged to do the right and avoid the wrong.

But no motive was assigned, why he should shun evil and do good. All was vague and shadowy. After he arrived at adult age and felt the responsibilities of manhood, he conceived an inordinate desire for money, the gambling frenzy took possession of him, and he schooled himself in all the arts of self-control, that is, control of his emotions, and unscrupulous deception to gain the end he had in view.

To quiet the stings of conscience, he soon began a careful study of materialism. He was not a well educated man; his range of reading and study had been very limited, he studiously avoided giving any attention to refutations of materialistic theories, for he sought, what he found in the ridicule of religion, encouragement for his disordered and deceitful life. He had succeeded fairly well in quieting his disturbed conscience, by the theories of uncertainty about human accountability to God, and a future life. His excuse for not giving more serious attention to thoughts of religion when under sentence of death, was that his mind was at rest, he felt no certainty about future punishment for sin, no certainty about the existence of God, and why should he disturb his few remaining days with sad reflections upon what was passed or upon serious consideration of an uncertain future.

The past could not be undone, the dead were beyond recall, his conscience accused him of no wrong, inasmuch as those whom he had sent out of life had suffered no pain, had sustained no loss; were in fact perhaps better off in another existence, if another life is known beyond the dark and silent grave.

Hayward was not a keen or close reasoner, he had made a special study of all the objections against religion and carefully ignored any refutation of these, to him, consoling theories. His shallow mind was easily satisfied with the half truths he had learned, and his corrupt heart was gratified with the specious defense of his reckless life, which the alleged uncertainty of the future offered. If there be no God, and if man has a well founded doubt about his existence and consequently about absolute right, justice and an inflexible standard of morality, the selfish interest of man naturally impels him to seek the good of which he is certain and not to take any chances about obtaining the good which may have no existence.

This reflection only forcibly reminds a thinking man of the infamy into which the corrupt heart of one hardened in crime can sink an intelligent being. There can be no morality without law. There can be no law without a law-giver. A law-giver, capable of framing laws for the direction and guidance of reasonable beings, must have some end in view in making his laws, as well as the right and power to enforce them. If the laws of my being, the laws of nature and the written law of human society forbids or enjoins certain actions, these laws must have their root in authority, or I am not bound to obey them. If there be any doubt about the authority and the consequent binding force of the law, I am not in duty held to observe it, for a doubtful law is not binding.

Individual contempt of the law, or personal doubt of its binding force, does not, of course, exempt a responsible agent from its pro-visions. But if the doubt be reasonably well founded, if it cannot be removed, the conscience of man is not held to the binding force of a doubtful law. This is sound reasoning, but sound reasoning, like wholesome food or medicine, may often be erroneously applied. This was the leading difficulty with Harry Hayward. He had not properly digested certain elements of truth, and carefully avoided to mingle correctly sound elements together. He had caught up the phrase that a man's conscience is his guide. A man makes no mistake in following the direction of his conscience. His conscience, he asserted, accused him of no crime, gave him no unrest, for he had always held that it was no more of a crime, in itself, to kill a human being than to kill an animal. The human being had no more right to life, he claimed, than had the brute. If man has no soul and there be no God and no future life, and all is ended when the body is cold in death, can anyone claim that Hayward was wrong? "It all depends on how you look at it," he claimed.

His maxim was, that pleasure was the highest good in life, and pain the only evil. The reason of man, as well as his selfish inclinations, suggests to him to strive for the highest, greatest good. Money could purchase pleasure, money could soothe pain, hence Hayward longed for money, with which to gratify pleasure. He claimed it had always given him pleasure to inflict pain upon others, or deceive or mislead them, by his cunning arts. Hence he gratified his desire for pleasure to the extent of satiety and "had his day." The clutches of the civil law he alone feared, as the power of the civil law was the only power he knew, but he had eluded this so long that he had become foolhardy and reckless concerning it.

The poison of false principles had entered Hayward's brain. The blight of irreligion had withered the good impulses that had once taken root in his heart, and the callous, unrepentant, defiant destroyer of human life was the result. He was abnormal, in the sense that every man is abnormal who surrenders his will to the dominion of passion, and resigns the liberty with which God endowed him, to the caprice of pleasure.

His abnormal conduct could in no way have excused him from the full consequences of his criminal career, for he voluntarily "took his chances," as he termed it, in this life, and for the life to come. The wholesome food of sound principles is the only saving antidote for such insidious poison dimmed the light of Hayward's reason. Elevating, religious influences can alone counteract the immoral tendencies, the irreligion fostered in the heart of man. Every man's mind, therefore, should be well nourished with the strengthening food of true principles, and his heart fortified by salutary environment, that he may be safely guarded against the influences that led Hayward to the scaffold, when he fancied that he had "fooled the world."

REV. J. M. CLEARY.

17

BELLE SORENSON GUNNESS, SERIAL KILLER (DECLARED DEAD, 1908)

Belle Sorenson Gunness, born in Norway, is thought to have murdered between twenty-five and forty people in the United States, including her husbands, several children, and most of the men who showed a romantic interest in her. To a large extent, she was apparently interested in collecting on a series of life insurance policies. She was also suspected of burning several structures for the insurance money. Her ultimate fate is unknown.

MRS. BELLE GUNNESS, THE ARCHFIEND WHO REQUIRED A PRIVATE GRAVE-YARD FOR HER NUMEROUS VICTIMS, BUT WHO WAS SUBSEQUENTLY MUR-DERED AND CREMATED WITH HER THREE CHILDREN.

Belle Paulsen was born in the little town of Christiania, Norway. Her father, Peter Paulsen, was a traveling conjurer and magician, and when Belle was a mere child she participated in the exhibitions by dancing on the tight-rope.

They prospered and through their frugality they were enabled to retire when Belle was still in her teens, and the father purchased a little farm in their native land.

Belle then came to the United States, and about two years later she married a Swede named Albert Sorenson. They resided in Chicago, and in 1900 Sorenson died under most suspicious circumstances. While it was said that he died from heart failure, his relatives were positive that he was poisoned, and as a motive for the deed, pointed to the fact that the widow collected the life insurance of $8,500 as soon as possible after his death. It is stated that an inquest was ordered, but for some reason the body was never exhumed.

Mrs. Sorenson then moved to Austin, Ill., and a short time afterward her home there was burned. A question arose as to the origin of the fire, but in the absence of proof of fraud the insurance companies were forced to pay the insurance.

She then returned to Chicago, where she conducted a confectionery store at Grand avenue and Elizabeth street, which was subsequently gutted by fire. This mysterious fire resulted in another investigation by the insurance officials, but they were forced to pay her claim.

Shortly afterward she purchased a farm about six miles from La Porte, Indiana, and married Peter Gunness a few months later.

In 1904, a meat chopper is said to have fallen off a shelf and split his head open, thus ending his existence. The weeping widow described to the coroner's jury how it fell from a shelf and struck her "poor husband's head," and in the absence of proof to the contrary, the statement was accepted as true.

At the time of the death of Gunness, she had three small children, named Philip, Myrtle and Lucy. She also had an adopted daughter named Jennie Olsen, who was fourteen years of age.

In September, 1906, this girl disappeared, and Mrs. Gunness accounted for her absence by stating that she had sent her to Los Angeles to complete her education.

The woman then employed a man named Ray Lamphere to do the chores about the place. In 1906 she inserted an advertisement in the matrimonial columns of the leading papers of Chicago and other large cities, which read as follows:

Personal—Comely widow who owns a large farm in one of the finest districts in La Porte County, Indiana, desires to make acquaintance of a gentleman equally well provided, with view of joining fortunes. No replies by letter considered un-less sender is willing to follow answer with personal visit.

In May, 1907, Ole B. Budsburg, a rather elderly widower residing in Iolo, Wisconsin, saw the advertisement, and as it looked good to him he decided to make a nice, quiet investigation without telling his grown up sons, Oscar and Mathew, a word about it.

The poor old gentleman left his home but never returned, and the last seen of him was when he negotiated the sale of a mortgage at the La Porte Savings Bank and drew the money on April 6, 1907.

In December, 1907, Andrew Hegelein, a thrifty batchelor from Aberdeen, South Dakota, also corresponded with Mrs. Gunness. She replied that it would be advisable for him to come to the farm, and she suggested that he might sell out his business interests in South Dakota, as she was very favorably impressed with his letters.

As far as was convenient to do so, Hegelein, delighted with the headway he was making, complied with her request and repaired to her farm, arriving in January, 1908. He had been at Mrs. Gunness' place about two weeks when he accompanied her to the Savings Bank in La Porte and presented a check for $2,900, but as he was unknown there and as the bankers would not accept the endorsement of Mrs. Gunness for this amount, they left the check there for collection. In a few days the draft came and the money was delivered to him, which she must have obtained, for almost immediately afterward she deposited $500 in that bank, $700 in the State Bank, and also paid numerous large bills.

A few days later Hegelein disappeared, and Mrs. Gunness stated that he had drawn the money for the purpose of going to Norway. He had a brother named A. K. Hegelein in Aberdeen, South Dakota, and as the weeks rolled by and he heard nothing from his brother, he became alarmed and wrote to Mrs. Gunness regarding his whereabouts.

In her reply she stated that all the information she could impart was the missing man's own statement to the effect that he drew his money with the intention of going to Norway, but she expressed some apprehension over his failure to confide his plans to his brother, and she suggested in her letter that he sell out the remainder of his brother's stock along with his own, and come to her farm, so that she might join him in an extensive search.

At 3:30 a. m. on April 28, 1908, Mrs. Gunness' home was burned to the ground and in the ruins the charred remains of a woman and three children were found. The bodies of the little ones were at once identified as the remains of Mrs. Gunness' children, but as the woman's head was burned or cut off, there was some question as to whose remains they were.

Ray Lamphere, the farm hand, left her employ on February 3, 1908, because of a quarrel with Mrs. Gunness, and procured employment on a farm owned by John Wheatbrook, a short distance from the Gunness place.

After Lamphere left Mrs. Gunness, he frequently intimated that he could make it interesting for her if he wanted to talk, but her only response to this was that Lamphere was "crazy."

As it was proven conclusively that he was on the ground at the time the fire started, he was taken into custody by Sheriff Smutzer.

The mysterious remarks made by Lamphere in regard to making trouble for Mrs. Gunness were recalled, and a most thorough investigation was instituted, with the result that five more mutilated and decomposed bodies were found buried in the back yard on May 5.

One was identified as the body of Jennie Olsen Gunness, the sixteen-year-old adopted daughter of Mrs. Gunness, who was supposed to be in Los Angeles completing her education. It is presumed that she was murdered because she knew too much regarding the death of Peter Gunness in 1904.

The second body was that of Andrew Hegelein from South Dakota. The third was the unidentified body of a man, and the fourth and fifth were the bodies of two eight-year-old girls. On May 6, four additional bodies of men were unearthed in the back yard.

In most instances the limbs were removed from the bodies in such a manner as to indicate that the amputations were performed by some one familiar with anatomy. The theory is that some of the bodies were too heavy for the woman to handle as a whole.

On May 9, two more bundles of bones, decayed flesh and clothing were found in the private graveyard, but the ravages of decomposition made identification impossible. On May 14, a few bones of one more victim were found in the ashes in the cellar.

In view of these discoveries a serious doubt arose as to the actual fate of Mrs. Gunness. It was suspected that in addition to murdering her children and several others, she had enveigled some unsuspecting woman into her home, and after killing her, disfigured her remains in such a manner that they could not be recognized, and after setting fire to the house, escaped; believing it would be taken for granted that the charred remains of the woman were those of herself and that no further search would be made for her. This theory proved incorrect, for on May 16 a lower jawbone was found in the ashes and was taken to Dr. Morton, a dentist in La Porte, for examination. Some dentistry work was plainly visible on the teeth which still adhered to the jawbone, which he positively identified as work done for Mrs. Gunness a year previously. Rings found on the fingers of the dead woman were also identified as the property of Mrs. Gunness.

There was a difference of opinion as to how Mrs. Gunness met her death. The theory of the prosecution was that she was burned to death, but Dr. J. Meyers gave it as his opinion that death was caused by contraction of the heart, probably due to strychnine poisoning, which was the poison used in killing Hegelein and several other victims.

Shortly after Mrs. Gunness' private graveyard was discovered, Oscar and Mathew Budsburg came to La Porte, as they suspected that their aged father, who had mysteriously disappeared from his home in Iolo, Wis., in May, 1907, might have fallen into this woman's trap. Their suspicions proved to be well founded, for they identified one of the bodies as that of their missing father.

Olof Lindboe of Chicago stated that his brother, Thomas, had worked for Mrs. Gunness three years previously, and the last letter he had received from him contained the information that Thomas intended to marry his employer. As Olof heard nothing more from his brother he wrote to Mrs. Gunness, who replied that Thomas had gone to St. Louis, but Olof never heard from him again.

On May 12, the surgical instruments with which the bodies were probably dismembered, were found in the ashes.

On May 19, Miss Jennie Graham of Waukesha, Wis., arrived in La Porte to inquire regarding her brother, who had left home to marry a rich widow in La Porte, but who was never heard from after that. As most of the bodies were badly mutilated and decomposed, it was impossible to ascertain if her brother's remains were among them.

Henry Gurholdt of Scandinavia, Wis., corresponded with Mrs. Gunness, and then took $1,500 with him to La Porte and was never seen again, but a watch found with one of the bodies was exactly the same in appearance as the one he wore.

Mrs. Marie Svenherud of Christiania, Norway, made inquiry through Acting Consul Faye of Chicago for her son Olof, who had written her that he was about to leave Chicago for La Porte to marry a rich Norwegian widow with whom he had become acquainted through the agency of the matrimonial advertisement column of a newspaper. The mother added that she never heard from her son again.

After the disappearance of Hegelein, Lamphere was seen wearing an overcoat which belonged to the former, and on May 18 a watch which was in the possession of Lamphere at the time of his arrest was identified by J. G. Ramden of Manfred, N. D., as the property of his half brother, John Moe of Elbow Lake, Minn., who left his home in 1907, ostensibly to marry a widow in La Porte, but was never heard from afterward. Lamphere stated that Mrs. Gunness had presented him with the watch.

When first interrogated as to his whereabouts on the night of the fire, Lamphere claimed that he was in the company of a negress named Mrs. Elizabeth Smith until 4 a. m., or one-half hour after the fire started, but he subsequently confessed that he burned the Gunness home but denied that he had committed murder.

Lamphere and a neighbor named Fred Brickman stated that they dug trenches for Mrs. Gunness at different times, but that they had no knowledge as to for what purpose they were used.

On May 22, 1908, Lamphere was indicted for the murder of the Gunness family by means of arson, and also on the charge of accessory in the murder of Hegelein. He pleaded guilty of arson and was sentenced to imprisonment for an indeterminate period of from two to twenty years. Immediately after his conviction Lamphere's health failed rapidly and he died from consumption on December 30, 1909.

On January 14, 1910, Rev. E. A. Schell made public a confession made by Lamphere shortly after his arrest, in which he admitted that he helped Mrs. Gunness to bury one of the victims and saw her chloroform another after felling him with a hatchet. He also confessed that he chloroformed the Gunness family, but claimed that Mrs. Smith, a negress with whom he had spent a portion of the night, assisted him, and that it was she who set the house on fire.

As there was no evidence to substantiate the charge against the negress she was never prosecuted. It is the opinion of Attorney Ralph Smith that the negress did not accompany Lamphere on this night.

★★★★★

Scenes at the Indiana Murder Farm

A coarse, fat, heavy-featured woman forty-eight years of age, with a big head covered with a mop of mud-colored hair, small eyes, huge hands and arms, and a gross body with difficulty supported on feet grotesquely small—such is the description of Mrs. Belle Gunness, the extraordinary creature who ran the "murder farm" near Laporte. Ind.

Murder for money was Bello [sic] Gunness's trade. She was a Scandinavian, came to this country when a girl, and married a fellow countryman. Max Sorenson, in Chicago, in 1883. He died mysteriously in 1890. Poison was hinted at, and exhumation suggested; but nothing was done. The woman collected $500 insurance money, and two years later married Gunness. In 1902 he moved to Laporte.

Before three months had passed she had become feared and hated among the neighbors. "She was more a devil than a woman," said one of them, whose farm adjoined her own. When Gunness was found dead in 1902, with the back of his head crushed in, every one believed that she had murdered him. Mrs. Gunness alleged that a sausage grinder had fallen from a shelf and struck him. Her statement could not be disproved. She collected $3,000 insurance, and began her systematic trade in murder. Everybody knew that she was advertising for a husband. Strange men met her at the railroad depot from time to time, drove back to the farm with her, and disappeared. But nobody cared to discover the mystery. Belle Gunness and her three children were left severely alone. There was only one companion, the hired man, Ray Lamphere, now under arrest, who worked on the farm, and he bore none too reputable a character. There had been another, Jennie Ilsen, an adopted daughter; but she was sent "to school in California" in September 1906. At any rate she disappeared from view.

It was the disappearance of Andrew Helgelean that opened up the mystery. Helgelean had read Mrs. Gunness's advertisement, drew $3,000 from his bank in Aberdeen, South Dakota, and told his brother Asle that he was going to Laporte to marry. After two weeks Asle wrote to Mrs. Gunness to learn his brother's whereabouts.

Dear good brother of the best friend I have in the world," the murdress [sic] wrote back, "it is with tears flooding in my eyes and my heart overburdened with grief that I write you about your dear brother. He is gone from me, I know not where. As I think of him my heart bleeds. May God bless him wherever he may be.

Sell off everything that he owns, get together as much of your own money as you can, and come here during the first part of May. We will then go and seek him. Bring the money all in cash. It will be easier to handle in this way. . . . I will fly to his arms and never, oh, never be separated from him again." Do not neglect to bring the money in cash.

This letter was written on April 23rd. Five days later Asle Helglean read that the Gunness house had been burned and that Mrs. Gunness and her three children had died in the flames. He took the train to Laporte, and told Sheriff Smutzer his story. Then Joe Maxson, a new hired man of the murderess, spoke about some "soft spots" in the garden. Digging began, and the first body turned up was the dismembered body of Helglean.

A few feet away the body of a young woman, supposedly Jennie Ilsen, was found. In all ten corpses were unearthed, three being of women. Whether Mrs. Gunness died in the fire or, as is believed, substituted a corpse, killed her children, burned down the house and fled, may be disclosed at the trial of Ray Lamphere.

Mrs. Gunness has willed her property, in reversion, after her children's death, to the Norwegian Orphans' Children's Home in Chicago.

18

BROTHERS FELIPE
NERIO ESPINOSA &
JOSÉ VIVIAN

Felipe Nerio Espinosa and his brother José Vivian were among the most notorious, and vicious, murderers in American history. Evidently they were bent on vengeance over losses of both family members and property they had suffered during the Mexican War. They killed at least thirty men, using guns, axes, and knives, often mutilating their victims in the most gruesome fashion imaginable. Several posses attempted without success to capture or kill the elusive Espinosas. In the spring of 1863, legendary scout, mountain man, guide, and bounty hunter Tom Tobin (whose father was an Irish immigrant and whose mother was Native American), hunting the killers alone, tracked them down and shot them at their makeshift camp. Tobin cut off their heads (as proof of death, so he could collect the reward). Army Colonel Sam Tappan, who had enlisted Tobin's help, gave him a Henry repeating rifle to show his gratitude.

The Story of Dead Man's Canon and of the Espinosas

As Told by Henry Priest to Elsie Keeton

I have heard so many different stories as to why Dead Man's Canon is so called that I am going to tell the true story about it. I came to Dead

Man's Canon with my parents from Buckskin, Colorado, on March 12, 1863. At that time there was no road through this canon. It was just a wide canon filled with majestic pines.

Henry Harkens, the man who was murdered a week later, met us in what later became known as Dead Man's Canon and piloted us to the place where we were going to live. This place was just below where the Fountain Water Works stand, on what is now the Mary Helen Ranch. We had known "Uncle" Harkens, as every one who knew him called him, for two years before he came down from Buckskin. He was one of the best and kindest of men, always ready to help anyone in trouble, and loved by all who knew him. At the time he came to Dead Man's Canon he was about fifty-five years old, and he was not murdered by his partner for his money, as I have often heard, nor by Indians, but by a couple of Mexican desperadoes by the name of Espinosa, who went through Colorado in 1863, slaying white men wherever they found an opportunity to do so.

Harkens and three other men, McPherson, Bassett and Judd, had bought a saw mill in Canon City, and were moving it to Dead Man's Canon, which was then called Saw Mill Gulch. Our house was just a mile from where they were setting up the mill. Two teams and seven men had come over with the first load of machinery and while here, the men had cut logs and built the cabin where Harkens was afterward murdered. Four of the men went back to Canon City after more machinery and their families, which left Harkens, McPherson, and Alden Bassett to work on the mill while they were gone.

On Wednesday, March 19, 1863, Harkens worked all day on the cabin, daubing it and hanging a blanket for a door. McPherson and Bassett worked on the mill, and my father and I worked all day on the hill near where Paul Dingel's house now stands, where we were building a road to haul lumber away from the mill when it got to running. At quitting time that evening McPherson and Bassett went to the cabin, got their gun and sixshooter, and told Harkens they were going down the canon to see how Priests were getting along with the road while he got supper, and as they left, Harkens threw down his trowel preparatory to getting the wood with which to cook supper.

As we found out afterwards, the two Espinosas had lain up on a little bluff about a quarter of a mile from where Harkens and the two men were working, and had watched them at work on the mill and cabin all day. They had their horses picketed there, and as soon as they saw McPherson and Bassett leave the cabin they had evidently mounted their ponies, rode down to the cabin, and murdered Harkens.

When McPherson and Bassett got in sight of the cabin on their return from the road, McPherson remarked, "I wonder what's the matter that the old man hasn't got a light?"

"You must remember he daubed the cabin today and hung a blanket for a door, so we couldn't see a light if he had one," replied Bassett.

It was getting dark when they reached the cabin, and the first thing that met their gaze was Harkens, lying dead within six feet of the cabin door, his head split open with the ax, and two ugly gashes in his left breast. McPherson thought the murderer must be in the cabin, so cocked his gun, and with the barrel cautiously pushed aside the blanket which served as a door. There was no one in the cabin, but everything was topsy-turvy. McPherson's suitcase had been slashed open with a knife and the contents were scattered about the cabin, and there was a great white splotch on the floor just inside the door, where the Mexicans had emptied a hundred pound sack of flour they found in the cabin. That frightened McPherson and Bassett nearly out of their wits, for they thought the woods were full of Indians and they fully expected to be scalped any minute, so they took to their heels and ran every step of the way to my father's house.

Father and I had quit work on the road and were preparing to sit down to supper when the door was burst open by McPherson and Bassett. They were so breathless from their long run they could scarcely speak, but finally managed to tell us that Harkens had been murdered, as they supposed, by the Indians.

Father wanted to go right over and put the body in the cabin where it would be safe from wild beasts, but mother and McPherson and Bassett were so frightened and so sure he had been killed by the Indians they would not let him go, so we stood guard all night and at daybreak father started down creek to the nearest ranch, five miles distant, for help. When he reported the killing there a man rode on to Fountain, which was five miles further, and reported the murder there, and by noon there were twenty-five men at our house, and we all went over to Harkens' cabin to see what had happened to him and whether there were any Indians about. We found Harkens had been shot in the middle of the forehead with a Colts Navy revolver, then the murderers had taken the ax and split his head open from the top to the mouth, and then, judging from the appearance of his head and the ax, they had hit him on each side of the head with the head of the ax, and two pieces of skull and his brains lay on the ground at the top of his head. He was also stabbed twice in the left breast; two four-inch gashes about three inches apart. He must have been killed shortly after McPherson and Bassett started down the canon, for he had not yet cut the wood with which to cook supper.

The murderers must still have been ransacking the cabin when they heard McPherson and Bassett returning, for judging from their pony tracks they had mounted them and hastily ridden away toward the red cliffs west of the cabin. They had ridden right through the pine tree tops, which were scattered about where the logs for the cabin had been cut, and in one pile of the tree tops we found a chunk of beef they had lost in their flight. They rode back to the red cliffs where there was a sheltered place in a gulch by a ledge of rock and here we found they had evidently cooked their supper; then they mounted their horses and had taken the old trail to Colorado City. This old trail passed within a few rods of father's house, and while we were standing guard the night of the murder the bandits must have passed right by us.

As we could find no more traces of the murderers, we prepared to bury Harkens. We chose a spot on a little knoll under a sheltering pine tree, and while the other men were digging the grave I stood guard up on a bluff where I had a fair view up and down the canon. While they were digging I spied two horsemen coming at a brisk pace down the canon and I hastened to tell the diggers. When the riders arrived they proved to be a sheriff and his deputy from Hardscrabble, and they told us the Espinosas had murdered an old man by the name of Bruce, at the head of Hardscrabble, the day before they murdered Harkens, and at about the same hour. The sheriff said Bruce had apparently walked to the door of the blacksmith shop and the Espinosas had shot him several times. The sheriff and his deputy did not stop long and were soon off again on the trail of the bandits.

We learned that the murderers had killed a beef on Turkey Creek, at what is now called Aiken's Spring. (This spring was once owned by Mr. Aiken, father of Charles, Jessie and Mrs. Fannie Aiken Tucker, all of Colorado Springs, and is on the Glen Cairn Ranch, now owned by Mr. A. N. Jordan of Colorado Springs.) The bandits had cut about ten or twelve pounds out of the ham of the beef and left the rest. The meat we found in the tree tops back of Harkens' cabin was without doubt a piece of the beef they had killed at Aiken's Spring.

After the sheriff and his deputy had gone, we resumed our sad work. My father took small logs, and in the grave they had dug he laid the logs as though building a cabin, only he fitted them together as closely as he could. Then we lined the box with fragrant boughs and in this rude casket we placed the body, covered the top tightly with little poles and boughs, then covered all with the soil, and on a rough headstone we carved the words:

"Henry Harkens, Murdered Wednesday Eve., March 19th, 1863."

The sheriff and deputy from Hardscrabble followed the Espinosas to Colorado City, up through Manitou and on up through Ute Pass, and were first to find two men the bandits had murdered after Harkens in Dead Man's Canon, and they returned to Colorado City and reported that murder there.

From there the Espinosas went to South Park and killed wherever they caught a man alone. They waylaid cabins, roads and mining camps and murdered ruthlessly wherever they found an opportunity to do so. Finally six cavalrymen were sent after them and chased them all summer, but never got a glimpse of them. When the bandits reached California Gulch and killed two or three miners there, it aroused the wrath of the whole camp, and twelve old miners shouldered their guns and took the trail of the bandits. They caught up with the Espinosas at Cripple Creek, at what is now called Espinosa Peak. The bandits were camped on top of that peak, and there the miners had quite a battle with them and killed the oldest bandit, but the younger one escaped. In the camp where Espinosa was killed the two bandits had nothing to eat except half of a beaver. On Espinosa's person the miners found an article of agreement that they, the Espinosas, were to kill six hundred whites in revenge for the loss of their money and property during the Mexican War. They had treated the older men they killed much more brutally than they did the younger ones, presumably because they reasoned the older men had had more to do with the Mexican War than the younger men had. Where Espinosa was killed they found all the bandits' camping equipment except what the one who escaped took with him. Espinosa had only two or three dollars on his person when killed, but among his effects they found Harkens' gold rimmed spectacle frames, McPherson's gold watch and chain (worth about $25 or $30), his old-fashioned satin vest with embroidered flowers on the front, and his day-book. They also got the bandits' guns, revolvers, bowie-knives, ponies and saddles.

The younger bandit went back to Mexico, got his nephew, a boy twelve years old, and started out again.

The State offered a big reward for their capture, and Tom Tobin, an Irishman and an excellent marksman, killed both of them near Fort Garland, Colorado, and got the reward, though in small installments, receiving the last payment on it shortly before he died.

"And that," said the old-timer in conclusion, "is the story of Dead Man's Canon."

So the reason the name of Saw Mill Gulch was changed to Dead Man's Canon was because Henry Harkens was murdered there, and there, within fifty feet of the Colorado Springs-Canon City highway, where the morning shadows of Indian Head Ledge fall cool and deep, and the afternoon sun silvers the needles on the pine that has guarded it so faithfully all these years, is Harkens' grave; a totem faintly scrolled along the trail of the pioneers.

19

THE LOOMIS GANG

The Loomis Gang was a family of criminals who operated in central New York State (especially Madison, Oneida, Otsego, and Onondaga Counties) for decades until about 1866. The numerous sons of George Washington Loomis and his wife Rhoda formed the nucleus of the gang, which had powerful connections and many confederates in the area. Rhoda raised her children to be criminals and to steal, punishing them only for getting caught. Specializing in the theft of horses and livestock (they sold countless stolen horses to the Union Army during the American Civil War), the Loomises also committed robberies and burglaries and fenced stolen goods. The Loomis Gang grew very rich from their ill-gotten gains, and if any member were arrested and charged, he or she always seemed to have the best legal representation that money could buy. Frequently evidence of their crimes mysteriously disappeared, witnesses fell silent, and bribed local officials saw to it that convictions were exceedingly rare. Because George and Rhoda had so many children, there are also many descendants of members of the Loomis Gang, some of whom were perversely proud of their criminal ancestors. Others tried to distance themselves. One of these, famed poet Ezra Pound (originally Ezra Weston Loomis Pound) changed his name to avoid the association with some of his forebears.

The history of the Loomis family has never been written. For over sixty years they set the law at defiance, and were at last uprooted only by the strong arm of a vigilance committee. A report of the Prison Association, made to the Legislature in 1865, says that the family have grown rich by thieving. Their children are educated in the best and most expensive seminaries. They dress genteelly, their manners are polished, and they appear to good advantage in society. They rule the counties of Oneida, Oswego, Otsego, Madison, Chenango, Schoharie, Delaware, and Sullivan with a rod of iron.

They have numerous well-trained confederates in all of these counties, who are ready by day or night, at a moment's warning, to ride off in any direction for the sake of plundering or for the concealment or protection of associates who are in danger of falling into the meshes of the law. These men have been indicted times without number in the above named counties, but none of them have ever been convicted, nor have any of them been in jail for a longer time than was sufficient for a bondsman to arrive at prison. There are farmers, apparently respectable who belong to the gang and share in its profits. Whenever bail is needed, substantial farmers come forward and sign the bonds without regard to the amount of the penalty. The family exert a great political influence, and are always ready to reward their friends and punish their enemies, both at the primary conventions and at the polls.

Although they have been repeatedly indicted, the number of their indictments bears but a small ratio to the number of their depredations. It usually happens that any one who is particularly active in bringing any of the gang to justice has his barn or dwelling burned, or horses are missing from the stable, or his sheep or cattle from the pasture. These things have been done so often that cautious men are careful how they intermeddle by seeking to bring the members of the gang to justice. If a man so intermeddling happens to have a mortgage on his property, it is very soon foreclosed. If he has political aspirations, thousands of unseen obstacles interpose to prevent the fulfillment of his hopes. If he is a trader his custom falls off. If he is a physician malpractice is imputed to him, or other stories are circulated to his discredit, and at length matters come to such a pass that his only resource is to quit the country. All who make themselves conspicuous as opponents of the family are in some way made to feel the effect of a thousand blighting influences.

Although the law has been powerless when exerted against the gang, they have been in the habit of using its energies with great effect against those who stood in their path. We are told with great circumstantiality, by men worthy of confidence, of numerous instances in which, under skillful manipulations, the forms of law were used to punish innocence and shield robbery.

The finest horses stood in the barnyard night and day saddled and bridled, ready for use at a moment's warning. In early times they were the Kentucky Hunter stock, but were afterwards changed for Black Hawk and Morgan stock.

A relative of the family says the old lady was quick tempered. At times she was very devout, and spent hours reading the Scriptures. She frequently boasted how many times she had read through her Bible. One of her sons-in-law says that she set her face against all wrong doing; but this does not agree with accounts given by neighbors. They accuse her of inciting young visitors to petty peculations and crimes.

The [sic]were led to the house by Wash, who invited them to ride behind his fast horses, and studied their characters. If they were licentious, the attraction was blooming girls who had been brought to the mansion as servants on promises of good wages, and started upon an infamous career. If they were given to drink, the best liquors were set before them. At night the teams were harnessed, and the whole party sped away on a lark. The young fellows were on the road to crime before they knew it. When they were about to leave the house, the old lady would place her hand on their arms and say: "Now, don't come back without stealing something, if it's nothing but a jackknife." The first time they might return with the carcass of a sheep or lamb, or a tub of butter. Their dexterity was praised and the fruits of the marauding were placed upon the table. There were generally from three to half a dozen young men from 17 to 20 years old about the house. Sometimes they served as pickets, and gave timely warning of the approach of strangers and officers of the law. The most of the thieving and barn burning was done by these young rascals, the Loomises acting as receivers and disposers of stolen goods. They did the planning, and their young pals carried out the work.

The Big Search

The first authentic legal scrape involving the boys was in September, 1848. Allen Abbey had a country dance at Brookfield. Grove and Wash got a crowd of hop pickers together and drove over. The wagon body was filled with clubs. They entered the ballroom without tickets, insisting on dancing, and wound up in a bloody fight. Several heads were broken, and Abbey was nearly killed. Wash was indicted for an assault with intent to kill, and brought before James W. Nye, then County Judge and afterward United States Senator from Nevada. Nye admitted him to bail and repeatedly postponed the trial. Soon afterward old Dan Douglas, of Sangerfield Center, had Wash indicted for stealing a saddle and bridle. Things became so hot that Wash was forced to skip his bail, and put for California.

What is known as "the Big Search" occurred in 1849. Burglaries were of nightly occurrence. Clothes lines were robbed, farmers lost their sheep and horses, and there was a multitude of petty thefts. The farmers became thoroughly aroused, and accused the Loomises of the thefts. A large crowd drove up to the house in sleighs and made a thorough search of the premises. They found a great store of goods, including log chains, umbrellas, whiffletrees, neck yokes, buffalo robes, and an almost inconceivable variety of articles. Square holes covered with boards, and filled with stolen goods, were discovered in a hay-mow. Much of the property was taken to Waterville and identified. A guard was left in the house, but were frightened by the brothers, who fastened them in a room, and spent the night burning and destroying the goods that remained. Some of the family were arrested, but conviction seemed impossible. While all were satisfied that they were a family of thieves, no one could identify the one who stole the goods. Tangible evidence against William was unearthed, and he served a short time in jail. All the others escaped.

Wash remained in California several years. At one time it was reported that he had been hanged by a vigilance committee. In his absence old Douglas died and Abbey froze to death, so that it was an impossibility to convict him on either indictment. He returned from California before the death of his father. His return is said to have been accelerated by the dispute with one Burns over some pasture land. There were high words.

"Are you fixed?" asked Burns.

"I am," Wash replied.

"All set," said Burns, "let's go out and settle it."

They drew their revolvers and went out. On the way Wash tried to settle the dispute by shooting Burns in the side. The wound was a slight one, but Wash's treachery told upon the community. They gave chase with a rope. He escaped into a canyon and was followed by a friend on horseback. Wash rode the pony over two hundred miles pursued by Burn's comrades. It is even asserted that they tracked him to New York.

The old man Loomis died February 26th, 1851, aged 71 years, and the boys were left to their own resources.

[Their escapades and the high numbers of animals they had stolen, secreted, and traded away over the decades led the Loomis Gang to at various times to be in possession of horses of some local repute: one known as the California mare, another called Flying Cloud, and another by the name of the Wygart Mare, the latter one named for the family whose farm from which she was apparently stolen.]

The constable who gave the gang the most trouble, and finally destroyed the [sic] was James L. Filkins, a blacksmith [who stated that he remembered] that Bill Loomis was arrested on the charge of passing a counterfeit bill on a peddler. The peddler swore positively to both bills, but through some hocus pocus, engineered by Wash, Bill escaped. Wash was a genius. He would train a witness in manufactured evidence until he actually made him believe that he was telling the truth.

Robbery on the Highway

In June, 1858, so many sheep were stolen from the farmers that they organized a party, and began to follow the clues that led to the Loomis farm. The Loomis boys became alarmed. They joined the farmers, saying that they also had lost sheep, and had trailed a drove to the farm of Jeremiah Clark, in the town of Hamilton. The party went to Clark's place and found many of the missing sheep. The Loomises gathered the sheep which they claimed, and drove them off, after a severe fight with Clark, who told the farmers that the boys had sold him the whole flock. Clark charged Wash, Grove and Plumb with highway robbery, and they were indicted. The three men retaliated by putting Clark under arrest for stealing the sheep. They manipulated the law to suit themselves. The indictment for highway robbery was never tried but Clark was sent to State prison.

Filkins was one of the constables who served the warrants on the Loomises for arrest on this charge of highway robbery. It was his first service. With seven men he surrounded the house early in the morning. Plumb tried to reach the swamp through the tall grass, but Filkins outran him, jumped upon his back, and handcuffed him. This unusual treatment alarmed Plumb and he shouted murder. The constable threatened to brain him if he didn't shut up, and Plumb said he was afraid of him. Long Sile Clark, one of the gang, for whose apprehension Constable Keith had a warrant, reached the swamp. Filkins said he counted fourteen different men in and around the house, all spruce young fellows. Plumb only was captured. They took him to Keith's hotel in Brookfield.

He had not been there an hour before Grove rode up mounted on the California mare. A short club swung from his wrist, and he was armed with two revolvers. He demanded Plumb's release. Keith stepped into the house, and Grove, after a moment's hesitation, dashed away. He afterward said that he was afraid Keith had gone to saddle a famous horse that was more than a match in speed for the California mare. That night Plumb was put to bed on the upper floor, handcuffed to a special officer. In the morning the window was open and he was gone. He had slipped his handcuffs.

SCENES AT THE LOOMIS MANSION

In September following they were indicted. The bench warrants were sent to Filkins with letters from the Sheriff and District Attorney, urging immediate arrest, and charging him not to let the next slip through his fingers.

Filkins reached the house early in the morning with two men. It was snowing. He saw Wash, Grove and Plumb in the barnyard. They espied him, and were rushing for their horses. Grove mounted a trained horse without saddle or bridle, and put him through the woods over the face of the hill back of the house. Plumb got into the swamp, but Wash, unwittingly, ran into Filkins' arms, and was taken to Morrisville, where he was quickly bailed.

On Nov. 15, 1858, Filkins made a third attempt to capture the game. He approached the mansion at 5 A.M. with nine men. The constable and one of his assistants were mounted. The dogs barked. In the first flush of morning they saw a vedette in the road. He turned his horse and fled. It was Plumb. Filkins gave chase, and shots were exchanged and the vedette was wounded. Plumb ran into a posse on foot, headed by Ephraim Conger, who had come up from the opposite direction. He turned short, and Conger fired at him. The shot broke the leg of the horse, and he fell to the ground. In an instant Plumb was on his feet and off for the swamp. They tracked him some distance through the snow, stained by his blood, but he made his escape. In the confusion Grove and others of the gang became alarmed and got away without trouble. Grove and Plumb then quit the country, and did not return until Clark was imprisoned and matters were satisfactorily arranged.

On their return Plumb wanted the Grand Jury to indict Filkins for an attempt at murder. When the work of the jury was done one of the jurymen said: "Filkins, we came very near indicting you for not killing Plumb."

"The only apology I can make," said Filkins, "is that it was so early in the morning that I could not see very well."

About this time Grove was indicted for passing counterfeit money in Oneida County. The Loomis boys heard that District Attorney Munger carried in his pocketbook the twelve ten-dollar counterfeit bills which had been taken from Grove, and which were to be used as evidence against him. Before the trial the District Attorney was met on the street after midnight, and robbed of these bills. Without them the indictment could not be sustained, and Grove escaped punishment.

THE LOOMISES PUNISHING FILKINS

Filkins was made a Deputy Sheriff in April, 1855. He made so many raids upon the gang that they determined to punish him. In May, 1860, they went to Higginsville, Oneida County, and got a warrant from Justice Samuel Marsh for the arrest of Filkins and party on a charge of assault and battery. It was claimed that the offense was committed while the officer was endeavoring to make an arrest at the Loomis house. Filkins stood in his shop when Denio rode up with a Madison County officer, a friend of the Loomises, and served the warrant. Denio and the officer wanted to iron Filkins, but the officer would not consent. They drove to a crossroad in North Brookfield, where they met Wash, Plumb and William. They had Filkins' old posse in a wagon. The prisoners were shackled.

Filkins then had the Loomises indicted in Madison County for assault and battery. Judge Mason quashed all but one of the indictments, on the ground that Wash alone struck him when they dragged him from his house at night. The jury found Wash guilty and the Judge stultified the effect of their verdict by fining him $25.

Disgusted with this result, Filkins moved to Oneida County. His reputation had preceded him. He was nominated for constable by both parties, and despite the efforts of the Loomises elected by a large majority. He says he accepted the nomination on the promise of the people to stand by him in his efforts to uproot the gang.

At that time he says he could enumerate seventy persons in the town of Sangerfield alone who either affiliated with the Loomises, or stood ready to harbor or bail them. Many were land holders, and nearly all were of fair standing in the community. Filkins was elected March, 1862. When Plumb heard of it he swore that if Filkins ever came upon the premises to arrest him he'd shoot him.

A Beautiful Girl Murdered

Wash made money during the war by forcing the most worthless of the gang into the army and taking their bounty money. He knew their runways and scared them into enlistment by stories that Filkins was after them. In 1862 there was a sad tragedy in the Loomis mansion. In 1854 Wash had formed an intimacy with Anna Wright, a beautiful girl of German descent. She lived with him in the house and took an active part in the management of the farm. She was shot and killed by one Mott, a member of the gang. A coroner's inquest proved that Mott was near the mantel cleaning the barrel of a gun. The stock had been removed, and the barrels were capped and loaded. As Anna was passing he dropped them in the fireplace. One of the barrels was discharged, and the shot entered the girl's thigh, severing one of the arteries of the leg. She lingered several days, and died leaving Wash a son, who is still living and working as a farm laborer in Madison County. Filkins says that Mott entered the army soon afterwards, and told a comrade that Plumb and Denio promised him $50 to kill the girl, as they were jealous of her influence with Wash. They cheated him out of the money.

Plumb's threats against Filkins led the latter to get out a peace warrant. The warrant was served with one held by Officer Beardslee. Plumb made an effort to escape but was caught by Albert Root, one of Beardslee's posse, and now a dentist at Hamilton. He was taken to Waterville and promptly bailed. He then got out a warrant against young Root, charging him with drawing a revolver and threatening his life. He claimed that Root did not properly belong to the posse, and Beardslee, for some reason refused to swear that he did. Two trained witnesses swore in Plumb's favor, and the law kept Root from the stand. Plumb, however, swore too much. He knew the revolver was loaded, for he could see the points of the bullets when it was pointed at him. The revolver was then produced, and when loaded the points of the bullet could not be seen. Root was discharged. He denied the charge in toto.

THE OPERATIONS OF THE GANG

There were numerous petty thefts in 1862. Messrs. Montgomery and Eastman, the latter a brother of the late Mayor Eastman of Poughkeepsie, drove up to the American Hotel one evening at about dusk. In a few minutes they missed a valuable skunk skin robe. The landlord had seen old Beebe and several members of the gang in the streets. Montgomery made the remark that it was a dark night, but it might be lighter before they got home. Old Beebe lived over a hill a mile from the Loomises. His son, Lavergue, was one of the most daring and active of the gang. That night the Beebe barn was burned. The old man rode over to the Montgomery place and accused the young man of incendiarism. Mr. Montgomery kicked him out of his yard, and that was the end of it. While the barn was burning one of the clapboards fell off, and out dropped a store of revolvers, stolen from G. W. Tallman, a Government contractor in Utica. About the same time a shoe store in Hubbardsville and a tailor in Leonardsville were robbed. Filkins visited the Loomis place with a search warrant. The gang had become so bold, and had burned so many barns belonging to persons who had taken part against them, that the residents were frightened, and Filkins found it impossible to raise a posse. He went to the house alone and found Wash at home. The house was searched. Scores of saddles and bridles were unearthed. Among the things, Filkins found a half dozen of Tallman's revolvers, a lot of new shoes, and Montgomery's skunk skin robe. Whips and blankets were found including some of the stolen goods from Leonardsville. Wash was caught trying to secrete the robe, and Filkins arrested him. Wash submitted after a protest, and Filkins took him before Justice Church, who said "Why do you bring the infernal scoundrel before me? Why don't you hang him?" The Justice held him. During the examination, the Leonardsville tailor saw one of his coats on the back of a spectator, who proved to be George Peckham, who Filkins says was one of the gang living in Hamilton. He said that he bought the coat from John Hall, another member of the fraternity. Wash was indicted but never put on trial.

Farmer Brown missed some sheep, and got out a search warrant. Filkins visited the Loomises on the day after Wash was bailed, to look for them. As he neared the house, Plumb and Denio mounted their horses and prepared to fly. "You needn't run," said the constable, "I've no warrant for you." Wash received him with the utmost politeness, and ordered the sheep driven up to the yard, so that Mr. Brown could see them. Brown identified his sheep, and Wash said "There's a d--d sight of iniquity in this county. Now, John Hall probably stole those sheep and put them in our flock to cast suspicion upon us." Grove backed up Wash and told Brown to ask any neighbors who had lost sheep to come and look their flock over. Brown took his sheep and made no further complaint.

Assassination

Up to July, 1863, Filkins visited the place on business every week. Scores of indictments were found against the Loomises. At midnight on July 22, there was a knocking at the door of Filkins' house in

Waterville. His life had been so often threatened that he observed the utmost caution. His wife was attending a sick child. Seizing a revolver, Filkins approached the kitchen window and asked what was wanted. A voice replied "I'm Mr. Clark's hired man. Last evening he came by Van Dee's and saw Jack Van Dee at home, and asked me to come up here and let you know." Van Dee was a noted Loomis rascal, whom Filkins had vainly tried to arrest. Satisfied that the voice was that of Plumb Loomis, the officer stepped back. He was in the act of cocking his revolver, but a double-barreled shotgun loaded with slugs and pieces of nails was discharged through the window. Filkins was shot in the right arm and left hand. His hands dropped. The wife screamed, "James are you hit?" He replied: "I'm wounded," and she heard the blood pattering on the floor. He started for the bedroom, and two more shots were fired through the bedroom window. The blinds were shattered, and the lower part of the sash torn out. The bedroom door was filled with buckshot, and there were fourteen shot holes in the mantel. Seven buckshot and forty small shot had riddled the bed curtains. Filkins became faint with the loss of blood. The neighbors were aroused and his assailants retreated. The floor was covered with blood. Hundreds of persons visited the house on the next day. Filkins exhibited the following letter, which he had received two months before the attempt on his life, and there was much excitement:

"J. Filkins--Dear Sir: As a friend to you and all mankind I set down to write to forewarn you of danger. That gang has offered one of their associates a good sum of money to kill you at some convenient time, and he says he doubts whether they will pay him if he should do so. He is a daring and bold robber. I dare not sign my name."

Early in the morning Filkins requested an officer to go up to Beebe's house and look for a double-barreled shotgun that had recently been discharged. The public terror was so great that no one would leave town. When he got well however, he dug up enough evidence to secure indictments against Plumb, Wash, Lavergne and Ezra Beebe, and Thomas Mott. In May, 1865, he went to the office of the District Attorney to see what had become of the skunk's robe indictment. He found that a nolle pros. [i.e, nolle prosequi, filed to cancel a suit] had been entered, and that the same course had been taken with the indictments for attempted murder. He says he asked Hiram T. Jenkins, the District Attorney, that it was his last term, and he had an agreement with the Loomises to see them clear of everything before he want out of office. He wanted too make his word good, and asked me to help him."

Burning a Court House

About this time one of the Loomises outraged a girl 14 years old, the daughter of a respectable farmer. He was taken before Justice Ira B. Crandall of South Brookfield, and bound over. Bail was given. On the following night the justice's docket was stolen. The thieves did not find the bail bonds, because the Justice had mailed them to the County Court.

The girl was then kidnaped to prevent her from going before the Grand Jury, but testimony of the father, mother, and physician secured an indictment. After this some constables got upon the track of the girl and found her in the Loomis mansion. She was taken home, but her terror was so great that she preferred to stay in jail two years as an assistant in the Sheriff's family instead of remaining at home. She believed that the Loomises meant to put her out of the way.

Loomis jumped his bail bond. When the authorities threatened to come upon his brothers for the amount of the bonds, he came forward and pleaded not guilty to the indictment. D. C. Pomeroy, his counsel, urged a postponement of the trial Judge Mason, a brother of Congressman Joseph Mason, denied the request. One of the other brothers pleaded not guilty to an indictment, and was about to be forced to trial.

In this dilemma both brothers ran out of the court room, and sprang into a cutter driven by Dan Geer. They had not gone many miles before they were overhauled and brought back. Meantime the Judge had discharged the jury, and the cases went over. He declined however, to admit Loomis to bail. He was afterwards taken before Judge Le Roy Morgan, of Syracuse, on a writ of habeas corpus, and that Judge took bail for his reappearance. An industrious farmer was induced to go upon his bond. Loomis fled to Canada, and the farmer was forced to pay his forfeit. He did so, and then committed suicide. In Canada, Loomis took the name of Theodore Goodenough, and overlooked the interests of the family at that end of the line.

In September, 1864, the brothers deemed it necessary to clear themselves of certain indictments in Madison County, on which they feared to stand trial. It is rumored that after entering the engine house in Morrisville and cutting the hose, the gang fired the Court House. Anyway it was burned to the ground. Wash was in town when the fire occurred and took his turn at the brake of the engine. He seemed to be utterly astonished when some one told him that the hose had been cut, and said: "It's a d--d outrage, and I would like to help hang the man who did it."

Afterward, fancying that the indictments might have been destroyed, Wash and his counsel called for a copy of a certain indictment. The copy was given. Wash then learned that the indictments had been removed to the office of the County Clerk, before the Court House was burned. This was a fireproof building. In the same week it was broken open, and indictments, deeds and mortgages were burned in a stove that stood in the office. Every indictment against the brothers was destroyed, and as the statute of limitations had expired, new indictments could not be procured. Among the papers burned was an indictment against someone not a Loomis. Wash afterwards called upon him and told him his assessment for this work was $199. The man borrowed the money and gladly paid him.

DESTROYING INDICTMENTS

Meantime similar indictments were pressing the brothers in Oneida County. The District Attorney's office was rifled, and all his papers, including the indictments were carried off. The District Attorney is said to have paid Wash $250 for the return of the papers other than the indictments. They were afterward found mixed with leaves in a dooryard and returned to him. Many indictments were found against the family, but, except in one instance, no conviction was effected. At one time thirty-eight indictments were pending in which Filkins was a material witness, but hardly one of them was brought to trial.

The destruction of the indictments emboldened the gang. Robberies were of nightly occurrence, and Filkins found the gang operating far down in Delaware county. He took from them a horse said to have been stolen in the county, and the gang had him arrested for stealing the horse. He was a witness in one of Beebe's trials for stealing, and the old man had him arrested for perjury. When he was discharged it was getting dark, and his lawyer did not dare to ride back home with him. Ephraim Conger took an active part in reclaiming a stolen wagon; on the next night hes [sic] barn was burned. Maurice Terry made disrespectful comments on the Loomis family, and on the following night his barn was ablaze. No one who intermeddled with the family in any way was safe. A meeting was held in the Baptist church in North Brookfield to devise measures for protection. A committee on organization was appointed. At the next meeting by-laws were passed making any one who paid a dollar a member of the organization. Thereupon Wash and Grove gravely appeared, extolling the organization, and saying they were afraid of thieves, and wanted to become members. They planked down their dollars and crushed the life out of the association.

NEMESIS

At 1 A. M., October 29, 1865, fourteen persons were asleep in the Loomis mansion. There was a knock at the back door. Wash was called out and murdered. His body was found behind some barrels in the woodshed. Grove was the next victim. He was badly beaten and covered with oat sacks and blankets, which were afterward saturated with kerosene, and fired. His sister, Cornelia, saved his life. The barn was burned, and many valuable horses perished. The coroner held an inquest over Wash's body. Louisa Yates, swore that she was awakened by a rap on the bedroom window, and that someone called "Wash." Wash went to the window and asked what was wanted; that the reply was, "Come to the back door. I want to speak to you a minute." Wash went out. A second afterwards Filkins entered the room with a candle. Wash followed him, saying, "Filkins, I don't want you in here. Come out. There's nothing in here you want." Filkins looked under the bed, and then turned toward the door, saying, "No, there's nothing here, but Wash, I want you." Wash said, "Very well," and they walked out in the back kitchen, shutting the door.

Louisa then heard a "dreadful jar that shook the house." Just after this someone went upstairs, and in three or four minutes they came down with Grove. She heard Grove say, "Filkins, I want to see Wash a minute." Filkins replied, "You can't see Wash. He's not there." They then took Grove into the back kitchen and shut the door. She heard Grove screaming, and went to the kitchen door and tried to open it, but someone held it and she could not get in. She went back to her room and screamed while dressing. When she went back again she found Grove on the floor all on fire. He was covered with bags, blankets and his overcoat. They were saturated with kerosene, and the room was ablaze. Cornelia and herself threw the bags into the fireplace, and saved Grove from burning to death. A minute afterward the barn began to burn.

Grove corroborated this story. He swore that Filkins rapped on his door, and he replied that he would be there as soon as he could dress. Filkins said he was in a hurry and couldn't wait. Grove opened the door and went out. Filkins caught him by the collar. "I'll go with you, Mr. Filkins." Filkins shook him saying, "I know you will." They met two or three men with guns on the stairs. The men followed them into the back kitchen. According to testimony, Filkins struck him on he head six or eight times as fast and as hard as he could. The others pitched into him, and he defended himself as well as he could. Filkins then struck him several times with a slug shot. He also shot at him with a revolver, and the ball went into the fireplace. He then struck him twice with the revolver, breaking it in two pieces. Grove fell to the floor, and Filkins jumped on him two or three times, kicking him in the head and neck. Filkins then said: "Boys, he's dead. Let's burn him up." The kerosene was then poured on him and fired. Such was the testimony.

Nellie Smith and Cornelia, Grove's sister, both swore that they saw Filkins. When they tried to enter the room where Grove lay on fire, Filkins shoved them back with the words, "Get out of here. This is no place for women." Others in the house swore that they found a broken revolver on the floor, near where Grove was picked up. One man said that he found a pair of handcuffs in the meadow near the barn, and Grove swore that Filkins was inquiring for these handcuffs before he struck him the first blow.

Wash lived but a few hours. His skull was broken and he was beaten to a jelly. The jury returned a verdict that according to the testimony, Washington L. Loomis came to his death by the hands of three or more persons, and that one of these persons was James L. Filkins. Filkins informed the coroner that he was ready to deliver himself to the authorities. The coroner replied that he would let him know when he wanted him. Meantime, William Loomis swore out a warrant before Justice G. W. Cleveland, of Waterville charging Filkins with the murder of his brother. Filkins was arrested, and at the request of the prosecution, the examination was postponed two days, Filkins being discharged on his own recognizance. The same counsel appeared for the Loomises who had acted for them during the inquest.

On Nov. 6 Filkins again appeared before Justice Cleveland. Loomis's counsel, Mr. Lamb, again asked for a postponement until the 8th. This was granted. On the 8th neither Loomis nor the subpoenaed witnesses appeared. The complaint instead of serving the subpoenas, had put them in his pocket and gone to his home in Verona. The real design was manifested. The Grand Jury was to meet on the 13th; the object was to throw the case over, so as to put Filkins in jail until the February Court. Lawyer White told the Justice that the District Attorney had given instructions to postpone the case. The Justice, however, issued new subpoena, directing immediate service. Plumb Loomis appeared at 4 o'clock, and wanted the case postponed until Lawyer Pomeroy came. He said he had telegraphed for him. The Court refused any further delay, and called Plumb to the stand. Plumb asked to step out a minute and then ran away. Soon afterward Mr. White entered, and said he had dispatched from Mr. Pomeroy and the District Attorney, informing him that they could not control his actions, and issued attachments for the witnesses. Later in the day L. D. Bixby, who slept in the house on the night of the murder, was caught and put on the stand. In the morning the prosecution examined Nathan Gates, who swore that Filkins had asked him to assist in cleaning out the Loomises. With this testimony, Mr. White rested the case for the people.

THE DAY OF RECKONING

The second attempt to kill Filkins exasperated the public. Deputy Conger returned to Morrisville. One of the Judges threw some documents before the Sheriff, and told him it was his duty to serve them on the Loomises at all hazards. After the Judge retired the Sheriff took a revolver from a nook in the wall, and said that that was the only document he would serve on the Loomises. A Vigilance Committee was organized. They resolved to burn the Loomis mansion and hang every person found within it. The Sheriff and a strong posse went to the place early on Sunday morning, June 17, to serve half a dozen warrants. He was followed by over sixty persons well armed. The house was surrounded before day break, and the inmates were warned to make no resistance. Most of the family were handcuffed. The house was searched and silks, satins, furs, dress goods, and other stolen property were found. While the Sheriff was searching the barns and out houses the vigilants fired the house, and it was burned to the ground with all its contents. Cornelia and the old lady tried to save some of the valuables, but they were summarily taken from them and thrown into the flames. All the outbuildings but the negro shanty on the hill were destroyed. The only things saved were a valuable horse belonging to Grove, and some beds for the old lady and Cornelia, who retired to the shanty on the hill. Those caught in the house were Grove, Plumb, the old lady, Cornelia, a son of Wheeler, John Stoner, John Smith, Elizabeth Calkins, Adelaide Glasier (now Plumb's wife), Hester Crandall, and Nellie Smith. Plumb and John Stoner were hanged to the limb of a sugar maple fronting the house to extort a confession. Plumb was hanged twice. Having been resuscitated with much difficulty, he promised to tell all he knew and lead an honest life if his life was spared. He said the Maurice Terry's barn and Ephriam Conger's building were burned by Tom Mott, and that he and his brothers paid him to do it. He declared that Mott was the man who shot Filkins the second time. He was then taken to Morrisville jail, convicted of stealing, fined $100 and sent to jail for ninety days. The family afterward sued the county for $22,000 damages, and recovered $1,000.

After Wash's death the gang went to pieces. Grove retired to a little farm on the edge of the swamp and Plumb remained on the homestead. I paid him a visit. The bark was peeled from the limb on which he was hanged, and the blackened cellar and rusty farm implements told the story of retribution. Everything had gone to rack and ruin. He declared that the house was plundered before it was burned. He said the mob brought a keg of powder with them, and wanted to lock the whole family in a room and burn them alive and that there was not a decent man among them. They stole $585 in money from his sister, and carried off $386 belonging to the girl Crandall. No papers were served and "the Sheriff went back on the hill when the rope was put around his neck." Grove died a year or more ago.

20

JIMMY LOGUE AND ALPHONSO CUTAIAR, CAREER CRIMINALS (1850–1880s)

Jimmy Logue was a notorious robber and thief, especially in the Philadelphia, Pennsylvania area. But he also committed robberies in New York State, Massachusetts, and elsewhere. He was first convicted when he was only fifteen years old, and continued his pilfering ways his entire life, except during intervals when he was imprisoned. Jimmy's third wife, Joanna, disappeared in Philadelphia while Jimmy was away in Boston, helping out in a bank heist. Jimmy was suspected. Her body was not discovered for many years, and his stepson (or perhaps nephew—accounts vary) confessed to her murder.

STRANGE STORY OF CRIME

PHILADELPHIA DETECTIVES UNRAVEL A MYSTERY.

Sixteen Years Ago the Wife of Logue, the Bank Robber, Disappeared—Three Years Ago Her Skeleton Was Found Under the Floor of a House in Philadelphia—Last Month Logue, a Fugitive from Justice, Surrendered—Now the Son of Another of His Former Wives Is Arrested for the Murder.

Philadelphia, April 28.—While the larger portion of Philadelphia's population was attending church today there lay on a desk in a dingy little room down town the skull of a murdered woman. Around it were grouped a half-dozen newspaper men, two doctors and Coroner Samuel H. Ashbridge and Detective Geyer. There was unfolded a story of crime. The central figure in the story is James E. Logue, known to the police departments of the continent as "Jimmy" Logue, burglar, bank robber, and one of the most notorious all-round crooks in the annals of crime. The case turned upon the murder of one of this man's wives—Johanna Logue—but it was a fitting climax to a story that proved that he was not her murderer. On the night of February 22, 1879, Johanna Logue vanished as suddenly and as completely as if the earth had opened and swallowed her. The newspapers at the time were full of it, rewards were offered, and no one was more indefatigable in his efforts to locate the woman than Logue. But there was no trace of her, and gradually the case faded from memory. On October 16, 1893, fourteen years afterward, a carpenter repairing the house at 1250 North Eleventh street tore up some boards in the kitchen, and there found the skeleton of a woman. Clinging to the bones of the throat was a handkerchief, tied in a knot, and next to the mouldering bones lay the soles of a woman's shoes. This was all that remained of Johanna Logue. When it became known that Logue and his wife had lived in the house suspicion at once pointed to him as the murderer, but all search for him proved unavailing.

White-haired Fugitive Surrenders.

On the evening of March 5th last the door bell of Coroner Ashbridge's private residence rang, and, answering it in person, he was confronted by an old white-haired man, who said, abruptly:

"I am Jimmy Logue, and I have come to give myself up."

That was all he said in relation to the case, and the coroner handed him over to the police under an assumed name. From that time on

Coroner Ashbridge and Detective Geyer worked together in secret, until they had unraveled the complete story, which culminated a few days ago in the arrest of a man whose identity was not revealed until today.

He is Alphonso C. Cutaiar, Jr., the illegitimate son of one of Logue's former alleged wives. He is locked up at the City Hall on the charge of murder, while in a neighboring cell is Logue, held as the star witness.

Cutaiar's crime—for he has made a confession, in which he acknowledges causing the woman's death, though, he asserts, involuntarily—is best understood from a brief recital of Logue's career.

LOGUE'S LOVE AFFAIRS.

He was already a notorious character when, in 1858, he was married to Mary Jane Andrews. With her he lived two years, when, without the formality of a divorce, he was wedded to Mary Gahan, who, though she had not before been a wife, was the mother of an eighteen-months-old child, Alphonzo Cutaiar, Jr. Logue and Mary had not lived long together, when he became enamored of her sister, Johanna Gahan, whom he established in a separate household, paying all expenses until, in 1869, Mary died. Meanwhile, Logue, who had been working hard at his "profession," fell into the hands of the police for a series of burglaries. On May 23, 1811, he was arraigned at the Central Police-station for sentence; but before the case proceeded, he asked Magistrate Smith to do him a favor first. He wanted to be married to Johanna. The magistrate complied, and Logue, standing in the dock, was married to the woman. Then he was sentenced to seven years in the penitentiary. During this term Johanna boarded in this city, and promptly, upon his release in 1877, Logue came for her.

They went to New York, where for a time he operated with the equally notorious Peter Burns, who died some years ago in jail in

Florence, Italy. Logue raised money in some way, for not long after his release he bought $20,000 worth of government bonds. In February, 1879 Logue and the woman came to this city. Meanwhile, young Cutaiar had become a barber, and Logue bought for him the business of his former employer, William Matthews, at 1248 North Eleventh street, and later bought the adjoining property for $3,150, and fitted it up as a shop for Cutaiar, Logue and Johanna living with him in the dwelling portion, which was expensively furnished.

JOHANNA'S DISAPPEARANCE.

A few days after this Logue and the woman went to New York for a visit. There Logue fell in with another burglar named George Mason, and on the evening of February 20th the two men left for Boston, telling Johanna they would return shortly. The following Tuesday Logue returned and found his wife gone. He came to Philadelphia and went to his home. There he found Cutaiar, his journeyman, Fritz Eckert, and a young apprentice, named Harry Fricke. Cutaiar told him that the last he had seen of Johanna was on the preceding Saturday. She had come from New York, visited some friends, and spent some time at the barber shop. At seven o'clock in the evening she opened the door of the shop, cried "I am off," and was gone. He had noticed that she was intoxicated, and called to her to wait until he was at leisure, so that he could escort her to the railroad station, but she did not wait. Logue at once thought that she had eloped with Peter Burns, but it was found that Burns had sailed alone for Europe, and all trace of the woman was lost. With the assistance of her brother, Peter Gahan, Logue searched the country for her, but to no avail.

The next event was when he was caught, with Johnny Irving, in a store in this city in 1879, and was sent to prison for three years and nine months. This sentence was at once followed by two years for robbing houses in Reading, and again on August 2, 1836. he was given six years for another burglary. His last sentence was ten months, Imposed on June 22, 1892, for robbery, and after his release on April 22, 1893, he was lost sight of until he gave himself up to Coroner Ashbridge.

A WOMAN'S MONEY AND JEWELS.

At the time of her disappearance the woman wore jewelry worth $2.000, and had in the bosom of her dress four $1,000 government bonds. When they moved to the Eleventh street house, in 1879, Logue had secreted seven of these $1,000 bonds under the carpet of the stairway, telling no one but Cutaiar where they were. When he returned, he found that Cutaiar had stolen one of the bonds and sold it to Drexels for $1,045. Of this money, he gave $1,000 to Sallie E. Camp, who afterwards became his wife: but upon Logue's threats, he got the money back and returned it to him. Cutaiar and his wife lived at the house for a year after Johanna's disappearance, when foul odor coming from under the kitchen floor, made the woman so sick that they were compelled to move away. After that the house had numerous tenants up to the time of the discovery of the skull.

The warrant for Cutaiar's arrest was sworn out by Logue on April 6th of this year, and six days later he was taken into custody. Then search was made for Eckert, the journeyman, and at first it seemed like a hopeless hunt. The police of every city were put on the trail to no avail; but finally Detective Geyer found him in a barber shop on Houston street, New York, where for a long time he had been shaving from twenty to thirty Metropolitan policemen a week. Fricke was found in Philadelphia. His mind soon after became unhinged from fright, and it became necessary to send him to the insane department of the Philadelphia Hospital. After he had been sent there, it was found that by some strange fate, the superintendent of the ward in which he was lodged was Alphonzo Cutaiar, stepson of the accused murderer, and Fricke was hurriedly transferred to another ward. The former owner of the house 1248 North Eleventh street, where Cutaiar's first shop was, committed suicide some time ago, and Coroner Ashbridge has become almost prostrated from the arduous labor of tracing out the numerous clues.

Cutaiar's Confession.

After Cutaiar's arrest, several attempts were made to extort a confession from him, and he narrated a number of detailed stories of the crime, naming Logue as the perpetrator; but eventually he broke down, and on April 17 he told the true story. He said that when the woman signified her intention of returning to New York she was intoxicated, and he induced her to wait until he could accompany her to the station. He took her up stairs and made her get into the bed, with her clothes on. Then, he avers, to prevent her from getting away before he could go with her, he bound her hand and foot. This was at seven o'clock in the evening. Four hours later he found her lying on her face, with her head under the bolster, smothered to death in an evident attempt to break her bonds.

The next day he buried the body under the kitchen floor. He admitted having taken her jewels. but denied any knowledge of the $1,000 bonds which she was said to have in her bosom. The original story told by Logue was borne out in every detail by the investigations of the coroner and the detective; but they further found that Cutaiar had for some years been pursuing a crooked career. He had robbed many persons for whom he had worked, including the Prudential Insurance Company, upon whom he tried to work a bogus claim, and had stolen large quantities of gold and silver from various places, melted it down and sold it. With these facts in view, his story of the woman being accidentally smothered is generally discredited, and it is believed he deliberately murdered her.

★★★★★

Jimmy Logue is Dead

Man Who Stole Fortunes Dies on an Almshouse Cot. Repented Of His Many Sins. Was Comforted by the Priest Summoned to His Death Bed. Story of His Long Career in Crime.

Worn out by excesses and years of confinement resulting from his long career in crime, Jimmy Logue, who is believed to have stolen more money than any other thief of his time, died on an Almshouse cot at 4 o'clock yesterday afternoon, unattended by any relative or friend except the physician and the nurse. He sought religious consolation before he died and repented of his sins, but his fear of death was pathetic.

He retained consciousness to the last. the death rattle in his throat being heard just after he had asked to be propped up in bed. The nurse arranged the pillows as comfortably as she could have done for a respected millionaire.. The aged criminal thanked her with a glance, but never spoke again. He was old in crime, but although he appeared like a man of 80, his age was only 62 years.

Sent to the Almshouse.

On July 19 of this year Jimmy Logue, friendless and penniless, appeared at the detectives' room in the City Hall and asked that he be sent somewhere where he could live in peace and forget his old companions and misdeeds.

Police Surgeon Andrews sent him to the almshouse, but in a few weeks he tired of the society of "bums" and even called on Mayor Ashbridge to secure his influence in getting him transferred to the hospital. He afterward entered the House of Industry, Seventy-third street and Paschal avenue, but returned to the almshouse on September 28 to die. He was then a very sick man. He was threatened with pneumonia, but it yielded to treatment, and not until Tuesday evening was death believed to be near.

Oedema of the lungs set in. His breathing was labored. and at his request Father McElhone, of St. James the Greater Roman Catholic Church, was summoned.

"I have been a terrible sinner." moaned the aged thief. "You must have done some good in your life, Jimmy, or you wouldn't be repentant now." replied the priest. "Do all you can to save me," was the response, and after the prayer the dying man seemed easier.

From some peculiar system of ethics Logue imagined that burglary was a more serious sin than theft, and he frequently protested that he never was a burglar, but always a sneak-thief. "I began at 17 years of age," he said to Dr. C. M. Bumstead. his physician. "It was born in me. I couldn't help it."

He related with some glee about how he stole two watermelons at Decatur. Ill., where the doctor lived, but he never spoke without bitterness of the murder of his Wife. "That scoundrel, Cutaiar, did that on February 22, 1869," he frequently asserted. The discovery of his wife's skeleton under the steps of his house a few years ago, and the subsequent trial and conviction of his stepson, Cutaiar, is still fresh in the public mind.

A few days ago a well-dressed elderly woman, whom no one knew, called to see Jimmy Logue, but it is not known whether he has either relative or friend to bury him. If not his emaciated body may go to the Anatomical Board, and the peculiarity of his make-up be a subject of study and levity for medical students.

[It is estimated that he at one time] had a fortune estimated from $300,000 up, all of it other people's money. His career in crime includes more than 20 years in the penitentiary, and comprises some of the most startling and skillful robberies known to the history of crime. He was one of the most adroit and yet one of the most cowardly and sneaking thieves in the country. The plan of operations he first adopted was to enter an unoccupied house in a row and thence by the roof he would enter the dwelling that he purposed attacking, coming through the trap generally when the family was at supper. His aptness displayed itself best in his ability in discovering where large sums of money were to he obtained. Of late years safe breaking had been his forte.

He was born in Philadelphia. In 1870 he was captured in Fridenberg's pawn-broking establishment with "Curly" Harris, but they managed to make their escape. He was connected with the robbery of the Catholic. Beneficial Saving Fund, at Twelfth and Chestnut streets, where a large amount of cash and securities were stolen. He was also in the attempted robbery of the Southwark Bank, and had a hand in the famous raid on the Kensington Bank.

In May, 1871, on the day when the Germans, by a grand parade, celebrated the ending of their countrymen's war against the French, James Logue. John Jenkins, Jr., and James Hanley went uptown to rob the National Security Bank, at Seventh street and Girard avenue, while the watchman—a German—was away looking at the procession.

A policeman took it into his head to arrest Logue as a suspicious character. The others took fright, and all were arrested. While at the Central station he was permitted to go into the Rogues' Gallery. He jumped from the second-story window, but fell on an iron railing and, although badly injured, was still able to run, but was finally captured by a citizen as he fell over a dry goods box in Tower Hall. He was sentenced by Judge Finletter to 7 years and 6 months for a robbery in which it afterward appeared he had no part.

WEDDING TOUR TO PRISON.

While in the Court House dock he was married to a second wife, Joanna Gantz, and his wedding journey was the trip to Cherry Hill, unaccompanied by his bride. The skeleton of the unhappy bride was the one found years afterward.

When Logue was released he next turned up as a suspicious character down in Chester, where he was arrested and quickly released. He made his way to Washington, and played his favorite game of sneaking through a roof trap.

His victim in this case was Naval Constructor Isaiah Hanscombe, and his booty amounted to $75,000. While trying to dispose on Third street of some of the stolen securities Tom Bartlett was arrested, and the Washington authorities issued a requisition for him. With the proceeds of the robbery Logue dressed his wife Joanna very handsomely and even decorated her with diamonds. With these gains he also purchased for $3300 a house on Eleventh street, above Girard avenue.

It is claimed that a part of the money was deposited in a bank, and that Jimmy's latter day poverty was due to his inability to remember the name of the bank.

SOURCES

1. THE COLT-ADAMS AFFAIR (1841)

The New York Tombs: Its Secrets and Its Mysteries. Being a History of Noted Criminals, with Narratives of Their Crimes, as gathered by Charles Sutton, Warden of the Prison, edited by James B. Mix and Samuel Anderson Mackeever, A. Roman & Co., San Francisco, 1874, Ch. VI, pp. 64–80.

2. DR. VALOROUS P. COOLIDGE

Remarkable Trials of All Countries, With the Evidence and Speeches of Counsel, Court Scenes, Incidents, &c. Compiled from Official Sources. Volume II, pp. 425–429. S. S. Peloubet & Co., Law Book Publishers, 1882.

3. THE BLOODY BENDERS FAMILY

"Devilish Deeds" May 15, 1873 & "The Devil's Kitchen; Further Particulars of the Butcher Bender's Den," May 22, 1873, *The Weekly Kansas Chief*, Troy, Kansas.

4. THE LAMANA KIDNAPPING AND THE NEW ORLEANS BLACK HAND

"Black Hand Kills Kidnapped Child," *The Washington Herald*, Washington, D. C., June 24, 1907, pp. 1 & 3.

5. THE MURDER OF GRACE MAE BROWN

"People vs. Gillette," trial/appeal transcript.

6. THE MANSFIELD WALWORTH PARRICIDE

The Walworth Parricide: A Full Account of the Astounding Murder of Mansfield T. Walworth by His Son, Frank H. Walworth, with the Trial and Conviction of the Parricide and His Sentence For Life to the State Penitentiary at Sing Sing, Thomas O'Kane, Publishers, 130 Nassau Street, New York, 1873.

7. LAURA BULLION AND THE WILD BUNCH

"Stolen Bank Notes Representing $7,000 in Satchel Of Bandit's Woman Companion," November 7, 1901; and "Laura Bullion Relates Her Career Among the Outlaws," November 8, 1901. Both from the *The St. Louis Republic.*

8. HENRIETTA ROBINSON, THE VEILED MURDERESS

Life in Sing Sing State Prison, as Seen in a Twelve Years' Chaplaincy, by John Luckey, Ch. XXIII & XXIV, pp. 309–337. N. Tibbals & Co., No. 118 Nassau Street, 1860.

9. THE MOUNTAIN MEADOWS MASSACRE

Roughing It, Ch. XVII & Appendix B, Mark Twain, American Publishing Company, Hartford, Connecticut, 1872; and *Recollections of the Mountain Meadow Massacre* by B.G. Parker, Fred. W. Reed, Printer, Plano, California, 1901.

10. RACHEL WALL, PIRATE (1789)

"Life, Last Words and dying confession, of Rachel Wall, who, with William Smith and William Dunogan, were executed at Boston, on Thursday, October 8, 1789, for high-way robbery." Boston-gaol, Wednesday evening, October 7, 1789. Printed broadside.

Paper regarding "Legislation in regard to Highway Robbery in Massachusetts," pp. 178–190. In *Proceedings of the Massachusetts Historical Society, Second Series – Vol. XIX*, published by the Massachusetts Historical Society, Boston, March 1905.

11. MADAME DELPHINE LALAURIE, NEW ORLEANS MONSTER

New Orleans As it Was. Episodes of Louisiana Life, by Henry C. Castellanos, A.M., LL. B., 2nd edition, 1905. The L. Graham Co., Ltd., Publishers, Perdido Street, New Orleans. Ch. IV., "A Tale of Slavery Times," pp. 52–62.

12. THE BEADLE FAMILY MURDER-SUICIDE

"A narrative of the life of William Beadle, of Wethersfield, in the state of Connecticut. Containing I. The particulars of the 'horrid massacre' of himself and family. II. Extracts from the Rev. Mr. Marsh's sermon at the funeral of his wife and children," publ. Bavil Webster, Hartford, Conn., 1783.

13. THE ANTOINE PROBST AX MURDERS (1866)

"Confession of Eight Murders," *The Anglo-American Times*, June 2, 1866, p. 4.

The *Life, Confession, and Atrocious Crimes of Antoine Probst, The Murderer of The Deering [sic] Family*. To which is Added a *Graphic Account of Many of the most Horrible and Mysterious Murders Committed in this and other Countries*. Philadelphia: Barclay & Co., 1866, p. 63.

The Philadelphia Police, Past and Present, written and published by Howard O. Sprogle, 1887. Ch. XIX, pp. 656–657.

14. SLOBBERY JIM & THE DAYBREAK GANG (1850s)

The New York Tombs: Its Secrets and Its Mysteries. Being a History of Noted Criminals, with Narratives of Their Crimes, as gathered by Charles Sutton, Warden of the Prison, edited by James B. Mix and Samuel Anderson Mackeever, A. Roman & Co., San Francisco, 1874; Ch. XXXV, pp. 64–80.

15. ABRAHAM LINCOLN'S REMARKABLE CASE (1841)

"A Remarkable Case of Arrest for Murder" by Abraham Lincoln, published in the *Quincy Whig*, Quincy, Ill., April 15, 1846.

16. HARRY T. HAYWARD, THE "MINNEAPOLIS SVENGALI" (1895)

"Life, Crimes, Dying Confession and Execution of the Celebrated Minneapolis Criminal; other Interesting Chapters on the Greatest Psychological Problem of the Century." Calhoun Publishing Co., Minneapolis, Minn. 1896. Copyright, 1895–6, by E. H. Goodsell, J.T. Mannix and Frank T. Moody, Chs. XVI–XVIII & XXI.

17. BELLE SORENSON GUNNESS, SERIAL KILLER (DECLARED DEAD, 1908)

Celebrated Criminal Cases of America by Thomas Samuel Duke, Captain of Police, San Francisco. Published with Approval of the Honorable Board of Police Commissioners, San Francisco. James H. Barry Company, San Francisco, 1910.

"Scenes at the Indiana Murder Farm," *The Times Dispatch*, Richmond, Virginia, June 01, 1908.

18. BROTHERS FELIPE NERIO ESPINOSA & JOSÉ VIVIAN

"The Story of Dead Man's Canon and of the Espinosas," Henry Priest, *The Colorado Magazine*, Published by the State Historical Society of Colorado, Denver, 1930. Vol. VIII, pp. 34–38.

19. THE LOOMIS GANG

"History of the Loomis Gang" by Amos Cummings for the *New York Sun*, 1877. (The story was also picked up by several other upstate journals.)

20. JIMMY LOGUE AND ALPHONSO CUTAIAR (1850–1880s)

"Strange Story of Crime: Philadelphia Detectives Unravel a Mystery," *Baltimore American*, Monday Morning, April 29, 1895, Baltimore, MD.

"Jimmy Logue Is Dead," *The Philadelphia Record*, October 5, 1899, Philadelphia, PA.

ACKNOWLEDGMENTS

Regardless whose name appears on the cover, every book is a collaborative effort involving many hands, and this little volume is no exception. My heartfelt thanks:

To Keith Wallman at Lyons Press, who has guided this project with professionalism, patience, and good humor.

To production editor Lynn Zelem, for her excellent work and invaluable help.

To my former colleague, longtime friend, and editor and writer par excellence Tom McCarthy, for valuable help and advice.

A special thanks to Cindi Pietrzyk and her sharp eyes.

To Nick Lyons, for first opening the doors into the wonderful world of publishing. If not for Nick, none of this would ever have happened.

And last but certainly not least, to Eileen, without whom none of this would have been possible.

ABOUT THE EDITOR

Bill Bowers is a freelance writer and editor. He lives in rural New England with his wife and longtime collaborator, Eileen Bowers.